PRAISE FOR JILL SMOLOWE'S
AN EMPTY LAP

"Harrowing but ultimately joyous. . . . Smolowe tells her story with a combination of wit, emotion and skill. . . . The couple's mutual journey has a powerful effect."
—*Publishers Weekly*

"Touching. . . . What makes this book different from others is Smolowe's candor."
—*Arizona Republic*

"Smolowe's wonderfully clear writing puts you right alongside her."
—*St. Petersburg Times*

"Intensely moving and personal."
—*Adoptive Families*

"A richly detailed, brutally honest account."
—*Tampa Tribune & Times*

"An intimate look inside the head of a childless adult, written with vitality and wit. . . ."
—*Library Journal*

"[In] AN EMPTY LAP, the journey to parenthood joins the 'coming of age' book as a meaningful description of the passage from one stage of life to another."
—*Amazon.com*

"A touching and intensely honest memoir . . . also a poignant, revealing love story."
—*Big Apple Parent*

"Her revelations are as poignant as they are articulate."
—*Providence Journal*

"Smolowe has taken her life experience and her gift for words and written a book that will make you laugh, cry, recall your childhood, consider your relationships, and finish reading with a smile."
—*Child Welfare League of America*

An Empty Lap

One Couple's

Journey

to Parenthood

Jill Smolowe

POCKET BOOKS

New York   London   Toronto   Sydney   Tokyo   Singapore

POCKET BOOKS, a division of Simon & Schuster Inc.
1230 Avenue of the Americas, New York, NY 10020

Copyright © 1997 by Jill Smolowe

Originally published in hardcover in 1997 by Pocket Books

All rights reserved, including the right to reproduce
this book or portions thereof in any form whatsoever.
For information address Pocket Books, 1230 Avenue
of the Americas, New York, NY 10020

Library of Congress Cataloging-in-Publication Data

Smolowe, Jill.
    An empty lap : one couple's journey to parenthood / Jill
Smolowe.
        p.   cm.
    ISBN: 0-671-00437-9
        1. Interracial adoption—United States—Case studies.   2. Foster
parents—United States—Biography.   3. Childlessness—Psychological
aspects—Case studies.   4. Parenthood—Psychological aspects—Case
studies.   I. Title.
HV875.64.S66   1997
362.73´4´092—dc21
[B]   97-26214
                                                                  CIP

First Pocket Books trade paperback printing October 1998

10 9 8 7 6 5 4 3 2 1

POCKET and colophon are registered trademarks of
Simon & Schuster Inc.

Cover design by Lisa Litwack
Front cover photo by David Katzenstein

Printed in the U.S.A.

To Joe, Becky's wonderful father,
my cherished husband

Acknowledgments

Though loneliness is an inevitable and frequent companion on a journey of this kind, I most definitely was not alone. My thanks to:

Barbara Binswanger, Anne David, Jan Garten, Esme Gibson, Bruce Gilbert, Lisa Gornick, Denise Kilgore, Ken Reilly, Vicky Watson, Judith Weiss, my parents Dick and Greta, and my siblings Alan, Jonathan, and Ann, for gifts of compassion and counsel, insight and support;

Edward Barnes, Barbara Brittingham, Helene Campbell, Susan Caughman, Susan Freivalds, Lois Gilman, Emma Hughes, Kristen Kelch, Herb Lotman, Mary Moo, and Gloria Nelson, for their generosity and assistance;

Jim Gaines, Walter Isaacson, and Jim Kelly, for *Time* on and time off, as needed;

Gail Hochman, for the vision and energy that set this project in motion;

Julie Rubenstein, for the nurturance and interest that saw it through to completion;

Becky Treen, for her patience and hugs;

Joe Treen, for standing firm as my truest critic and staunchest ally throughout the writing of this book.

An **Empty** Lap

Prelude

BECKY AND I ARE IN THE CHECKOUT LINE AT THE A&P, finishing our weekly grocery run. After a year of practice, we shop in brilliant unison. I steer the shopping cart that carries Becky; Becky carries the list that steers our shopping. I throw essentials in the cart; Becky throws nonessentials on the floor. I pick up the tab; Becky picks up strangers. Right now, she's doing what I think of as her campaign thing. "Hi," she says to the shopper behind us, and waves. "Hi," she says, turning to the clerk at the cash register. "Hi," she says, waving at the candy display.

The shopper, a woman of perhaps thirty-five, bursts out laughing. "Well, hello." As she talks to Becky, she glances at me tentatively, as if she's sizing me up. I know what's coming. I've had the conversation scores of times. Out of habit, I smile and nod, a gesture that's meant to convey, Yes, you can ask.

"Your daughter's adorable," she says. "Where is she from?"

"China."

"How old was she when you got her?"

"Seven months."

"How long did it take you to adopt her?"

"Seven months," I answer, supplying the information I know she means. "That's from the time we signed with the adoption agency to the day Becky came home."

As I say it, I feel much the way I always do: like a starlet who, after years of slaving unrecognized in off-off Broadway houses, awakens one morning to find herself acclaimed an "overnight success." Usually, I can laugh as well as bridle at my own facile suggestion that yes, you, too, can have a Becky in just seven months if you pick up the phone and dial this number. But today I feel only the hurt, none of the humor.

Earlier this day in February 1996, I'd received a phone call from a woman who said she'd be leaving for China soon to pick up her new daughter. My conversation with the stranger roamed over the intimate territory familiar to adoptive parents. How long did you do the infertility stuff? How long have you been trying to adopt? What agency are you using? How many times did you get burned? Finally, we got to the point of her call: travel advice.

"Are you doing this as a single parent or as part of a couple?" I asked, meaning only to ascertain whether she'd be juggling the travel logistics alone or with help.

"I'm a single parent." She punctuated her statement with an unconvincing laugh. "My ex-husband and I broke up over the child issue."

That answer had caught me unprepared. Since bringing Becky home, I've fielded hundreds of inquiries from people interested in adopting from China. Their questions, their fears, their hopes, their anxieties, come at me by post and phone, by fax and E-mail. They come from as near as two blocks from my house in New Jersey and from as far as London and Buenos Aires. But none has ever come as painfully close to home as that comment.

"I'm sorry," I said.

I'd been aching ever since.

Joe and Jill. Weasel & Weasel. A partnership formed in 1982, incorporated before a judge in 1985, and blessed with good prospects for a long, happy life. We were each other's best friend. Favorite playmate. Most trusted confidante. Truest critic. Staunchest ally. Ours was a dialogue that, whether affectionate or combative, was always interesting, always in search of compromise. Even at our most divisive, we both knew that somehow, someway, we would find our way back to each other.

From the start of our relationship, we had been forthright about children. I was pretty sure I wanted them, Joe was pretty sure he didn't. Since we each perceived in the other some room for movement, the difference didn't worry us. Lots of couples started out that way. The distance between us seemed navigable.

Then priorities shifted, needs changed. My squishy feelings about children congealed into certainty. Over a period of years, I whittled away at Joe's resistance, first patiently with coaxing, then restively with an edge. Along the way, I inverted the age-old strategy of having a baby to try to rescue a failing marriage; instead, I upended a stable relationship to try to make room for a child. When Joe finally relented, we thought the battle was over.

But it had barely begun. After biology refused to cooperate, I nudged Joe into fertility treatment. Pressed him into counseling. Dragged him into the convoluted maze of adoption. If the distractions of the nursery are tailor-made to temporarily divert shaky couples from confronting uneasy truths about themselves and their marriage, the unsparing demands of the adoption process are designed to force spouses into immediate confrontation over priorities, prejudices, and values. What age? What sex? What ethnicity? What health condition? How much will you spend? Will you pursue an open adoption, knowing the biological mother may change her mind? Or will you hunt overseas, where your orphaned or abandoned baby may come without a birthdate, let alone a medical or family history? What risks are you willing to take? How much control are you willing to surrender?

As the challenges and choices grew more difficult, my desire for a child ossified into desperation, while Joe's resistance hardened into vehement opposition. We still loved each other. Still wanted to be together. Still saw in each other a best friend, playmate, confidante, critic, and ally. But what did that get us when compromise had lost all meaning? There is no halfway about a child. You either have one, or you don't.

By the end of 1994, we stared at each other across a distance that was no longer navigable. The partnership of Weasel & Weasel seemed headed for dissolution, and though I thought I could see what was coming, I was not at all prepared for what followed.

Becky's giggle stirs me from my reverie. "I'm sorry?" I say.

"I said, 'Seven months, wow, that's fast.'" Gently, almost cautiously, the woman behind me in the grocery line is wiggling her fingers in front of Becky, who rewards her with a winning smile. "How old is she now?"

"Nineteen months." Closer to twenty, actually, but I haven't the energy to correct myself. As it is, I'm laboring to sound enthusiastic. From the gold band on the woman's hand, I can see she's married. From her tentative manner with Becky, I can tell she's not a mother. Her interest may be fleeting, just so much chitchat in a grocery line. But if the inquiry is more than casual, I want to be encouraging. She and her husband may be debating whether to continue fertility treatments. Or call it quits. Pursue adoption or surrogacy. Or remain childless. See a marriage counselor. Or consult a divorce attorney. If she is a fellow traveler, I want to be respectful of her unspoken pain.

I don't need the particulars of her story to know that when Nature's most basic design fails a couple, the deaths accrue. The deaths of dreams. Of expectations. Of hopes. Of fundamental assumptions. If this woman is finding her way through that unmarked cemetery, she hardly needs me to tell her that "seven months" does not begin to answer how long it took to adopt Becky.

Still, just once, I'd like to answer that question. From start to finish. Extracting from my years with Joe only those pieces that, in hindsight, seem relevant to the final picture that emerged after our bruising journey ended.

First, though, three caveats. Although I'm entitled to infringe on my own privacy, I'm not entitled to trespass on anybody else's. So, all names, save those of family members, have been changed. The institutional names, however, are real. Also, though I'll rely on my journals from time to time to let my younger self speak for herself, my forty-one-year-old self feels the need to caution that the voice in those journals is almost uniformly distressed. Although turmoil could always move me to write during those years, contentment and happiness rarely had the same effect.

Finally, I want to remind that though two people may travel together, they never make the same journey. In places where I know that Joe's recollections diverge pointedly from mine, I'll give him a brief say. But this is very much my account, not his. Perhaps, one day, Joe will write his own. I'd like to read that book. Becky, I imagine, might someday like to read it, too.

I

IT IS THE POSTSWIM, PREDINNER HOUR, AND THE smallest members of the clan are restless. Inside my parents' house, I can hear my two oldest nephews bickering over a game of Go Fish.

"You can't put that there, Alex."

"Can so."

"Cannot."

"Michael! Quit it!"

Outside on the deck, I smoke a cigarette on a chaise lounge beside my sister Ann and sister-in-law Candace, watching the distant nightlights shimmer against the dark folds of North Carolina's Blue Ridge Mountains. I am fine, certainly far better than I was a year earlier when I'd arrived for my family's 1993 annual reunion reeling from a doctor's shock bulletin that Joe and I would not be able to conceive a child. I'd spent most of that week holed up in my parents' yellow guest room, hiding from everyone, particularly my five young nieces and nephews.

Joe had spent most of that week worrying about my alarmingly fragile state of mind.

Now, I'm able to play Aunt Jill again. I've spent the afternoon dunking Michael in the pool and executing antic leaps off the diving board for Jeremy. With Emily, I've outfitted my parents' golden retrievers in absurd costumes, while with Alex and Shaina I've tiptoed around the flower beds, searching for elves.

Suddenly, the silence on the deck is shattered by my youngest niece, who bursts through the screen door, shrieking, "Mommy! Mommy!"

"What is it, sweetie?" Candace answers.

"Mommy!" Shaina says more insistently, raising her arms to be lifted onto Candace's lap.

A moment later, Ann's two children appear. Jeremy climbs onto my younger sister's lap, puts a thumb in his mouth and nestles his head against her chest. Emily stands stroking Ann's thigh, then tries to wrestle a place for herself by nudging Jeremy. Without opening his eyes, he moans, "Emmy! Stop it!"

Thinking only to keep the peace, I say, "I've got an empty lap here. Who wants to sit on my lap?" Emily answers by burrowing her head into Ann's stomach. After an uneasy silence, Ann whispers something in Emily's ear. My niece scrunches up her face quizzically, then walks toward me. Wrapping her arms around my waist, she murmurs, "I love you, Aunt Jill," then scurries back to Ann's embrace before I can finish saying, "I love you, too."

Then we all sit quietly. The mothers stroking their children. The children nuzzling their mothers. And me, wondering who will fill my empty lap.

It wasn't always this way, this obsession of mine with babies.

Once I was a rational, optimistic person who thought she had a pretty good handle on maintaining some balance in her life. The daughter of a man who'd built a thriving dress-manufacturing business on the philosophy, "You create your own 'luck,'" and a woman whose ever-present lists reinforced her favorite maxim, "You plan your work, then you work your plan," I believed that results rewarded effort. I wasn't afraid to go after the things I wanted, confident that if I exercised forethought and patience, steeled myself for disappointment, and didn't try to make too much happen at once, I could eventually build a life that had it all.

My "all" was reasonable, I thought. Not too overreaching. I wanted to build a writing career. Find a loving mate. Establish a solid marriage. Move to a house in the burbs. Raise some kids. So I found it baffling when friends and family would say, "You're so directed. You always know what you want." Sure, I knew what I wanted. But it wasn't like I had a clue what key this would play out in or what notes would be struck. I just knew the leitmotifs and was trying to compose a life, one movement at a time.

Maybe it was my concentration that fooled people. I have great concentration. It didn't occur to me that was anything unusual until my junior year at Princeton, when my older brother and I met at Grand Central Station to ride home together to Connecticut. After we learned the next train to Westport wouldn't leave for another forty minutes, I sat down on the floor of the noisy main terminal and went to work on a term paper. When I looked up to check the time, I noticed Alan standing over me, laughing.

"What's so funny?"

"Look around," he said. "Do you even know where you are?"

It took me a moment to get what he meant. Then I laughed, too.

When Alan recounted the absurd scene in the train station, some family member joked that I was "tunnel-visioned." The adjective became a staple in one of those quick profiles that parents like to trot out for strangers, and children like to insist are untrue. Mine goes: "Jill is the most studious of our four children, the one with tunnel vision. She can be demanding of others, but she's hardest on herself. We never had to worry about punishing Jill. She always did that herself. She has a capable, tough exterior, and a soft, rather fragile interior that she hides from the world." Though I thought the tunnel-vision bit implied a narrowness that was unfair, I regarded my concentration as an advantage—that is, until I experienced just how dark and cramped the tunnel could be.

I've always had an aversion to tight physical spaces. On the day I was born, I was apparently so eager to escape the womb that my mother almost had me in the hospital elevator. Three years later when I accidentally locked myself in a friend's closet, I was so panicked I'd never get out that my mother heard my frightened screams an eighth of a mile away. I still hate situations that make me feel trapped. If a subway car has the packed look of a cattle car, I'll wait for the next train; if a party threatens to be one of those affairs where people sip cocktails pressed nose to nose, I'll find an excuse to stay away.

I'm the same way about tight psychic spaces. Most of the time my instincts help me steer clear of them. I cruise along, adjusting to what is, ignoring or shrugging off what isn't, and relying on peripheral vision to keep my gaze from settling on any one aggravation for too long. On those occasions when a problem is so absorbing that it narrows my range of vision to a single point, my mind will start racing round and round in search of an exit. Almost always, I find the escape within weeks, if not days.

Only twice has a problem proved so intractable that it dragged on for months. In both instances, the longer I couldn't find the exit, the more desperate and uninterrupted my mental thrashing became. Over time, I lost my capacity to look around. See where I was. Laugh. As absorption gave way to obsession, I was propelled into the darkest and tightest tunnel of all: depression.

One of those times, the issue was babies.

But let's leave babies out of this for a while. Let's talk instead about Weasel & Weasel. Once I get going on babies, they'll overrun these pages, just as they overran the space in my life that was once reserved for Jill and Joe.

Funny.

That should have been Joe's line.

When I first fell for Joe, I was twenty-six and very much focused on building my career. Marriage was an idea that teased more than tantalized. Children were, as yet, a distant hypothetical. I felt directed, secure, in control of my life.

I was, of course, grossly deluded.

I'd joined *Newsweek* in June 1981 as a writer for the international editions. When I reported for work the first day, a lanky editor with a touch of gray in his hair and a hint of Tanqueray on his breath escorted me to a windowless office in sorry need of a paint job.

"There's an empty office with windows," he said, his tone at once apologetic and defensive, "but we're holding that for Joe Treen, a reporter who's coming over from *Newsday* after the summer. He's got a lot more experience than you. It's only fair."

At the time, I didn't care. Fresh from four years of clerical and reporting duties in the cavernous newsroom of *The New York Times*, I thought it a great treat no longer to have to lock myself in a bathroom stall to secure a few minutes of privacy. But as the months passed and that windowed office remained vacant, I began to resent the alleged hotshot from *Newsday*. By the time Joe showed up in October, I was primed to detest him. As we shook hands and introduced ourselves, I smiled pleasantly and thought, "Schmuck."

Joe quickly dispelled my preconception of a prima donna. Though he was older than the rest of the international writing staff and more seasoned, having covered everything from Evel

Knievel's jump over the Snake River Canyon to the Yom Kippur War in the Middle East, he was amiable and unpretentious and had the deepest laugh I'd ever heard. The confidence that he exuded was offset by a shyness that seemed as uncalculated as Joe's nescience of his anchorman-style good looks. Though his chiseled cheeks, thick mass of hair, and warm smile screamed, "Camera-ready," he seemed not to hear it.

Almost immediately, we gravitated toward each other, tugged initially by our mutual newspaper backgrounds. We had plenty of time to talk since the trade-off for delivery from daily deadlines was a killer of a weekly closing that held us captive in the office from Friday mornings until the predawn hours of Saturday. Typically, that meant long stretches of downtime waiting for edits and layouts. As our conversation extended over weeks, we came to know a lot about each other.

I'd grown up in a close, private family, the first daughter in a boy-girl-boy-girl lineup. Security seemed a fact of life. I'd spent my entire childhood in the same prosperous suburb, same sprawling ranch house, same excellent school system. If life was never boring, it was also never unplanned: ski weekends followed the school week, summer camp and jobs followed the school year, college followed high school graduation. My parents turned up for both sons' Little League games, both daughters' piano recitals, all performances of all kids' school plays. Because they made each of us feel loved and special, I still cannot recall any sibling rivalry, despite the four of us having been born within five years. "It was my parents' greatest magic," I told Joe. "I remain very tight with my siblings."

Though rules were few, my parents' expectations were clear, consistent and unflinching. Major Jewish holidays were for family, no excuses. Bickering and screaming were not tolerated, period. And though discussion and debate were encouraged, once my parents made up their minds about something, they were a united, unyielding front. It was assumed that my siblings and I would go straight from college to work. It was anticipated that each of us would eventually heed my mother's injunction, sometimes humorous, sometimes earnest, to "get married, have babies." It was hoped that, like our parents' bond, our commitment to our partners would be paramount and permanent after we married. As yet, none of us had.

Joe told me that his parents were a similarly devoted pair, who held weekends in reserve for Joe, his younger sister Esme, and each other. Initially, family time meant attendance at Episcopal church services. After the Treens began breeding dalmatians, it meant dog shows.

Despite his family's stability, Joe had felt unsettled during most of his youth. A "corporate brat," he'd hated the periodic relocations to new states and new suburbs that had attended his father's ascent through management ranks. Although early on he'd been a reluctant loner who constantly felt disliked and displaced, by his teens, Joe had emerged as a gregarious prankster who wielded his humor and wit to make fast inroads at three different midwest high schools.

Upon completing his undergraduate work at the University of Wisconsin, Joe fled east, vowing never to return to either the Midwest or the suburbs, both of which he found stifling. After earning a masters degree in journalism from Syracuse University, he joined the reporting staff of *Newsday*, the daily on Long Island, where he remained for the next twelve years, minus an unexpected eighteen-month stint at Fort Eustis after his army reserve unit was mobilized during the Vietnam war.

Thirteen years my senior, Joe had done a lot more living than I. He'd married in 1965 while in grad school, divorced five years later, rebounded into a second marriage, then divorced within a year of that. Joe's life, I thought, sounded bold and unconventional. Certainly far more adventurous than mine.

Even so, we found much in common. A love of theater. A passion for travel. A twin devotion to writing and introspection that found expression in the keeping of journals. Each of us tended toward self-deprecating humor, and away from pretension in ourselves and others.

Serial monogomists both, we were each involved in years-long relationships, he to an outgoing secretary with a flare for throwing elaborate dinner parties, I to Marc, a fellow *Times* journalist, whose keen intellect, unwavering kindness, and talent for remaining calm, no matter what the circumstance, I much admired. Though Joe and I adored our current mates, neither of us quite saw in them a life's companion.

After months of these late-night chats, Joe admitted with a modesty bordering on embarrassment that he had written a few plays. When I asked to read one, I discovered a wonderfully imaginative writer whose words made me laugh out loud. I gushed. Joe blushed. It was around then that I stopped thinking of him as just another colleague. Our discussions became more flirtatious, more playful, more intimate.

One night, Joe confided that he felt out of place at *Newsweek.* "Everyone is younger. So ivy league and preppy."

"I may be younger and ivy league, but at least I'm not a preppy. Besides," I scoffed, "you're midwestern white bread. That amounts to the same thing."

"Anyone can be a preppy," he countered. "You just have to own plastic ducks."

"Well, there you have it. I don't own any plastic ducks."

The next day I found an inch-high yellow plastic duck standing on my desk with a note that read: "Zap! You're a preppy!"

After that, we touched hands in a darkened movie theater. We kissed in a park. We tangled on the floor of his apartment. I shared my favorite joke with him: "Why did the monkey fall out of the tree? Because it was dead." We laughed so hard that we clutched our sides, tears rolling down our cheeks, our eyes locked on one another as we gasped for breath.

We were, it appeared, in love.

In July 1982, Joe and I broke off our respective relationships, each of us feeling wrenched and guilty, but eager to see if our mutual infatuation could evolve into something more enduring.

From the start, I sensed with Joe the potential to forge the kind of connection I hoped for in a marriage, a love memorably described by Milan Kundera as a "constant interrogation." Affectionate and unafraid to show vulnerability, Joe was blessed with a great gift for intimacy. His eagerness to question, listen, and engage made him interesting and made me feel irreplaceable. His determination to keep growing ("relentlessly self-improving," I teased) promised to keep both of us from settling into complacency. His insightful observations, I thought, would challenge me to probe deeper and confront unexamined truths about myself.

In other words Joe wouldn't put up with my bullshit.

But the same Joe who could inspire was also capable of wielding his candor to devastating effect. The first time Joe erupted over some minor matter, I fled back to Marc, befogged with fear that I'd given up a comfortable, secure relationship for a fling with a madman. Soon, I was back with Joe. Then Marc. Then Joe.

My behavior, heartless and inexcusable, was a heedless expression of the debate raging within me. I felt I was choosing not only between two very different men, but between two very different versions of the me, as-yet unformed, who might emerge from each of those relationships.

I thought Marc reinforced many of my natural inclinations; Joe challenged me to exercise muscles that were atrophying from disuse. Where Marc massaged my intellect, Joe stimulated my emotions. In Marc I saw devotion, reliability, aversion to change; in Joe, excitement, spontaneity, unpredictability. Marc, who'd once told me, "You're the sanest woman I've ever known," inspired confidence and contentment. Joe, who early on maintained I was "as fragile as a China doll," aroused my creativity and passion. If my four years with Marc had been a soothing, warm bath, life with Joe promised to be a hot whirlpool.

By the time I stopped bouncing back and forth, Joe and I were as wary of each other as we were smitten. Joe mistrusted my intentions, I mistrusted his temper. Though we were cozily compatible when all was calm, we were badly mismatched when the peace shattered. Joe's battle style was confrontational and loud, with a quick recovery time. My own weapons, honed in a family where voices were never raised and grievances were seldom addressed frontally, were better suited to the style of warfare known as psychological operations. Edgy silence. Sniper attack. Rapid-fire rationalization. Then withdrawal and days of pouting.

"Why must you inflate every unintended misdemeanor into a premeditated felony?" I'd demand after his explosions.

"Why must you overreact to everything I say?" he'd counter. "When I get angry like that, just tune me out and give me twenty-four hours to calm down."

It was sound advice, but in those days Joe's mood was so variable that I seldom knew whom I'd encounter from one hour to the next. At work, would my E-mail be answered by supportive Joe, who could lighten any office irritation with his humor, or snappish Joe, who didn't want to be disturbed? When I returned from dinner with a friend, would I be greeted by playful Joe, dancing to Joe Cocker with a pair of socks dangling from his ears, or jealous Joe, demanding to know why he hadn't been invited? If I proposed a weekend outing, would the RSVP come from best pal Joe, who loved to go exploring with me, or frustrated Joe, who accused me of conspiring to steal time from his playwriting?

Though Joe told me repeatedly that he was "significantly depressed" about the approach of his fortieth birthday, I was too young and too myopic to see what was needed. Instead of giving Joe room, I crowded closer, determined to convince him—and myself—that I wasn't all the things he said I was: rude, selfish, unfeeling, inconsiderate, demanding, intrusive, uncaring.

Then his anger would pass as swiftly as it had come. While he rebounded, I'd brood. "Why don't you ever see all I do to hold this relationship together?" I'd demand. "Why do you always feel you have to 'do' something?" he'd answer.

Soon, he'd say, "It's over," and try to tease away my glum mood. "It's over for you," I'd sulk. "It's not over for me."

Eventually, Joe could kid me out of anything. He'd sing (desperately off-key). Dance (a gyration that reminded me of the Freddy). Or bow-wow to one of my classical records (must have been all those dalmatians).

After we could laugh again, we'd hear each other out and try to sift the truths from the gross exaggerations. We'd make our peace, kiss, vow to do better.

In March 1983, Joe moved into my apartment on the fifth floor of a walk-up in Chelsea. Though Joe maintained a safety net by subletting his apartment, we told each other that we regarded this move as a prelude to marriage. For the first few weeks, we felt oppressed by each other. Small stuff that had never rankled before suddenly grated. When Joe would burst into guffaws while reading in bed, I'd stiffen, resentful that he'd disrupted my own reading. When I would complain that Joe's accumulating mounds of newspapers were a fire hazard, Joe would bridle that I allowed no room for him to be himself. I couldn't stomach his rock music; he found my taste in jazz indigestible.

Then, we began to settle in. I started giggling at the Calvin and Hobbes cartoons Joe passed my way; he started taking an interest in the literary novels stacked on my night table. We carved out "Jill-free zones" where Joe could stack and litter without fear of me straightening up behind him, and "Joe-free zones" where I could work without threat of his encroaching mess. I learned to tolerate Randy Newman, Joe came to abide Laura Nyro. Together, we discovered Art Tatum and Etta James.

Somewhere in there I stopped regarding Joe as Marc's antidoppelganger or my missing link and began to appreciate him for himself. Through the habits of daily life, I came to see his tenacity and determination. His attentiveness to family, loyalty to friends, generosity to strangers. In a city filled with poseurs, Joe remained spontaneous, natural, unaffected. As his depression lifted and his mood evened, I discovered not only a far nicer guy than I'd imagined, but someone more steady and reliable. Joe's anger, I came to see, was neither free-floating nor constant. Actually, he had a tendency to stockpile frustrations for long periods, then erupt in a single, confused outburst that could take him days, even weeks, to sort out.

During the work week, our rhythms were contrapuntal. I was a straight line of motion from bed to office to writing my week's story. Joe was more likely to jog, schmooze, and dally over the newspapers before settling down to work. On weekends, we were like that toy with a half-dozen metal balls hanging from a rack. We might collide as we flung ourselves at each other from opposite directions, but we'd quickly absorb the impact and soon be swaying, at the same speed, in the same direction. Sunday nights we'd groan, "I miss you, Wease," then steel for the week ahead.

The more uninterrupted time we had together, the more relaxed and in sync we became. Often we were at our best on the road, where there was never any question who was in charge. Early on, Joe had aptly dubbed me a "directional dyslexic." He thought my unfailing instinct to turn the wrong way was the product of a shoddy education in the East, where geography lessons lack the reverential rigor they enjoy in the Midwest. My own theory was that it was the difference in our heritages, mine Jewish, his part Cherokee. "Your people are trackers," I reminded him. "Mine wandered in the wilderness for forty years."

In Mexico, we roamed lazily through the vendor stalls in Oaxaca and discovered a compatible taste in art. During a trip to England, we clowned along the walls of York and in London discovered a shared taste for Alan Ayckbourne comedies. In the highlands of Scotland, we baaed at the sheep and discovered a mutual taste for nicknames. (Trust me. You don't want to know about the Weasel business unless you have an airbag handy.) No matter where we went, time alone together only made us crave more of each other's company.

Life with Joe was proving to be not only the constant interrogation I'd hoped for, but a far more pleasant give and take than I'd anticipated. I was increasingly certain that Joe was the person I wanted to and would marry. Joe gave every indication that he felt the same way about me.

We still had much to learn about each other.

In August 1983, my younger brother Jonathan became the first of my siblings to make his way to the altar. There were mostly Protestants on the bride's side of the aisle, mostly Jews on ours, and a red-carpeted swath of unease in between. Joe and I watched the ensuing drama warily. We'd often joked about writing our own wedding vows, things like, "No screwing around, no bow-wowing to Beethoven." Jonathan's wedding inspired more serious discussion. Whom was the wedding pageant for? Who could perform a service that would satisfy us, yet leave both sets of parents comfortable? What should the content of that ceremony be? Even so, I felt no urgency about marriage.

Five months later, my first journal entry for 1984 mentions elliptically: *Joe and I have entered "discussion" pending decision on the "big M": marriage. The conversations, few to date, have been mixed.*

A few weeks later on a chilly Tuesday morning, I awoke to discover all the blankets piled on Joe's side of the bed. "Goddamn it," I muttered, and gave the blankets a rude yank that awakened Joe. *I got the "You're a selfish bitch" spiel, but there was something more in it. Joe is talking of a breakup. This has come out of nowhere for me; clearly not for him.*

As winter snows turned to spring showers, our relationship plunged into free fall. Though the connection between our talk of marriage and his talk of leaving now seems obvious, at the time I thought we were squabbling about houses.

Our hunt for a country home had begun casually, an outgrowth of the driving and biking trips we liked to take through the Berkshire mountains. I thought I'd made clear that for me, houses were about planting roots, not staking assets. When we came upon a house that Joe wanted us to buy, he was surprised by my insistence that I wouldn't consider a joint investment of such magnitude until we were married. He grew angry, convinced that I'd deliberately misled him. I couldn't believe he was so irrational; he couldn't believe I was so inflexible.

Joe demanded that we see a marriage counselor. Soon we were facing each other in the office of a Central Park West therapist named Grace, going at each other like two guests on *Geraldo.*

"Jill expects all sorts of trappings to go with a house, including marriage," Joe fumed.

"I regard a house as a trapping to marriage," I shot back.

"You're buying two different houses," Grace said, slicing through our nonsense with admirable efficiency. "Jill is buying a home. Joe is buying a shelter."

Over the next three months in weekly sessions with Grace, I became a lot less relaxed about the issue of marriage. Though Joe had told me about his two marriages and his "fear of failing again," I'd assumed he just needed time to gain confidence in us. Now, I began to suspect that Joe might be content to remain single permanently. For me that was not an option. If, until now, marriage had seemed a distant someday appointment, it was nevertheless an appointment I intended to keep.

At our final session, Grace assessed us as a "compatible couple with no fundamental problems." We could talk through and resolve problems. We shared many interests. We had fun together. She described Joe as emotional, me as practical, and suggested we could learn from each other.

"But Joe," Grace said, "is going to have to resolve his own ambivalence about commitment." If he doesn't, she warned, he'd probably hit the same point in some other relationship two years up the road. "Jill," she predicted, "won't wait much longer."

In the meantime, she said to me, "It would help if you could learn not to take Joe so seriously."

I thought all aspects of Grace's analysis were sound, save one: the part where I wouldn't wait much longer. The prospect of a breakup filled me with dread. Every part of it. Particularly the part where I landed up alone.

Soon after that session, Joe confided to Richard, the colleague to whom he'd sublet his apartment, that we were heading for a bust up. Richard, he suggested, should start looking for a new place. Unfazed, Richard answered, "It sounds like you're getting married." Richard, appropriately, went on to a brilliant Hollywood career in TV comedy writing.

Throughout the fall, as Joe spoke more frequently of leaving, I became someone I barely recognized. I clung, I implored, I pleaded. I couldn't, wouldn't, let go. And Joe, as ambivalent about a breakup as he was about a commitment, wouldn't let go either. Bound by our mutual inability to move on, I began to despise him. Us. Most of all, me.

Then in early November, a well-liked *Newsweek* writer, just thirty-two years old, died of heart failure while swimming laps at a midtown health club. It spooked everyone in our department. Dana was there one day; he wasn't there the next. Dana had told me over a recent lunch that he and his wife had just bought a house and were about to adopt a baby. At the memorial service, Joe and I held hands, feeling closer than we had in a long time.

A few weeks later, my sister Ann announced her engagement to an architect named Jim. Ann and Jim's plans threw back at me our own indecision. Joe, I was now convinced, could fence-sit forever. Dana's death had been a reminder that I didn't have forever. None of us did. For the first time, I felt the weight of an approaching birthday, my thirtieth.

Suddenly, my impatience kicked in and my will came surging back with a vengeance. I reminded myself that I'd never been the sort of romantic who believed there was only one man in the universe for me. If Joe wouldn't give me what I wanted, then I'd get through the pain of a breakup and find someone who would.

Angry and determined, I set a date several weeks away. "I need an answer by then. Yes, we marry. No, I'm out of here." Then I waited out the weeks, silent on the subject of marriage.

When the day arrived, I waited nervously for Joe to say something. At the office, he offered no clue what he was thinking. We came home. Showered. Ate our standard mid-week dinner: a pint of Häagen-Dazs and a box of cookies. Sat on the couch, held hands, watched *Hillstreet Blues*. Still nothing.

"So," I said, as the credits rolled. "What's it going to be?"

"What's what going to be?"

"The marriage thing. Yes or no."

Joe looked at me with a twisted smile. After a long pause, he said, "No."

The smile threw me for a second. He was joking, right? Then, I got it: Joe hadn't taken my deadline seriously. "That's it," I said quietly. "You should leave."

We talked calmly for a time. But the longer we talked, the more apparent it became that he had no intention of going.

"Why am I the one who has to leave? Why don't you?" he asked.

"Because this is my apartment."

"It's my apartment, too."

He called me immature. I called him self-centered. He shouted that I was inconsiderate and impatient. "Why do we have to make a decision this minute?" he demanded.

I went to the bedroom, called my friend Beth, and packed a bag. Then I trudged down Eighth Avenue and stayed the night with Beth and her husband John in their Village apartment.

The next morning Joe came to my office door and asked if we could talk. Fine, I said. We went round and round. He told me I was the most "vibrant, interesting, and stimulating woman" he'd ever known. "I fear if we don't get married, I'll never marry again, but I need more time. Why can't you wait?"

"I've been waiting since last spring," I answered, unmoved. "How much longer do you suggest?"

" 'Til I'm ready," he snapped.

I put on my coat. "I'm leaving."

He looked stunned. I started to cry. We reached for one another. "Marry me," he said. "This is a proposal."

I pulled back. "Are you serious?"

"Marry me," he repeated.

Though we celebrated that night with champagne, I was so chary of his proposal that I told no one. Within a week Joe was saying that he didn't want to get married, but that he didn't want to break up with me either. Within two I was back at Beth and John's, waiting for Joe to move out of my apartment.

At *Newsweek*, I worked with my door closed and went the long way round to the ladies' room to avoid passing Joe's office. Three nights later, Joe called me at Beth's to say he would stay with a friend until Richard moved out of his apartment; I could return home. Calmly, we discussed how we would divide up our mutual purchases. Quietly, we agreed this was very sad.

When I got home from work the next evening, I couldn't sit still. I wanted every trace of Joe expunged. I put a Smokey Robinson album on the stereo, moved the needle to "Tracks of My Tears," and began decoupling our libraries. By two-thirty, I'd boxed an entire wall of Joe's books, dismantled his hanging walnut shelves, and spackled every hole.

The next morning, Joe walked into my office and closed the door. "Marry me," he said.

"Get out," I said, pointing toward the door.

"I mean it."

"Please. Just go away."

"Will you marry me?" Then he started to cry, something I'd never seen him do. "It was the spackling," he said. When he'd gone to the apartment that morning to get a belt, he'd seen the patched wall. "Until that moment, I hadn't believed we were really splitting up."

"I don't need this," I said.

"Marry me," he persisted.

"I have to work. Go away. I'll think about it."

Later, I went home, climbed into bed with my journals, and for the first time read every entry I'd written since we'd met, hoping the answer would become apparent. But as I moved from the first infatuated *G-d, I like you, Treen*, to the last fuming, *He always wants out—except when I want out; then he wants in*, I saw only that though there was ample evidence of the Joe who was unsettled and frustrated, the more frequent companion who loved and let me love was nowhere to be found in those pages.

I turned out the light and tried to see us as we really were. We emerged as contradictory as ever: critical and supportive, ill-suited and well matched, angrily embattled and intimately engaged. An imperfect couple, true. But trying, always trying, to understand each other better.

Pride advised, *Screw him if he doesn't know a good thing when he sees it.*

Reason reminded, *You'll never find everything you seek in one man.*

Fear warned, *The pain of a breakup will be short-lived, but the pain of a life with Joe will be enduring.*

The Calendar prodded, *You're almost thirty; it's time.*

And Love whispered, *Kundera never promised that a life of constant interrogation would be easy.*

At around ten o'clock, decided yet undecided, I called Joe and said he could come over. We talked and talked. Sometime around midnight, I said I'd marry him.

"Yes?" he said.

"Yes."

"She says, 'Yes!'" He picked me up and twirled me around.

After New Year's, we set an April date and began to make wedding plans. Neither of us had the time or interest to fret the details, so we made most decisions together and quickly. For the ceremony, we picked a judge and the UN chapel (both nondenominational), for the reception a Chelsea restaurant (spacious and funky). We picked a menu (brunch food), a band (schlock city) and a photographer (a *Newsweek* colleague). We picked invitations (black script on beige cards), a guest list (about one hundred people), and a musician for the ceremony (a classical guitarist whom I'd discovered playing in a subway station). Independently, I picked a maid of honor and the flowers. Independently, Joe picked a best man and the fights.

Six weeks before our scheduled appointment at the altar, he

demanded that I cancel the wedding. "We're only getting married because you're too chicken to tell people that it's off," he accused.

"You want to call it off? Fine. *You* call it off," I responded. "I'm planning to get married."

I began having jilted-at-the-altar fantasies. Then I went on the offensive, ginning up fantasies where I was the jiltee. I imagined myself saying, "No," if he glowered during the ceremony. If his "I do" lacked conviction. If he so much as looked nervous. Then Joe calmed down, and I decided I could live with nervous.

Our wedding day, April 21, 1985, dawned a bit hot, a bit humid. I was calm while my mother's stylist did my hair, calm while I posed for pictures with my sister, calm when, moments before noon, I stepped into the foyer of the UN chapel and took my father's arm. Then, I began to shake uncontrollably. My last thought before I started down the aisle was, *If Joe is smiling when I come through that door, we'll be okay.*

The door swung back, I stepped into the chapel and looked down the rows of pews. When my eyes found Joe's, he burst into the most beatific smile I'd ever seen. It was a glorious smile. A joyful smile. A smile that said, "You look beautiful! I'm so glad we're doing this!"

When I reached his side, he took my hand, then, feeling how badly I was trembling, placed his other hand on my back.

The judge smiled reassuringly and tried to ignore the photographer, who was tackling the assignment with news-gathering gusto. After a brief greeting, the judge said, "Usually on occasions like this, I offer some words of encouragement for the bride and groom. But, as you know, you can't tell journalists anything." Then, as our guests laughed appreciatively, our judge, the stand-up comedian, launched into the standard interrogation. "Do you, Joe—" "Do you, Jill—"

"—You may kiss the bride." Self-consciously, Joe and I

pecked one another on the lips. We started to back away, then impetuously grabbed each other and locked in a kiss that had the intensity of a Vulcan-mind probe, inspiring a noisy ovation from family and friends.

From that moment forward, Joe never again mentioned his ambivalence about marriage.

II

SO, WHERE IN THAT WAS MY HUNGER FOR A BABY? Where was the appetite so rapacious that it would devour all other parts of my life, putting my career on stall, my mind in disarray, my marriage on the line? Where was the craving so insatiable that I would search four continents for a child I could call my own?

My friends, family, and husband would say that it didn't exist. And they would be right. They would maintain that I wasn't one of those women poised to hit a biological land mine and get hysterical. And I would agree. Some of them would even argue that I had no intention of having kids. But there, they would be wrong. I knew I wanted kids. Not just one. Two. Parents are, by definition, neanderthals; every kid, I believed, needs an ally.

But wanting children in the abstract and wanting them in the flesh are two different impulses entirely. If anything, I felt uncomfortable around small children, awkward and tentative, embarrassed to show affection. When a baby would squawl on an airplane, I was one of those unknowing people who'd roll my eyes and shoot dark looks. I could ogle a baby, play patty-cake, make a child laugh. But the moment that smile turned to tears, I'd hand off the infant, muttering, "What *is* it about me and kids?" I found it irritating when children interrupted adult conversation, and I thought parents who couldn't stop their kids from screwing up the VCR buttons lacked in the discipline department.

When I would talk with female friends about children, we tended to exercise our minds, not our hearts. How long, we asked each other, would we need or want to stay home before returning to work? Three days? Three weeks? God help us, three months? How would we juggle the demands of babies and bosses, households and husbands? Would our mates pull their fair share of the load, or would we have to nag them into compliance?

This last issue was a particular sticking point with me, and had been ever since an unsettling exchange with Marc at the peak of our relationship, a good year before I met Joe. At the time, Marc was polishing his Spanish skills and reading up on foreign affairs in hopes of being posted overseas. Since I could no more imagine giving up my job to follow a man's career than I could imagine asking a man to follow mine, both activities pissed me off.

After months of stewing, I finally demanded, "If we went overseas, what would *I* do?"

"I don't know," Marc answered, his tone unconcerned. "Maybe that's when you'd raise the kids."

" 'The kids?' They'd be your kids, too. What makes you think I'd want to stay home anymore than you would?"

"I've always assumed that if we had kids, you'd stay home."

I looked at him blankly. "Why would you assume that?"

"Well," he said, "why would anyone want to have kids if they didn't want to stay home to take care of them?"

"I don't hear *you* talking about staying home."

"Children need their mothers."

That conversation made a deep impression. Marc was very much a professional woman's man, supportive of women's careers in general and his female friends' in particular. If *he* could harbor such arcane assumptions, I felt, then women in general and I in particular must approach family with romantic blinders off and reality lenses sharply focused.

But throughout my twenties, I had little interest in what that reality might be. Unprompted, my thoughts seldom strayed into child territory. The journals I kept during my first three years with Joe mention children just seven times; most of those references are no more than a sentence or two. Perhaps because I regarded children as one of life's givens, I was poised primarily to take. "I want to have kids," I always wrote; never "I want to be a mother." My main reason for wanting to have kids was an uneasy certainty I would live to regret it if I didn't. Though I entertained no reveries of rainy-day snuggles, I had no trouble imagining myself in widowed old age, yearning for the companionship of a grown son or daughter.

The first musing about kids comes just four months into my relationship with Joe, when I was still reeling from the breakup with Marc. Convinced that Marc and I had waited too long to level on too many important issues, kids among them, I resolved to tell Joe that I eventually wanted children. This required a summoning of courage that women who spent their twenties raising kids or mentally decorating the nursery will find incomprehensible. To me, it seemed an admission of weakness, a sneak preview of the ordinariness of my soul.

"I'm gonna want kids," I said one day. "Not now, but someday."

I don't remember Joe's exact response. My journal notes only, *We talked about children. He sounds ambivalent*. I do recall, however, that the exchange was brief. That Joe didn't freak out at the mention of children. That his answer struck me as nothing to worry about. And that I changed the subject quickly.

During Joe's moody period prior to his fortieth birthday, I sounded a few brief alarms about his potential fitness as a father. Things like, *I worry what kind of example he would be, always up and down.*

Only once was my concern kindled by an actual encounter with a child. Shortly after we moved in together in 1983, Joe and I traveled to Mexico for some serious vegging out in the tiny coastal town of Puerto Escondido. During the first four days, nothing disturbed our shared solitude or disrupted the routine we fell into effortlessly. Up at dawn with the roosters for a sunrise walk along the beach. Breakfast. A morning by the pool reading and swimming. Lunch. A nap. Back to the pool for chilled beers and more reading. A sunset walk on the beach. Dinner. X-rated stuff. Sleep. Next day: repeat.

On the fifth day, as we were settling down with our novels, the hoards began to descend. Puerto Escondido, we now learned, was a popular weekend retreat for Mexico's urbanites. The chairs around the pool filled. The splashing in the pool intensified. The noise level ratcheted up about a billion decibels. And this one kid, about age eight, slowly began to drive us crazy. First with his shouting. Then with his splashing. Then with his frisbee. Joe and I exchanged a lot of meaningful looks and tried to escape back into our books.

"Is there capital punishment for murder in Mexico?" Joe joked before giving up on his book and climbing into the pool.

He was looking the other way when the kid misaimed his frisbee and conked Joe on the head. "No!" Joe shouted, and flung the frisbee onto the deck. For a brief moment, everyone stopped to look at the angry gringo. Joe hurried out of the pool and came toward me, looking for reassurance I couldn't give.

What Joe would take from that incident was a memory of my failure to support him in a moment of need and a recollection that he later apologized to the boy's father. What would stick with me was the image of him flaring at a child. *I was appalled. Is that how he's going to deal with our children?*

Twenty months would pass before the next mention of children. This time, the inspiration would be our impasse over marriage. "I've been talking with my sister," Joe said. "Esme says, 'Given Jill's age, she'll want to have kids right away.'"

"I don't think that's true," I answered.

"I can deal with marriage, but not kids."

"Well," I said, "I can't guarantee that I won't want them eventually."

After sleeping on that, I raised the subject again. *I told Joe that I thought he was using the child issue as an excuse not to get married. He didn't disagree.*

On the night we decided to get married, I asked Joe to promise to keep an open mind about children. He said he'd try. That was good enough for me. I figured that if Joe could overcome his ambivalence about marriage, he could do the same about kids.

After that, more than four years would pass before I felt sufficiently roused to write about children again.

During those years, Joe and I worked hard and played hard. We became infatuated with each other all over again. It helped that the day after we returned from an idyllic three-week honeymoon in Greece and England, I started a new job.

After we'd gotten engaged, I'd launched a job search, seeking to carve a greater distance between our offices. By doing the same job in the same department at the same magazine, Joe and I were unable to escape work. Too often our home discussions lapsed into shop talk, perhaps an inevitability given that we shared not only the same colleagues, same work headaches, and same office intrigues, but similar assignments as well. Once our romance became known, editors tended to regard us as interchangeable. "Treen's not available? Okay, what's Jill doing?"

A few weeks before the wedding, I landed a position as a foreign affairs writer for *Time*. When we returned from our honeymoon, the mound of mail included a clipping from the *New York Post*'s gossip page. The item featured a judge who had performed three wedding services in a single day, the last of them involving a Broadway celebrity couple. Joe and I were mentioned because our ceremony had been the first of the judge's tripleheader. The item identified Joe as working for *Time*, me for *Newsweek*. My new editor at *Time* had scrawled in the margin: "Hey, which one of you did we hire, anyway?" The *Post*'s screwup seemed an appropriate coda to my *Newsweek* career.

Now, with me across town at *Time*, Joe and I no longer strained against one another. When a friend asked us, "How's married life?" Joe responded, "Very quiet. We can't talk about work until both magazines are put to bed. And we're not fighting over whether we're getting married. So, we have nothing to say to each other." That answer cracked us up and became our stock response.

The greatest distance between us was the degree of enthusiasm each of us had for urban living and for our jobs. After eight years in the same cramped apartment, I itched to move to more spacious quarters, preferably in a town with trees. Joe was all for roomier accommodations, but couldn't imagine living anywhere but Manhattan. As for work, while I was delighted by *Time*, finding the atmosphere collegial and my assignments challenging, Joe was growing increasingly impatient with the weekly grind. He wanted to write a novel.

A year into married life, we agreed that this was the optimal time for him to do it. We had no financial burdens, no obligations to kids; we could make do on one salary. To keep his hand in journalism and make pocket money, Joe signed on as a freelance reporter for the *Boston Globe* and a commentator for a radio station in Australia. Then in February 1986, he left *Newsweek*.

The following autumn, we finally bought a country house. We were driving north through Pennsylvania on I-81 to visit my brother Jonathan in upstate New York, when our aging Toyota Tercel emitted a metallic grinding sound, then sputtered to a stop. Conveniently, the car had died within feet of a sloping exit ramp with a gas station at the bottom.

"It's a rear wheel bearing," a mechanic said. "It'll take about three hours to replace."

While roaming through a nearby shopping mall, we noticed that the houses pictured in the window of a real estate office advertised prices half that of Berkshire properties. Every year that I'd delayed our purchase of a country home, prices had leapt another twenty thousand dollars. These pricetags suggested that we might yet land up with something larger than a heated tent.

Soon we were cruising the unpaved backroads of the Endless Mountains. Plush with a thick canopy of oak, ash, and maple foliage and an understory of fern and wild berries, the region was less developed than the Berkshires. Stay alert, the realtor said, and we might see deer, wild turkey, fox, even black bear. That day, we saw three houses that convinced us to explore further.

When we returned the following weekend, we saw maybe ten houses. As we drove up the long driveway of the last property, I knew before we even entered the house that this was the one. The grounds, bordered along one flank by a steep, wooded hill, offered the privacy I sought. When we walked through the front door into a large, airy kitchen, then spotted the spacious living room with a ceiling too high to touch, Joe and I traded a look that told me he was sold, too. Veteran house hunters, we telegraphed cool interest while the realtor prattled on about how the owners, two school teachers, had left the eight-year-old house in mint condition.

As Joe conducted his ritual inspection of the utility room, I surveyed the two-point-five bedrooms upstairs. The point-five was a small room with a sharply sloping ceiling. Perfect for children, I thought. By that I meant nephews and nieces; already, Jonathan had a son, and he and Candace were planning future additions.

We placed our bid that day. Five weeks later, we were proud home owners. As we drove from the bank closing to the house, Joe pointed out every rundown trailer and piece of litter along the way that might drive down property values. "Wease," he gasped, clutching his throat. "I think I'm becoming a Republican."

When we entered the house, we carried on like little kids, whooping, dancing, and taking running jumps to try to touch the living room ceiling. Never mind that for years to come, we'd be known among the town's four hundred residents as "the people who live in the teachers' house." At last, we had a house. A home. A place that was truly ours. And I had my escape from Manhattan.

Rare was the weekend we didn't take off for the Endless Mountains. Everything about our place appealed to us. The quietude. The puttering. The undisturbed time together. Even the three-hour drive had its pleasures. We'd catch up on each other's weeks. Listen to music. Bask in companionable silence. Sometimes, we'd play name-that-baby. We'd pluck town names off the road signs and try them out. Scotrun Treen? Baby Netcong? Or we'd look for the conjunction of names that would drive Joe's Episcopal parents and my Jewish ones most crazy. Xavier Myron? Rivka Christiana? We debated whether Rachel or Deborah was the nicer name, and if William should be shortened to Bill or Will.

Not that we were planning to have a baby anytime soon. With

Joe earning only pocket money from his freelancing, babies were not a consideration. This was fine with me. We were married now. We had time.

Our parents didn't see it that way, though they rarely signaled their impatience. Joe's mother let her interest slip just once. On a warm summer evening in the Endless Mountains, as we sat outside feeling the floating effects of the heat and our predinner cocktails, my mother-in-law asked me, "Are you planning to have any children?"

"I don't know," I said. "We're not sure."

"Then what the hell did you get married for?"

Though I've always appreciated the measured distance my in-laws keep from Joe and my personal affairs, I savored that rare intrusion. I'll be damned, I thought. She wants to be a grandmother.

With my parents, the "get married, have babies" refrain of my childhood had, by my mid-twenties, become an infrequent but more earnest, "You're not getting any younger." By the time I married and passed thirty, they no longer mentioned children. I figured they were biting their tongues, knowing how bristly I could be if I thought they were interfering.

One night, Joe and I were reviewing our investments with my father, our financial guru. "This is good," I responded to a piece of advice. "But when there are kids—"

My father bolted forward in his chair and cut me off. "Are you planning to have children?"

I was puzzled by my father's surprised expression. "Well, of course. I mean, not right this minute. But, you know, somewhere down the road. You knew that."

He shook his head. "Your mother and I had given up on your having children."

"Come on, Dad. I've always said I wanted kids."

By then, my father had tuned me out, his expression soft and wistful. He was off somewhere in grandpa land.

* * *

Actually, I was growing ambivalent about kids. By now, several of my friends were parents. It was obvious and disturbing to me that the women shouldered a disproportionate share of the child care. I was still holding out for parity.

As yet, I saw little reason to hope that Joe would be any different from those of my male friends who were now fathers. Most of them, it seemed to me, shared an adoration for their kids and a deep-seated assumption that while their own busy schedules could not expand to accommodate child duties during the work week, their wives' could. As I watched Joe burn up the computer at all hours, I wondered where in his schedule there would be room for children.

I also wasn't convinced that this was the right time to ask. Joe was working harder than ever as he wrote and rewrote a novel, coscripted a screenplay, and oversaw the production of one of his plays in an off-off Broadway house. How could I think to disrupt his creative momentum with kids? Besides, work was absorbing for me, too. I was writing weekly about Nicaragua and El Salvador, hot stories at the time, and making occasional reporting trips to Washington, Mexico, and Central America.

During this period, I belonged to a weekend reading group in the Endless Mountains. Several members were mothers of small children, and whatever novel we selected was often the only book they had time to read between our monthly sessions. To me, that hardly seemed a glowing endorsement for parenthood.

One member, Donna, was a doctor who'd quit her medical practice to "try to get pregnant." I'd never heard of such a thing. How could "getting pregnant" be a full-time commitment? As the months had expanded into years and Donna's failed in vitro fertilizations had accumulated, her body had begun to show the toll of the fertility drugs. One Sunday, she grew uncharacteristically agitated, pounding her critique of a book exhaustively, her voice rising to a shrill pitch.

Watching everyone shift uneasily in their seats, I thought, It's those damn fertility drugs. I'd never do that to my body. If I couldn't get pregnant, I'd take it as a sign, even be grateful. At least then the child question would be resolved.

As 1988 drew to a close, I began to feel restless. I thought my agitation reflected an inability to break the rhythm of my school years. After four years of high school, I'd spent four years at Princeton, four years at the *Times,* four years at *Newsweek.* Now, as I neared the four-year mark at *Time,* my editors were nudging me toward editing, a job to which I did not aspire.

Yet, I plainly needed a change. For eight years, I'd been taking the reports of foreign correspondents and fashioning them into what writers at both newsweeklies call "seamless narratives." I'd stitched my way through the rise, fall, and rise of Poland's Solidarity movement; the decline, fall, and stall of the Soviet empire; the disintegration of Eastern Europe and the reintegration of the Germanys; the subversive wars of Central America; and the subversive policies of the Reagan years. Brezhnev, Andropov, Chernenko, Gorbachev, Jaruzelski, Honecker, Duvalier, Somoza, Ortega, Duarte, Aquino, Thatcher, Reagan had all come and gone—yet I had gone nowhere.

At home, I was growing impatient for Joe to return to a salaried job so we could afford a larger apartment. After eleven years of hiking up and down five flights of stairs, I'd had enough. Joe and I had initially agreed that he'd freelance for one year. But at the end of that year, he'd been well launched on a complicated techno-thriller, and we'd agreed he should finish the book. Now another year had passed, his book was still unfinished, and Joe was still making no more than pocket money. Vaguely I wondered how we would ever have kids, given our space and financial constraints. Aloud I griped about my restlessness.

Joe was the one to suggest that I consider an overseas assignment. I found the idea striking. "Are you serious?"

"If you wanted to go abroad, I'd consider it," he answered.

A few weeks later, I learned that the top slot in *Time*'s Johannesburg bureau was coming open. South Africa, I thought. A fascinating story. Fixed borders, a defined territory. I wouldn't be on the road all the time, away from Joe. He could finish his novel, then freelance. We could get by on English. Perfect.

When I raised the prospect with Joe, he asked, "Is all of this a big disguise for your wanting to have a baby?"

"I don't know. Maybe."

"I've always assumed that the quid pro quo for your supporting me would be a kid."

I was surprised and pleased by the twin implications of his statement: Joe not only recognized that he "owed" me, but he was thinking, however dimly, about children. Still, I was a pragmatist. "That can't happen until you finish the novel and get a salaried job."

"Then go for Johannesburg," Joe said.

"If I open the door and they offer it to me, then I have to go through that door. You understand that, right?"

"Right."

Two months later, I was offered the post. I accepted on the spot. When I called home, excited and nervous, expecting a "Wow, Wease, we're really going!" Joe's response was chilly. By the time I got home, he was furious. "How could you even think of accepting the job without consulting me first?"

"But I thought we agreed that if they offered the job, we would go," I said, confused.

"That's ridiculous. Everyone takes at least twenty-four hours to think it over."

I felt like an idiot. Of course, they did. "You're right. Sorry." It'll blow over, I thought.

The next day, I asked if he was feeling any better about Joburg. "Goddamn it," he answered. "Stop putting pressure on me, Jill."

Not Wease? This was worse than I thought.

Though I'd been promised four months to relocate, within days I was bombarded by questions, requests, and demands from administrators and bean-counters, editors and bureau staff. All required immediate attention, including instructions to visit Johannesburg right away to find a residence. When I applied to the South African embassy for tourist visas to go house hunting, I learned that Joe and I had to submit papers now for the longer term work visas if we hoped to be in place by June. Joe's application, I was told, must include letters from each publication that planned to run his work. Joe wouldn't be permitted to add to that list once we got to South Africa.

Understandably, Joe found this timetable absurd. "Essentially, I have to line up jobs in the next two weeks or I won't be able to work." When he began to call newspapers and magazines, it quickly became apparent that freelance opportunities were thinner than we'd assumed. "What the hell am I supposed to do over there?" he demanded. "I'm not going to be Mr. Smolowe."

My way of coping with the mounting pressure was to try to impose order on the logistics of the pending move. Joe felt I was fretting about our two residences too much; I felt he was worrying too little. Small, testy exchanges were blown into cosmic truths. Joe's refusal to discuss what we were going to do with our apartment and country house became, to my mind, evidence that he wasn't going to help in the relocation. Joe became convinced that I intended to strand him, impoverished, in Johannesburg, while I jaunted off to play correspondent.

Soon, Joe was asserting that we couldn't pack up either residence until he was ready to move. "You go ahead alone and stay in a hotel," he ordered. "I'll join you when I finish my novel."

"And just when do you think that might be?" I snapped back.

"I don't know. Sometime around August."

"Come on, Joe. You know as well as I do it won't be before December at the earliest."

"Okay, December. God, Jill, will you just get off my back."

Initially, my anger matched Joe's. Where was the adventurous man I thought I'd married, the one who would help me court change and take risks? I also resented the bind I felt Joe was putting me in at work. If I backed out of the assignment, it might demolish the goodwill I'd built up over the years.

"It was never my intention to go abroad alone," I fumed. "I never would have contemplated an overseas assignment if you hadn't raised it first."

Then my own aversion to change began to gain on me. Did I really want to move overseas? Leave my family and friends? Put children on hold for another three years? I imagined answering the phone in my Johannesburg hotel room one night and hearing Joe announce that he wasn't coming at all. Once that prospect entered my head, I could think of little else. As I felt the tunnel narrowing, my mind began searching feverishly for an escape. I could see only one exit.

"This isn't worth destroying our marriage over," I said ungraciously. "You and I are obviously incapable of making this move, so let's not go."

As soon as I ceded defeat, Joe shifted and suggested Johannesburg would be exciting. Then the debate started all over. As we continued to volley back and forth over two weeks, I began to perceive only trouble ahead. My most optimistic scenario, the one where Joe came at all, envisioned a husband resentful of my travel schedule, my access to sources, my every breath. I saw but two options: risking the derailment of my career at *Time* or ruining my marriage. When it came down to that stark calculus, my priority was clear.

I declined the post. My editors proved understanding beyond all expectation. This happens all the time with dual-career couples, they assured me. Within days, marital calm descended and I put South Africa behind.

After the turmoil subsided, I began to rethink the future Joe and I were likely to share. Twinning Joe's antagonism to a relocation with his earlier antipathy to marriage, I concluded that I'd been mistaken about his capacity for adventure; he was even more resistant to change than I. The way the two episodes had unfolded had also shown me that Joe, so resolute on daily matters, was much more tentative about decisions of lasting import. His first, second, even third soundings could not be trusted. At the same time, his statement about kids being a "quid pro quo" suggested that he was less resistant to starting a family than I'd assumed.

Over the next year, I salved my restlessness by writing a novel and thinking hard about starting a family. To my college friend Evan who lived in California, I wrote: "My sister Ann is pregnant with her second. My sister-in-law Candace is pregnant with her third. Two friends just had babies; two others are pregnant. The wives of two editors here just had babies. BABIES, Evan! Do I think of babies? Tick-tick-tick. Joe will be 48 on his next birthday; I'll be 35. Tick-tick-tick."

When Joe and I would discuss children, a dialogue invariably initiated by me, both of us tended to posit children as a disruption, rather than an enhancement, to our lives. How would we manage work schedules? Finances? Space constraints? Discipline issues? The monologue in my journal raised other doubts that I chose not to share with Joe.

I worry that Joe will be too old; that he'll be, say, 70 when the child is 20. I don't worry as much about me. I'm a lot more patient and tolerant now than I would have been in my 20s . . . Though I now play with children with attention and interest, I don't so much actively want them as think that if we don't have them, we will have missed out on something very special. It seems an inverted way to approach children. I have little confidence any longer that my ambivalence will give way to a crushing desire to have a child, as happened with marriage. It seems if Joe and I ultimately decide to have a child, it will be impulsive. We'll pull the plug and take the plunge ... I'm afraid that we'll delay too long. When I can't have a child, only then will I discover that, yes, it was children that I really wanted. Then the vacuum. The void. The disappointment. Again, a pretty convoluted reason to have a child.

In April 1990, *Time*'s chief of correspondents asked if I'd like to head the Miami bureau, with responsibility for the magazine's South America coverage as well. The offer surprised me. When I'd turned down Johannesburg a year earlier, I'd assumed I was trashing any chance of another posting. I was flattered. Interested. Wiser.

"Let me talk this over with my husband," I said.

Our discussion over the next month reprised the South Africa debate, only now I was fourteen months more restless, fourteen months more sick of our apartment, fourteen months more impatient for Joe to finish his novel and take a salaried job. During our tense negotiations, female friends cautioned that if a decision didn't go my way soon, I'd grow even more resentful and angry. A male friend offered a different perspective. "Joe's self-image will take a battering if he feels he's disappointed you, but doesn't offer anything in return." He suggested that Joe and I make a joint five-year plan, advice I took to heart.

Joe and I mapped out a plan, at least short-range, I wrote the same day I declined the Miami post. He'd have until December to settle his career situation. Within the next year, I'd get pregnant. From there, we'd consider a move [to a new apartment].

Six years later, Joe would tell me, "I don't remember that plan at all."

I do. Vividly.

I not only clung to it like a life raft to relieve my treading but began to arrange my career plans around it. Soon after I turned down Miami, I was again invited to give editing a try. Though I now found the offer more tempting and suspected that I might be squandering the final ounce of my editors' goodwill, I demurred. Soon, I reasoned, I wouldn't have the extra hours to give that editing requires. I'd be raising a child.

As I thought about starting a family, I discovered that not only my ambivalence, but my unease around small children, had dissipated. By now, Jonathan had two sons, and Ann one daughter. I would watch my nephews and niece endlessly, fascinated by their energy, curiosity, and quirky way of seeing the world. I was particularly entranced by toddlers around the eighteen-month mark. Children in that brief interregnum between helplessness and willfulness could rivet my attention for hours with their joyous smiles, clownish antics, and determined exploration.

Somewhere along the way, I'd stopped thinking of kids as an insurance policy against lonely old age. Children, I now knew, could reach parts of me that no adult could touch. I felt ready, very ready, to probe that largely untapped part of myself.

But was Joe ready? For years I'd blithely rested my hopes on our name-that-baby games, telling myself that Joe wouldn't continue to indulge this whimsy if he truly didn't want kids. Now I watched more closely when we came into contact with children. Although it was obvious that Joe didn't share my degree of interest, he was great with kids in twenty-minute spurts. Inventive. Playful. Cheerful. Afterward, when I would comment how well children responded to him or what a great father he would make, Joe would get an embarrassed, self-conscious grin, one that I knew signaled his pleasure.

When I scanned back through the years, I also saw ample and sustained promise of a wonderful father. For oldest nephew Michael, Joe had invented the "Great Snake," an adventurous reptile who delighted in stirring mischief in the world's hottest spots. Haiti. Eastern Europe. The Bronx. Each time we saw Michael, Joe would spin a new tale, then respond good-naturedly when Michael pestered him for more details. To Alex, who shared Joe's birth date, Uncle Joe sent annual birthday letters that over the years exhorted our younger nephew to ever-escalating heights of outrageousness.

Most memorably, there had been two occasions, years apart, when we'd hosted the teenage daughters of friends. Remembering my own teen years, when I'd often regarded the attentions of adults as synonymous with interference, I'd suggested, "Let's just give them a key so they can come and go as they want." Joe had agreed, in theory. In practice, he'd been vigilant, concerned, strikingly parental. He'd not only kept track of the girls' whereabouts at all times, but he'd arranged activities he thought would interest them, listened intently when they recounted their adventures, seemed genuinely concerned that they have a good time.

It's like the marriage thing, I decided. If I stop catering to Joe's ambivalence and insist that it's time to start a family, he'll come around. Once we have a child, his sense of responsibility and commitment will kick in. Then he won't look back.

Quid pro quo. Quid pro quo. Where the hell is the quid pro quo?

It's March 1991, almost a year since the Miami option gave way to the baby option, and I'm in a rage. Joe's novel finally finished, he's about to start a writing job at *People* magazine. Though it's a temporary post, we're so optimistic it will turn into a staff position that we've begun hunting for a larger apartment in Hoboken, a New Jersey town that is our compromise between Joe's need for concrete and my own for trees.

Our second outing has turned up an airy, spacious duplex with high ceilings. I'm having the same gut reaction I had when we first saw our country house: I want it. But Joe's stalling.

"Moving and starting a new job are two of life's biggest stressors," he's arguing. "Why can't we wait to do this until I've been in my new job a month?"

"Because the apartment will be gone by then."

"There'll be others."

It's a reasonable position, but I'm in an unreasonable mood. "I've supported you for four years," I say between clenched teeth. "When the hell is it my turn? You didn't give me South Africa. You didn't give me Miami. Now you're telling me that you're not going to give me fucking Hoboken. For chrissake, Joe, when are we going to get on with our lives and have kids?"

"We've never discussed having kids."

My eyes widen, stunned, disbelieving. "What are you talking about! How many times have you told me, 'I always assumed the quid pro quo for supporting my book would be a baby.'"

"I don't want a baby," Joe answers just as vehemently. "We're not going to have a baby. If we ever have a baby, it will be *your* baby."

To my ear, this is a perfect articulation of Joe's ambivalence. There will be no baby; but there will be a baby; but it will be Jill's baby.

I know all about Joe and ambivalence. I also know that I'm far too furious to hear his needs, desires, or excuses. "We need to see a marriage counselor," I say, and call Grace.

Seven years have passed since we last faced each other from the black leather chairs in Grace's office. Like the last time, the surface issue is real estate, but the real issue is far more profound. I'm so angry that I risk blurting out my grievance in an incoherent jumble, so I've prepared a three-page, single-spaced typed statement that I now read aloud.

"Joe and I are at a point in our marriage that I feel is very dangerous. I do not think he perceives the gravity of the situation . . . I have gotten a clear impression that Joe does not in the least appreciate anything I've done for the sake of the relationship and his work: not the four years of financial support, not the rejection of two jobs I wanted, not the deferral of having a baby. To him, the issue of the apartment emerges from a vacuum, and on that score, I am being 'precipitous' . . . I feel that I have demonstrated again and again that I hold our marriage as my top priority and that I am willing to compromise and bend my own interests to keep the mutual interests of the marriage at heart. Joe's only priority seems to be Joe. This leaves me feeling not only angry and hurt: I am also beginning to feel used."

"So," Grace says, after a moment's silence, "you're afraid if you don't meet his needs, he'll leave you."

"No," I respond. "What I fear is that my anger will become so deep that *I* will leave."

Grace turns her neutral, inquiring gaze to Joe. The apartment, he says, is no big deal. He'll come around. Probably already has. "But Jill never gives me a chance to think things through." He pauses, then adds, "She thinks a lot faster than I do."

Grace laughs. "I know."

Her laughter breaks the tension. Joe and I both laugh, too, relieved to be poking fun at our collective self. By the end of the session, we've agreed to take the duplex in Hoboken.

Though our sessions over the next two months explore a range of issues, the main focus is children. To my ear, Joe's concerns are no more convincing than his earlier reservations about marriage. He's worried that kids will distract from his writing. That he isn't getting any younger. That he'll be a lousy father, long on discipline, short on patience. That parenthood will be a reprise of his uncomfortable stint as a stepfather to preadolescent twins during his brief second marriage.

"That's not at all the same as raising your own child," I

object. "Those kids saw their father every weekend, so they didn't need you. In their eyes, you were just an interloper. And you inherited them at the worst possible age. I was a camp counselor; I know that age. All adolescents are nightmares."

"So, ours will be a nightmare, too." He offers a little smile that says, Gotcha, Wease.

"Well," I say lamely, "presumably by the time he or she is a teenager, we'll love him or her so much that we'll be willing to put up with it."

We end our visits to Grace, the child issue unresolved. Though Joe has said nothing I haven't heard before, I feel I've heard him better—though apparently not well enough. Years later, Joe will assert, "Over and over, I said my biggest fear was that I would have to raise kids by *your* rules and wouldn't be allowed to be myself."

That August, I take it hard when my sister moves to Oregon. In recent years, she's become one of my closest friends. The geographic distance, I fear, will destroy our intimacy. I'm also reluctant to see her children go. Jeremy, my third nephew, is a human waste pail at age one. Whatever he sees goes in his mouth. Sticks. Dog hair. Cigarette butts. It drives Ann crazy. It delights me to watch him drive her crazy. Emily, at two and a half, is mesmerizing. Every question is answered with a vampy, "Oh, yes," that sounds like Marlene Dietrich. Her mispronunciations are a riot: Cousin Alex is "Ahyix"; Candace is "Aunt Penis."

Their last week on the East Coast, my sister is a wreck about moving so great a distance from family and friends. Emily, too, is jittery about the relocation, fretful that her toys won't make it cross-country. The way she both clings to and tries to protect Ann moves me. "Stop crying, Jeremy," she lectures her brother. "It's making Mommy sad."

The day after Ann leaves for Oregon, I drop in unannounced on Caren, a country friend. After my nephews and niece, hers are the three small children I know best. I want to hear them shout, "Hey, Jill! Watch this!"

"I need company," I tell Caren. "My sister just left for Portland."

Caren looks at me, her expression a peculiar mix of excitement and guilt. "I don't know how to tell you this," she says, "but I think we're moving to Seattle." Within weeks, Caren, her husband, and three kids are gone.

After that double whammy, I know that being an aunt or a special friend is never going to be enough. I want my own child to love without reservation or restraint. I want a child who will jump off the edge of a swimming pool into my arms with the same trust that Emily hurls herself into Ann's. I don't want to have to hand a child back to its mother or father to slow a cascade of tears; I want *my* arms to be the remedy.

I'm way beyond knowing I want to have kids.

I want to be a mother.

We're making love when Joe whispers, "I want to have a baby with you."

It's February 1992. Two years since we made our plan to start a family. One year since we consulted Grace. Nine months since each of us gave up hope of seeing our novels published. In the six months since my sister's move west, I've said nothing about children. So, this invitation is initiated entirely by Joe. I smile in the dark, pleased but cautious. I know Joe: for every reaction, a counterreaction. Restraining my impulse to catapult out of bed and remove my diaphragm, I hug him and say nothing.

Within a week, we have a blowout over nothing in particular. No surprise there. Just bad timing. Valentine's Day.

After another few weeks pass, I ask, "Were you serious about having a baby?"

He doesn't say yes. He doesn't say no. Instead, he gets that self-conscious grin that I know to be an affirmative.

"Then let's wait 'til summer," I say, shifting instantly into planning mode. "That way, I'll deliver in the spring and won't have to carry all that heavy weight through a hot summer. And there's the added bonus that I'll have the summer off with the baby." Joe agrees.

A few days later I have lunch with Lynn, a clinical psychologist and writer who has been the keeper of my secrets since our freshman year together at Princeton. She confides that she may be pregnant.

"No! Joe and I are finally ready to have kids, too!" We both laugh, delighted but not really surprised. So often during the long trajectory of our friendship our lives have taken parallel turns. "Actually, we're holding off until summer," I say.

"You know," she says after I tell her our plan, "you probably don't need to wait until summer. It doesn't always happen so quickly. I mean, it could take a while."

"The way things work in my family," I respond, "I'll probably get pregnant the minute I unplug my diaphragm. My mother. My sister. Both of my grandmothers. They barely had to blink to get pregnant."

"Okay," she says, not sounding totally convinced. "Did I tell you I cancelled my ski trip to Utah?"

"How come?"

"You're not supposed to be at altitudes over ten thousand feet when you're pregnant."

"Jesus," I say. "What I don't know about pregnancy."

"This will be so great," she says. "We'll be able to go to the park together with our babies. Who knows? Maybe we'll have them together in the same hospital. Joe and Kevin can pace the lobby together."

It's such a pretty fantasy. Us. Our husbands. Our kids. We beam at each other.

That night, Joe and I laugh about Lynn's cancelled ski trip. "I bet Kevin is furious," I say. "I vow not to be so fastidious when I get pregnant."

"You're gonna have to quit smoking, Wease."

"I know." I roll my eyes, then click off the light.

"I mean it, Wease."

I squeeze his hand. "I know, I know."

Then I lie beside Joe in the dark, marveling. We're really going to do this. We're finally going to have a baby.

III

I STILL REMEMBER IT AS GIDDY, THE FIRST TIME WE make love without protection. It's a rainy Saturday in early April 1992, the sort of lazy afternoon without obligations that only a childless couple can indulge. Joe and I are planning to go see *Basic Instinct* when we have a change of mood and disrobe instead. I don't know why it is that after seven years of marriage and nine years of shared living, real sex suddenly seems more appealing than a steamier screen simulation. But later I'll like to think we were propelled toward the bed by the prospect of conceiving a child together.

"Is it okay?" I whisper. "I'm not protected."

"Let's make a baby," he murmurs.

That night, we catch a showing of *Basic Instinct* in Jersey City, then rush back to our Hoboken apartment to make love again. I'm pretty sure that second time had little to do with making babies.

The next morning as I awake, my hand goes to my stomach and I smile. Joe apparently has the same thought. He puts his ear against my abdomen and with a grave expression says, "I hear the baby. It's doing this." When he simulates my smoker's cough, we both crack up.

"If there's a baby in there," I say, "you should sing. Music is good for a growing fetus." Usually, I have to flirt to get my tone-deaf husband to sing. I beg, he demurs. "Come on, Wease," I cajole. "Just one song?" He looks at me disdainfully, says he could have been a reggae star if his mean, evil parents hadn't made him go to college. We consider the life that might have been. He looks wounded; I sympathize. Then, finally, he sings. On this morning, though, Joe needs no further urging to launch into his Top Hits: "Buffalo Soldier" by Bob Marley, Sade's "Diamond Life."

As he tortures the high notes of the chorus—"I'm a smooth operator. SMOOOOOOTH operator"—I feel an unexpected stir of optimism. This man, my mate, whose attitude about children has seesawed over the years between good-natured ambivalence and agitated opposition, for the first time seems unconflicted, even inspired, by the prospect of a baby.

"Let's not tell anybody," Joe says. He means, of course, our families. To inform any one member is to tell them all, and neither of us wants the pressure of excited expectations.

"Come on, Wease," I laugh. "Don't you want to tell the world, 'We're trying to get pregnant'?"

"Not until you've cleared the three-month mark." We've heard too many sad tales of miscarriages.

As we negotiate the terms of our pact, our intimacy and excitement deepens. Joe jokes about his "he-man sperm." I insist that I have a strange feeling in my stomach. We're both pretty much convinced that I'm already pregnant. We dub the phantom fetus "Junior" and begin hatching absurd schemes for his or her future.

When Joe goes to get the papers, I lean out a living room window to smoke what I vow will be my last cigarette. After so many years of restraining my desire for a child to keep pace with Joe's resistance, I now let my fantasies off their tight leash for a romp.

I imagine the phone call to my parents, announcing the pregnancy that they've long since given up on. I think about whom I want at my baby shower. I debate amnio, thinking that perhaps it would be best to know the gender early on, so that I don't imprudently build up too much hope for a girl. I think about how we'll have to rearrange furniture to convert the second bedroom, currently Joe's office, into a nursery. And wonder if there's any hope of coaxing Joe to move to a house in the suburbs before Junior's arrival. I try to recall the names Joe and I have considered over the years. I wonder how we will diplomatically steer clear of *bris* expectations if it's a boy and pink outfits if it's a girl. I deliberate about how much time I'll want or can afford to take off from *Time.* I can't imagine anything less than three months.

I guess what astounds me is how easily Joe and I are transitioning into this possibility, for the first time very real. He doesn't seem at all freaked by the idea. He seems to be enjoying it. When he had his head on my stomach and was pretending to cough, I just felt relieved, grateful that, yes, if there's a pregnancy it could be a fun one, not me having to struggle to hold my sanity against his anxiety and anger. I guess all of this means we're ready . . . I hope I AM pregnant. Nine months already seems awfully far away.

When I think back on that day, it sets off a mental litany that echoes the Yom Kippur atonement service. God, we were confident. God, we were smug. God, we were naive.

Neither of us is particularly surprised when my period is late. I'd never doubted that I, like generations of women on both sides of my family, would conceive quickly. During all the years I'd been so scrupulous about contraception, never once playing baby roulette, I'd had an almost talisman-like belief that my diligence would be rewarded the moment I pulled the plug. As for Joe, though he was approaching his half-centenary, he was as fit as a man ten years his junior. Moreover, for years he'd been turning his head leftward and coughing on command for doctors without incident. Obviously, everything was in working order.

As the days go by, my anticipation becomes tinged with dread and guilt. What if I *am* pregnant and the baby is born sickly, underweight, or deformed because of my smoking? Joe is thinking the same thing. In addition to chiding me about cigarettes, he starts issuing humorous injunctions about coffee and alcohol. I'm so pleased he's taking an interest that I bite back sarcastic reminders that I seldom drink more than a glass of wine a month and that we'd vowed not to be hypervigilant parents-in-waiting. Everything is so merry.

Then it isn't. Joe begins picking at me for walking too fast, an old complaint that resurfaces whenever we're emotionally out of sync. He complains that I don't laugh at his jokes anymore, and absurdly accuses me of nuking one of his friendships because I'd failed to reciprocate a dinner invitation. Annoyed by the escalating carping, I retort that his relationships aren't my responsibility. "You want to hold a dinner party, then you make the plans."

"I grew up in a world where women make the social arrangements."

"We've been together ten years," I snap. "Get over it."

Joe's rare allusion to the difference in our ages should be a tip-off, but I'm too distracted by the rocky dynamic between us.

We go along for weeks, months, with everything seeming great. Feeling lucky that we get on so famously. So companionable. Such great playmates. Then, boom. I haven't any idea what set Joe off.

After my period arrives, Joe's good humor revives. I quit smoking. Then we try again.

In late June as I count down the days to my period, Joe's

edginess returns. I write off his mood to work frustrations. In recent days, he's been talking about wanting to quit his job at *People*. Having recently sold the TV rights to an article he'd written about a murder, he thinks there might be a book to be done as well. I've been countering with arguments that Joe doesn't want to hear. The murder was a copycat version of an already-celebrated case, so a book is unlikely to find a large audience. And his steady income is critical right now; I may be pregnant.

On a hot, sticky Sunday after a long road trip in our unrefrigerated car, we go to war, ostensibly over whether to turn on the apartment's fan or air conditioner. As the decibel level crescendoes to record heights, Joe yells, "You might as well start smoking again since we're not going to have a baby."

Finally, I get it.

"Grow up, Joe," I retort.

The crack about babies was a low blow. Using a baby as a weapon in a fight bodes ill for the future. We've settled on—or at least it's felt like we've settled on—having a child; we've even started talking about moving to the burbs. But this raises doubts about having a kid with a man who's so quick to throw out cracks like that. Will he be there for us?

Despite such angry scribings, I'm not really concerned that Joe will forsake his obligations to a child. His habit of vacillation is infuriating, yes. But I know Joe. Once he makes up his mind to do something, his resolve is unshakeable. It's the quality that makes him such a good reporter, such a reliable friend, such a steadfast mate. What I still can't predict is whether Joe's acute sense of responsibility will extend to shouldering his share of daily baby-care chores or allowing himself any space to experience the joy a child can bring. At this point, though, I'm not sure I care anymore. I've waited long enough for a baby.

I put my happy fantasies back on a tight rein. Away go the short-lived daydreams of Joe and me giggling our way through

Lamaze class. Back come visions of Joe ranting that the baby's crying is disrupting his work and me raving that he isn't handling his fair share of the diaper detail.

Better, I think, to be girded for the worst.

By my thirty-seventh birthday in late July, we are again companionably settled into the business of making a baby. On a clammy morning, as we drive to the Endless Mountains, I have a bizarre craving for a hamburger. One of the fast-food variety, thin and greasy, topped with ketchup, lettuce, and tomato.

"You're pregnant," Joe says, pulling off at the Clark Summit exit and steering us into a Burger King.

"No. You really think so, Wease?"

"Trust me, Wease. You're pregnant."

I'm not.

After five months of failed attempts, I decide it's time to help the process along. Realizing that I know nothing beyond the obvious about procreation, I make my maiden visit to the infertility shelves of Barnes & Noble's health section. After thumbing through several content pages, I find a promising chapter heading: "How To Get Pregnant Fast!" I like that exclamation point. It exudes confidence.

When I flip to the appropriate pages, I find a variety of tantalizing subsections dealing with body temperature, mucus texture, saliva, and sexual positions. There are tips on when to make love with the lights on and warnings to make love with the electric blanket turned off. Jeez, I marvel. Who would have thought it could be so complicated?

That night I read the chapter and highlight the portion that makes the most sense to me. It deals with something called Basal Body Temperature, which, the text instructs, will help establish a fertility curve. By taking my temperature first thing each morning, apparently, I can track the fluctuations of my reproductive hormones. A sharp drop indicates ovulation is about to occur; a subsequent steep rise means I've ovulated. The trick, the book instructs, is to make love within the twelve- to twenty-four-hour period between the drop and the rise.

No problem. Well, one. I can't read a mercury thermometer. After a pharmacist assures that a digital thermometer is just as reliable, I place one on my bedside table alongside a pad and pen, and begin to chart my monthly cycle.

Initially, this seems like a grand scientific experiment. Each morning, Joe lies beside me while I take my temperature, then together we read the numbers. Ninety-six? Yippee! We burrow back under the sheets and proceed, assiduously avoiding the positions under the subhead "How *Not* To Make Love." No matter how tired we are, we repeat at night. Just to be sure.

After a few more cycles, I begin to pay closer attention to some of the less appealing instructions. I check for the position of my cervix. (Is it firm and does it have a pointy shape— whatever that means.) I inspect my cervical mucus. (Is it thin, slippery, and stretchy—whatever that means.) I also begin a postcoital exercise, lying for twenty minutes on my back with my knees drawn to my chest to assist the swim of Joe's mighty sperm toward my fallopian tubes. I have great faith in this maneuver. Not only have I read about it in the book; I've seen it on *L.A. Law*.

Soon, our lovemaking ceases to be about pleasure. Sex is now a means to an end, dictated by the thermometer. I read off the numbers, like the coordinates on a battlefield map, then summon Joe to action. Ever the good soldier, Joe never fails in his duty.

By September 1992, agitation is my constant companion. Though the wall calendar indicates that Joe and I have been trying to conceive for only seven months, my internal calendar dates my active attempts to start a family to the day in May 1990 when Joe and I agreed that the quid pro quo for Miami would be a child. I date my more passive campaign to soften Joe's resistance even further back, to 1989. Perhaps, I muse, South Africa, Miami, even my fiction writing, were all attempts to sublimate my desire for children while I waited for Joe to come around. Am I finally facing the truth?

Or am I concocting bullshit rationalizations for the mounting aggravation I feel at work? My intermittent restlessness of recent years is fast-hardening into churlishness. In recent days, I'd become entangled in overheated office debates about the pending presidential election. The one-year anniversary of the Anita Hill–Clarence Thomas showdown had been marked by a bruising exchange about racial issues with one of my favorite colleagues. I'd responded to another colleague's usual arrogance with a snippy rejoinder.

I feel increasingly out of control and unhappy at work. No matter which way I look at it, I don't see anything there that would make me happy.

In the years since declining the Miami offer, I've come to feel sidelined at the magazine. I know I have only myself to blame. When I'd turned down the last editing opportunity, I'd suspected that it might be called a strike, the third after South Africa and Miami. I'd been willing to risk the out, confident that I would soon be out of the rotation, watching from the dugout with a baby on my lap. By the time I realized I was no longer perceived as a power hitter, I was too preoccupied, first with fiction writing and then with our efforts to sort out apartment and baby issues, to mind very much. After we'd finally agreed to give Junior a chance at bat, I'd stopped minding at all.

But as the weeks of trying to conceive had stretched into months, I'd begun to mind. First, a little. Then, a lot. Now, too much. My work life was beginning to feel like a sick twist on my favorite sick joke: Why did Jill's career fall out of the tree? Because it was dead.

In another sick twist, now Joe is the one who never knows what partner he'll encounter from one hour to the next. When I seek his guidance on an office matter, will fragile Jill respond to his suggestion that I'm overreacting with pleas for further reassurance or will boorish Jill snarl that he doesn't understand? When he responds to requests to read my stories, will insecure Jill heed his every editing suggestion or will defensive Jill insist that his instincts are all wrong? When he needs to discuss his own office life, will supportive Jill listen intently or will impatient Jill balk that he talks too much about work?

My sense of confidence and direction fast eroding, I start to second-guess myself. Have I become too distracted from my career? Too lax about my job at *Time?* Should I have pursued one of the editing opportunities? I begin to regard Joe's rapid ascent at *People* as a rebuke. While he's moved quickly from a writing slot to an editing position, I've stagnated.

In hopes of restoring my standing and revitalizing my interest, I've requested a transfer to one of the magazine sections that handles domestic news. Such a shift would offer greater opportunity to report my own stories; immersion in an unfamiliar setting might pull me out of my self-absorbed brooding. But I'm not terribly hopeful about the transfer. Why should anybody give me what I ask after I've squandered so many wonderful opportunities?

I'm also not completely persuaded that a job change will make much of a difference. The malaise I feel at work is beginning to permeate all areas of my life. Nothing feels right. Unable to identify the locus of this widening and uncharacteristic discontent, I diagnose myself to be suffering a "spirituality vacuum," though I'm not sure what exactly I mean by that. When the Jewish high holidays roll around, I feel drawn to synagogue services for the first time in years. As I fast and try to pray, tears roll down my cheeks. I find this both embarrassing and fascinating. I almost never cry.

What's making you cry? I ask myself.

Nothing. Everything, comes the answer.

In late October during a routine checkup, I mention to my gynecologist that Joe and I are trying to get pregnant. Dr. Lowell smiles with the delight of a man whose motto should be Babies 'R Us.

"How long have you been trying?"

"Seven months."

"Remind me," he says. "How old are you and your husband?"

"I'm thirty-seven. Joe will be fifty next month."

Lowell nods. "Given your ages, you should proceed as quickly as possible."

He suggests that we run a standard battery of tests on Joe's sperm. "No point in wasting time." He also says there are cysts on my uterus. "They're benign, but sometimes cysts can block attempts to get pregnant. Why don't we take them off."

We do the cryosurgery right there, right then. I leave his office, crampy but unworried about my pregnancy prospects, though I'm concerned that Joe may balk at the sperm tests.

To the contrary, Joe makes the appointment right away.

Over the next few weeks, I'm too distracted to think about babies. Not only are rumors swirling at *Time* that a management change is imminent, but I, the reluctant hostess, am staging a surprise party for Joe's fiftieth birthday. I'd assumed that most of the invited out-of-towners would attend only in spirit by responding to my request for written anecdotes about Joe ("the more embarrassing the better"). Instead, people are flying in from as far away as Milwaukee, Los Angeles, San Francisco, even Moscow. I'm scrambling to find accommodations.

The people who gather in a French restaurant in Greenwich

Village on the evening of November 15 are a remarkable assemblage, representing most phases of Joe's life. When Joe walks through the restaurant door, he stares, then his hands come slowly to his face, his expression shocked and embarrassed. Like a sleepwalker, he moves between the tables, greeting friends and hugging relatives. I burst into tears, moved by the wealth of people who love this man, my husband.

Everything is right. The food. The wine. The flowers. But what makes the evening special are the people, who chat and laugh familiarly, as if they've all known each other as long as Joe has known all of them. The director who staged the readings for Joe's first play swaps theater notes with the director of his second play. High school friends trade favorite Joe stories with college friends. Book packagers talk shop with authors. My confidante, Lynn, now eight months pregnant, exchanges mommy tips with Joe's confidante, Kathryn, the mother of a toddler. The journalists amuse one another with horror stories about editors. And through it all, Joe sits, stunned, barely able to talk.

It is a wonderful night, a sublime one. As it happens, these will be the last happy or lucid moments I'll have for a long time to come.

Two days later, a message from the corporate enclave on the thirty-fourth floor of the Time & Life Building ends weeks of speculation. *Time* is getting a new managing editor, a company insider, but an outsider to the magazine. Like virtually everyone on the staff, my first reaction is, What will this mean for me? My request for a department change is still pending.

My mind is buzzing with the morning's announcement as I ride the B-train to the Upper West Side for my lunchtime appointment with Dr. Lowell, a follow-up visit to the cryosurgery. I figure it will be a brief trip to the stirrups, then I'm out of there. So something in me startles when I enter Dr. Lowell's office and see him leafing through the contents of a manila folder.

"Please sit down," he says, his eyes and tone oozing far too much sympathy. "Joe's sperm results have come back from the lab. Both the volume and motility are low."

A numbing tingle begins to emanate from my solar plexus. Automatically, I take out a reporter's notebook and start to jot notes in case I fail to absorb what's being said. Joe's sperm motility, Lowell explains, tested at 31 percent; it needs to be 50 percent. As for volume, Joe gave one milliliter, where the normal ejaculate is between two and six mls. Within that small sample, however, the number of sperm per ml was 113 million, a count within the average range. There is a sperm specialist whom Lowell wants Joe to see.

There's also a test for my fallopian tubes, a hysterosalpin-gogram, that Lowell wants me to undergo right away. And there's a procedure called intrauterine insemination that he wants us to do later in the month when I'm ovulating. That will be assured, he says, because he's going to put me on a drug called Clomid.

I try to look intelligent as he describes an IUI. Somewhere between days twelve and sixteen of my menstrual cycle, I'll ovulate. Instead of making love those days, Joe will go to a lab and ejaculate into a plastic cup. The sperm will then be "washed," and the most motile sperm separated out. Within ninety minutes of this onanistic exercise, he must race, specimen in hand, to Lowell's office, where Lowell will inseminate me with Joe's sperm.

He smiles encouragingly. "Why wait?"

I feel like I'm hearing the sound of my future shattering. Please, I think, just get me out of here before I start to cry.

As soon as I reach the street, the tears flow. Low motility? Low volume? How will I break this to Joe without offending his sense of masculinity, his virility, his manhood? What if he refuses to see this sperm specialist whose name and number are tucked in my purse? As I walk down Central Park West, I can already hear his irritated, "I don't have time for this, Wease."

Even if he agrees, what about the IUI business? It sounds so clinical, so unromantic, not to mention complicated for two people with conflicting work schedules. Joe's longest, busiest days are Monday and Tuesday; mine are Thursday and Friday. Suppose I ovulate on a Tuesday, closing day at *People,* and Joe can't find the time to jerk off into a cup? Or on a Friday, when I can't break from a late-closing story at *Time?* What if I ovulate on a weekend, and Joe refuses to forego a weekend in the country? And do I really want us running marathons between two doctors' offices to get me pregnant?

The questions accumulate through the afternoon and into the evening. By the time Joe gets home, I'm a mass of anxiety, steeled for just about every reaction, save the one I get.

"What! Not macho sperm?" he says with mock indignation.

Far from being upset, Joe regards the volume problem as insignificant. He hadn't realized he was supposed to fill up the dixie cup. "They want volume? Next time, I'll give 'em volume," he laughs. As for the motility deficiency, he dubs it "Lo mo!" and teases a laugh out of me with talk of his lousy swimmers.

"Don't worry, Wease," he says. "I'll do the motility exercises, or whatever it takes."

He is less enthralled by the prospect of an IUI. "That sounds premature." He tells me that he lunched that day with Aaron, a friend visiting from Israel. "I told him about our trying to get pregnant, and Aaron said that it takes a year." I'm heartened to hear that Joe has been discussing this with Aaron. If he's confiding in friends, that means children are on his mind, not just when I put them there.

When we consult our calendars, the decision becomes easy.

We're going to be in different cities around the time of my next ovulation, and we'll probably be out of town at the time of the one following that. Rather than try to fight the scheduling conflict, we agree to hold off on the insemination. Meanwhile, Joe will call the sperm specialist, a doctor named Edelson, and I'll fill the Clomid prescription.

"Maybe the Clomid will be enough," I tell Joe. "Lynn got pregnant after taking it for just two cycles."

After we get in bed, Joe hugs me. "Don't worry, Wease. This isn't a disaster. It's just a small blip."

I fall asleep, bolstered by his confidence and good humor.

When I awake the next morning, my expectations have done a polar reversal. Overnight, I've flipped from unquestioning certainty that I'll get pregnant to dark certainty that I won't.

Not now.

Not ever.

Instantly recognizing this irrational pessimism as a warning, I pick up the phone and dial a number I haven't called in years.

"Miriam? It's Jill. I'm in trouble."

Only once before in my life have I experienced such an overwhelming feeling of negativity. That once, precipitated by the unexpected breakup of a relationship, had made a profound impression. For three months, I'd trudged around in a dense mental fog, dazed and ignorant of what was happening to me. Eventually, I'd learned there was a name for my disorientation: depression.

After the cloud lifted, I resolved to get help so that I'd never suffer a recurrence. I sat through consultations with two psychiatrists, but was so put off by their shrinkiness that I chose not to pursue therapy with either one. It may have been the manner of those particular doctors, but far more likely it was me. I'd been raised on the maxim, "Psychiatrists and Girl Scouts are for people who don't have strong families."

Over the next four years, though the depression didn't return, my resistance to the idea of therapy gradually eased as I came to realize that almost every journalist I knew—and I knew a lot of them—was in or had at one time been in therapy. I couldn't decide if the pressures of journalism screwed people up or if screwed-up people gravitated to journalism, but I figured, Hey, I'm a journalist, I'm Jewish, I live in Manhattan; there'd be something wrong with me if I *wasn't* neurotic.

When I became anxious in late 1984 about whether Joe and I were going to get married, I decided, What the hell. Whatever the outcome, I could use some support. That's when I hooked up with Miriam, a psychologist recommended by a friend. After our first session together, Miriam rendered her diagnosis: "What you're saying is you want to develop a thicker skin."

Exactly.

Sensing a sympathetic and intuitive ally, I opened up to Miriam and soon became fascinated by the therapeutic process. This heady period of "self-discovery" ended without regret two years later when Miriam moved to Louisiana; by then, I felt I'd grown that tougher layer of epidermis. Even so, when the occasional crisis would erupt, I'd do a few phone sessions with Miriam, who would help me sift through the issues, identify my priorities, then make my peace with them. During the South Africa debacle, for instance, Miriam had helped me see that my sense of well-being was more anchored in marital stability than in a new work challenge. By the time I turned down the job, I understood it was a choice, not a selfless act.

Now, though, as Miriam says, "Tell me what's going on with you," I'm less hopeful talk therapy can help. Through the years, Miriam has seen me guilty, angry, anxious, but she's never encountered me depressed.

In a tangle of rushed thoughts, I bring her up to date. Joe's sperm test results. My free-floating sense of having lost both purpose and direction. The management change at work. My concerns about the department transfer. My deeper concerns that this will be just a temporary panacea. I tell her of the various ideas I've toyed with lately: applying for a year-long journalism fellowship, writing another novel, launching a job search.

"My mind goes round and round, searching for another plan if there are no kids," I say. "But all I do is reject every option I come up with."

"Your wanting a baby is the affirmative part," she answers. "You've been ready for some time to turn your main focus away from work to family. Your job seemed under control, a good place to be while you thought a baby was on the way. But that hasn't happened as quickly as you hoped or planned. Now, you're trying to reenvision your life."

"I'm impatient."

"Yeah," she answers. "You are." Miriam cautions me to slow down, then concludes, "You're not in crisis. You're overwhelmed by a lot of things happening at once."

I'm in dismal shape four days later when I travel to my parents' home in rural North Carolina for Thanksgiving. This is to be our last autumn get-together. With some of my siblings' kids approaching school age, we've decided to switch our annual reunion to the July Fourth week. I want to rally for this long-anticipated gathering, but I can neither halt nor control the depression that is swiftly descending.

I have to fight each minute to keep my mind up. I can't just move from activity to activity. There are no transitions . . . I hate this never being able to forget myself even for a moment. Worse is not being able to let my mind wander freely.

The smallest tasks feel enormous. On a trip to Walmart, I set out with three purchases in mind: a hair blower, a clock battery, a pair of party shoes for my eldest niece. As I push a cart up and down the aisles, I begin to feel like the Robin

Williams character in *Moscow on the Hudson*, daunted by the huge displays of merchandise. After what feels like hours, I grasp that the hair blower I want is not in stock. The shoes are nowhere to be found. The battery I purchase doesn't fit the clock. I leave the store convinced that this failed mission is a reflection of my whole life.

I spend most of the days in search of distraction, drifting from room to room, trying to glom onto others' conversations, activities, even facial expressions. I watch my nieces and nephews come and go and come and go. I play game after game of Candyland with Emily.

You begin to appreciate how it's the very small things (kids smiling, laughter, a moment of unexpected support) that make life worthwhile. You escape into the small moments to escape the pain, and learn they are life.

Each day I go for long walks with one or another family member, up steep inclines to the wooded spots with the best views, down sloping hills to the fields where my parents' llamas, sheep, chickens, and burro graze. Walk after walk, talk after talk, no one can make sense of my depression. Until now, they haven't known that I've been trying to get pregnant. Most of them don't believe this could really be about children. Not Jill. Must be about job. I get lots of well-meaning career advice.

After my walk with Ann, she asks Joe how he feels about children. He answers with a story. "I have this Australian friend, Frank Rogers," he begins. "I bumped into him at a party when his wife was pregnant. He went on and on about how he didn't want kids. 'I don't know what the big deal is. Women in China do it all the time, then go right back to the rice paddies the same day.' Several months later, I ran into Frank on Seventh Avenue. This time, he was gushing about fatherhood. Couldn't stop talking about his son. 'It's incredible, mate. When the little tyke's lying on the changing table, his piss almost hits the ceiling!'"

Joe is laughing. Ann is laughing. "I just assume that something happens to men," Joe concludes. "I figure you feel differently when it's your own kid."

Ann shoots me a glance that says, Come on, that was funny. My answering smile is as unconvincing as I find Joe's story. The first time I'd heard Joe tell it in Grace's office, I'd felt reassured. So he *does* understand that when a child returns your love, it's different. Now, though, I find the anecdote irritating. How can he make so light of so tortured a subject? Is it a Wasp versus Jewish thing? A man versus woman thing? A Joe versus Jill thing? Does anybody buy that he feels so carefree about all of this?

As the reunion draws to an end, I feel guilty for having been such a drag on the festivities. I feel dread at the prospect of returning to work in such a fuzzy mental state. I feel anxious about the Clomid I will soon start, worried that if I don't get pregnant, I may sink deeper into despair.

Yet, I haven't lost my optimism entirely. As the plane lifts off, I console myself with the thought that I'll be able to make amends for my miserable behavior at our next reunion, just eight months away. I'll be in much better spirits by July: I'll be pregnant by then.

"How's Joe handling this?" Miriam's voice comes at me across the phone line, soothing and intent.

"He's being wonderful. Patient. Helpful. He tells me he's felt this way, too. It makes me feel less crazy."

"I'm beginning to understand more and more why you married Joe," she says. "He has flaws and allows for them. Joe is human and willing to admit it."

I understand the significance of what she's saying. Over the years, Miriam has steadily exhorted me to feel more sympathy for my psychic aches, to accept my limitations, to stop making unreasonable demands on myself. Her efforts to replace my mental slave driver's unyielding "shoulds" and "oughts" with a more soothing "there, there" have dried up pools of guilt and

allowed a fuller range of feeling. But part of me still clings to
the idea that I should always be in control, able to contain my
pain and avoid the nastier human emotions.

I tell Miriam of my doubts there will ever be a baby. In all the
years I contemplated children, infertility is one possibility I
never considered.

"In all those years, I expected— No, wait, it's more than
that. I *assumed* that I'd have a baby," I say. "And now, no
matter how hard I may try, I can't make a baby happen. If it
doesn't, and if it's the absence of a baby that's making me
depressed, how can I be sure the depression will ever lift?"

I describe how my mind has been racing nonstop in search
of an alternative that might ease the anticipated blow. "I think
maybe I should resume tutoring junior high school students.
Or volunteer to work with inner city kids." I pause, feeling
sheepish. "You know me. Always a Plan A, a Plan B."

"So, if it doesn't happen, you'll make another plan," Miriam
says calmly. "Only one small piece of you is in pain. It's like
when you step on a nail. Your whole body may ache, but only
your foot is in pain." She pauses, then says more sternly, "It's
just pain. It won't kill you. You must learn to sit with it."

I want to, I really do. But the symptoms of depression are
descending so rapidly that I can barely keep pace with the
changed rhythm of my days. I have no appetite. I'm sleeping no
more than two, maybe three hours a night. I can barely
concentrate on anything except my misery. Time is beginning
to stretch; a single hour can feel like an entire day. I feel
trapped, and my mind is racing round and round in search of
an exit.

"There's this incessant dialogue in my head," I tell Miriam a
few days later, "me divided against myself in pursuit of a
logical explanation for this pain. Part of me insists, 'I've always
wanted kids!' That only a child will give my life a sense of
meaning, reward, and challenge. But another part believes this

depression is self-indulgent and within my control to stop. It's not as if I've built my whole life around having children. Sometimes I wonder if I'm just using kids as an excuse not to face what's happening at work."

"It's easier to think that," Miriam says.

"How do you mean?"

"You're trying to force the focus back on work because that feels more controllable."

It's one of those insights that makes the years of therapy seem worthwhile.

"Stop flailing," Miriam commands. "You know what Jung said about the unconscious?"

"What?"

"It's unconscious."

I laugh. That's very funny, coming from a shrink.

The friends in whom I confide, all of whom have known me since college days, none of whom seem to question the intensity of my desire for a child, also try to help.

"I remember what it was like to think I would never have a child," says Beth, her gift for empathy attuning her instantly to my distress. Now the mother of a little girl, Beth hadn't known at the time she married John if his vasectomy could be reversed. "It's so hard."

"Worst case scenario, you adopt," suggests Lynn, who's now counting down the weeks to her delivery.

"Look on the bright side," offers Valerie, an attorney with a prodigious memory who has more than once backstopped or refreshed my own recollections of Jill-and-Joe collisions past. "Joe is being supportive."

Yet nothing makes a dent until I speak with Jan, the most levelheaded and least sentimental of my friends. Like me, Jan's a childless, involved aunt. Unlike me, she doesn't worry that career and family aspirations may be part of the same zero-sum equation. "It's so basic, wanting to have a child and wanting to experience motherhood," she says. "That's why it's so disturbing. How could something so basic be so difficult?"

Of course. Why shouldn't I be thrown? Who wouldn't be?

After two months of relentless self-interrogation, the debate inside my head subsides and a mental space opens for me to see and accept the obvious. Whenever, whyever, however, for me a child is no longer a choice. It's an imperative.

IV

IT'S ONE THING TO WANT CHILDREN. IT'S ANOTHER thing to be obsessed by them.

Each day, every day, starts with the wan bleat of my digital thermometer telling me the day's reading is ready. Don Imus, my preferred morning radio fix, ridicules me with his tireless daily campaign to stamp out SIDS, Sudden Infant Death Syndrome. Who's my favorite male feminist talking with this morning? Anna Quindlen, the professional woman's favorite guide to motherhood. Flip to CBS and the local news lead is inevitably some child tragedy: baby dies in burning building, mother abandons baby in dumpster, abusive father beats baby daughter.

Once I hit Manhattan, the landscape mocks, no matter which direction I turn. The streets of midtown teem with women pushing strollers. Escape underground, and the subway platforms are crammed with females toting tots on their backs or in slings on their chests. Pick a car, any car. When the doors slide open, the first advertisement that greets features either a child in need of dental care or welfare services, or a discreetly worded message promoting abortion services. I never sit the length of my trip anymore; always there's some woman to offer my seat to, some woman with a stomach so swollen that I'm certain she'll fall down shrieking with labor contractions at any moment. If I flee to Central Park at lunchtime to try to walk off my pain, the tortures accumulate. Every bus shelter along Sixth Avenue in the seven blocks that lead from the Time & Life Building to the nearest park entrance sports a body-length advertisement for mineral water featuring a bare-chested mother hugging her wide-eyed, naked infant. In the park, school-age children jam the pathways, racing circles around the slow-moving mothers with their bundled infants.

When, please, did the world's most famous walking city become the city of mothers walking their babies?

With each passing day, my sense of yearning and urgency deepens. But the fertility maze is a complicated jigsaw. In each menstrual cycle, there's only one chance to get it right. Miss that moment, and you're stuck for another long month to cope with your pitiful hopes and pitiless despairs. Moreover, Manhattan is a town of frustrated Baby Boomers, impatient, even desperate, to worship at the altar of the fertility gods. You must queue up and wait your turn.

Joe, as promised, calls the sperm specialist the day after we receive his lo-mo test results. Dr. Edelson's receptionist says the earliest available appointment is in January. No good. Joe will be out of town on business. Next opening? Early February, three months away.

I, meanwhile, have the tubal patency test recommended by Dr. Lowell. On the appointed day, I cross town at lunchtime for the unpronounceable hysterosalpingogram, a procedure that involves flushing a woman's fallopian tubes with dye to test for blockages.

"You may experience some discomfort," the male doctor says.

As I lie on my side, I'm suddenly seized by an abdominal pain so wrenching that I gasp, then scream. The cramping sensation relaxes, grips, relaxes, grips. Is this what labor feels like? I wonder. Is this the closest I'll ever come to that experience? Far from minding the pain, I embrace it. Unlike my irrational depression, this pain is explicable, admissible, sane. It has a beginning and a middle. It has an end.

My tubes are unobstructed, but the news does little to hearten me. The test has cost more than three hundred dollars to verify what, to me, was never in question.

On the third day of my next menstrual cycle, which should start any day now, I'm to begin taking the 50-milligram Clomid tablets prescribed by Dr. Lowell. Lynn, who, both as a friend and a psychologist, can sense my emotional disintegration, is trying to bolster my spirits.

"Remember, Clomid worked for me," she says by phone. "Maybe it will happen for you, too."

A conflict in work schedules is our excuse for not getting together. But we both know I can no longer bear to look at Lynn's swollen stomach. Appalled by the meanness of my spirit, I apologize for my inability to share in the excitement of her approaching due date. Silently, I'm hoping she'll offer me a pass on her pending baby shower.

"I know this shower will be difficult for you," she says, "but I really hope you'll come. It wouldn't be the same without you."

"Of course, I'll be there," I say.

At lunch, I force myself to enter a midtown department store and press the elevator button for the babywares floor. A few years earlier when I'd heard that a friend was "expressing" her milk during the work day, I'd assumed that referred to the mode of transport, and conjured an image of a guy on a bicycle, wending his way through Manhattan traffic to rush the freshly pumped milk home to baby. When I'd passed along this bit of misinformation to Lynn, she'd answered with a fascinated, "Really," as impressed by the advances of modern motherhood as I.

Now, my thought is that Lynn and her baby are going to need all the help they can get. I tell a saleswoman that I want to assemble a baby starter-kit. "You know," I say. "The basic, essential stuff that no one else is likely to think of." With me tagging numbly behind, the woman plucks items from a variety of counters. Receiving blankets. Onesies. Tiny washcloths. Crib sheets.

I've vacationed with Lynn's mother and sister. I know her aunt and mother-in-law. Her sister-in-law and I threw Lynn's surprise wedding shower. I gave the toast at Lynn's wedding. This shower should be akin to a homecoming for me.

Instead, it's excruciating. As I sit through the festivities, my agitation mounts. Like Lynn and I, most of her friends are writers. As they talk on and on about their work, not even breaking from their chatter long enough to watch Lynn unwrap her gifts, I want to yell, "Shut up! Give this baby its proper due." Mentally, I align with the small clutch of mothers in the room who ooh and ahh over each gift.

On the way home, I get stuck in a traffic jam that ties me up on Ninth Avenue for nearly an hour. By the time I enter the Lincoln Tunnel, my patience is spent. I open my mouth wide and scream at the top of my lungs.

"—so he suggested I try boxer shorts."

Joe is making his nightly attempt to coax a smile out of me. Tonight, he's brought home news of a conversation with a colleague to whom he's confided that we've hit some conception obstacles. The guy had responded by asking if Joe wore briefs or boxers.

"What's underwear got to do with anything?" I ask.

Joe laughs. "I don't know. He said it has something to do with the temperature of the sperm."

"So, tomorrow you'll get some boxers, right?"

Joe looks at me like I'm crazy. "Wease. Lighten up. This is a joke. A *joke*."

"It sounds like it makes sense. Was he joking when he said it?" Joe shrugs uncertainly. "So, what's the big deal," I say, my voice rising. "Get some boxer shorts."

"I hate boxer shorts."

"It's okay for me to pump my body up with fertility drugs, but it's not okay for you to change your underwear?"

"This is ridiculous. I'm not going to wear boxer shorts. God, Jill, will you please calm down."

The expression on my face makes it plain that's not going to happen anytime soon. "Look," Joe says. "When I see Edelson, I'll ask him about the damn underwear. Okay? Are you satisfied?"

He picks up the remote and clicks on the TV. He's trying. He really is. But there's no dealing with me on a rational level. I'm getting crazier by the hour.

The day after the U.S. invades Somalia, I go over the top.

As I sit before my office computer, trying to write a late-breaking cover story about the three thousand American troops who have waded ashore in Mogadishu, I can't concentrate. Over and over, I read the words on the pieces of paper piling up on my desk, reports from *Time* correspondents, newspapers, wire services. On the TV, CNN correspondents natter on and on with minute-by-minute updates. On my screen, "You have a message" blinks again and again, with internal messages from editors requesting that I remember to tuck this and that into the story.

But I can't achieve the immersion I need to process all of this fast-moving information. My concentration is splintered into too many pieces. A part of me is focused on the desperate depressing thoughts that will not stop pounding in my head. A part is focused on the war I'm waging to train my attention on the jumble of news reports that keep accumulating and changing. Another part is tormented by the hitherto un-thinkable—not completing my assignment. And a part of me is actually writing against deadline. Though sentences are filling up my computer screen, I can't tell if these sentences link up to make coherent paragraphs and if the graphs link up to make a cogent narrative. As I race from sentence to sentence, I can neither remember what I wrote just moments before, nor where I meant the next sentence to head when I began the one I'm working on.

Toward evening, as I'm still struggling to complete the mental equivalent of a marathon in a gale storm with the winds blowing against me, something happens. Is it exhaus-tion? Strain? Mental collapse? Whatever it is, it's unlike any-thing I've ever experienced. I disintegrate, meaning the inte-grated parts of myself come apart. As my five senses attend to the business of finishing the story, my mind wanders off somewhere else entirely. This is something different, some-thing more scary than the feelings of despair and insignifi-cance I'm already battling. My mind, I realize, has quite literally taken leave of my senses. Since this is a first for me, I have no idea if once you take leave, you ever return. I'm terrified.

Around midnight, I press the computer key that sends my story on for editing, then I put on my coat and leave the building. Though it is pouring and I have neither a hat nor an umbrella, I start to walk. An hour later, I'm still walking. Round and round midtown Manhattan. Over to the Christmas tree in Rockefeller Center. Past the store windows, bright with holiday displays. Down the puddled streets. In an arcade, I come across three teenage boys flapping umbrellas and making noise. Instead of hurrying away from this unexpected midnight encounter with a group of overheated boys, I stop and watch them, struck by how joyous they seem. How playful. How incredibly normal.

I start to weep uncontrollably. Why must everything be so hard? Will I never have a clear-headed, single-tracked thought again? Will there never be relief from the litany of misery in my head? Am I cracking up? And if I am, what exactly does that mean?

When I return to the office, a researcher tells me the story went through with few changes. When I punch up my messages, there are praising notes from two editors. Then I call up the story and try to spot the editing changes, but I can't. I don't remember what I wrote in the first place.

Two weeks later, I'm pushing the food around on my plate, trying to make a convincing show of enjoying the Christmas turkey, when the phone rings in my sister-in-law's Pasadena condominium.

"Jill?" Esme says. "It's for you."

I take deep breaths, trying to steel myself as I walk from the earthquake-proofed dining room to the kitchen. I've been anticipating this call.

"Hi. It's Lynn." She sounds tired but happy. "It's a boy."

I can only hope that I asked all the appropriate questions. Details of Lynn's delivery. Length and weight of her son. Health of the baby. Health of the new mother. I can only hope that my expressions of congratulation and joy were convincing.

In a blur of pain, I return to the dinner table. "Lynn had a boy," I tell Esme, her husband Bob, my parents-in-law, Joe. I sit a moment, then say, "Excuse me."

I go into the guest bathroom, sit on the toilet and weep. We were going to share a hospital room, have our babies together. I feel both inconsolable and unworthy of consolation. As much as I loathe my unpregnant state, I detest even more the self-absorbed person I've become.

Friends and family step up their attempts to ease my pain.

"Almost everyone I know had trouble getting pregnant," says Valerie.

"Is there any chance of you and Joe getting away for a vacation?" my mother asks.

"Wease, I think you should be seeing a shrink in New York," Joe presses.

"I can give you a referral to get a prescription for an antidepressant," Miriam suggests. "There's no point in all this suffering."

None of it helps. Other people's pregnancy travails no longer reassure. A vacation can do little good, since I'd have to bring me along. And a change of therapists is out of the question; I don't have the energy to begin building a new relationship. As for antidepressants, a call to my gynecologist has confirmed my suspicion: if I go on medication, I'll either have to abandon my efforts to get pregnant or risk damaging a fetus. Neither option is acceptable.

As it is, I'm already battling a generic suspicion of doctors and their prescribed remedies. After I spiral-fractured my right leg in a ski accident at age twelve, a doctor had set the limb at the wrong angle. When the toe-to-thigh cast came off three months later, the leg was badly misaligned. Three orthopedists told my parents the leg would have to be rebroken. Instead, my parents tracked down a gifted homeopath who taught my father a painful technique for massaging my leg back into alignment. Months of my father's patient peanut-oil massages, in combination with swimming, had restored the limb to full health.

That experience had made my parents such strong proponents of alternative medicine, with its emphasis on a mind-body connection, that their tolerance for common ailments withered. "Smolowes don't get migraines," my father once told Valerie when she requested an aspirin for a pounding headache. Smolowes also don't get allergies. Colds. Certainly not depressions.

Yet, plainly, I have one. I want to believe Miriam when she says that my "suffering" can be relieved, but I'm convinced that my psychic eddy has no biological component. I've brought this on myself. Only I can make it go away.

Once again, it's a comment from my levelheaded friend Jan that makes a dent. "I think depression may be a side effect of Clomid. Have you checked a physician's handbook?"

I go to the reference section of the *Time* library and consult several drug manuals. One warns against taking Clomid if you're in a depressed state; another cautions that in rare cases Clomid can induce depression. This, I find very reassuring. The Clomid, I know, hasn't induced my depression. But it's possible, even likely, that the hormonal stimulant has played a role in stimulating my mind to the bizarre state of recent weeks. Just knowing there *might* be a biological explanation for my mental fragmentation calms me. The side effect will fade.

Until now, I've been thinking that to be happy, I must get pregnant, my last entry for 1992 reads. Learning of the Clomid, I instead think, No, I'm not willing to go through that to get pregnant. My mental health and stability is more important to me. That seems reassuring, claiming myself again, my own well-being. Not leaving it up to uncontrollable variables.

Poor Joe.

For almost two months, he's endured my anxiety, my depression, my acute need for isolation. Now, he's making a reasonable request. He wants to attend the New Year's party we've been invited to by our country friends Arthur and Ken. I don't want to go. I don't want our friends to see me so miserable. I don't want to put a damper on the festivities.

But Joe's patience is wearing thin. "Come on, Wease," he persists. "It'll be good for you."

I arrive at the party feeling tentative, as if I'm entering a room full of strangers rather than the home of two close friends. I hang along the fringes of the largest gathering in the crowded living room. At the center of the group, a forty-something woman named Shelly is talking animatedly, her smile so wide that her face can barely contain it. Her husband looks every bit as pleased. "She's pregnant," someone fills me in.

"Really," I say, trying to keep my expression neutral. "I didn't know they were trying."

"Oh, yeah. For years." Shelly and Gary, I learn, have conceived using the mysterious intrauterine insemination process.

When the circle thins, I approach Shelly hesitantly. During the nine months Joe and I have been trying to conceive, I've mentioned our efforts to no one, save family members and a few close friends. I also don't know Shelly well enough to know if my questions will be welcomed, or regarded as an invasion of her privacy. Briefly, I tell her that Joe and I may be doing an IUI.

"IUI babies," she laughs, "are a dime a dozen."

What was the procedure like? "It was simple," she answers. "The only thing that was hard was the months of Clomid I did prior to the procedure. It sent me up the walls."

"I just did a cycle of it and literally thought I was losing my mind," I say. "Did anything like that happen to you?"

"Oh, yeah. There were days when I was afraid to drive the car. Some days, I couldn't even leave the house."

Donna, the doctor from my now-defunct reading group, joins the conversation. While I knew that she was still trying to get pregnant, only now do I learn the extent of her efforts. IUI, IVF, ZIFT. The whole alphabet soup of assisted reproductive wonders. When others approach to congratulate Shelly, I draw

Donna into a cove off the living room and speak candidly about my depression. "Do you think the Clomid could have been what sent me off the rails?"

"Absolutely," she says. "These drugs are very strong."

Relieved to be talking to someone who can truly empathize, I brief her on our miniscule efforts to date. "Why, didn't your doctor have you try an ovulation predictor kit first?" she asks.

"What's that?"

These kits, she explains, measure levels of luteinizing hormone, or LH, to help pinpoint the most fertile moment in a woman's cycle. Why hadn't Dr. Lowell recommended that I try one of these noninvasive kits, available over the counter in any pharmacy, before mucking around with my hormones?

As Donna talks about some of the options and attendant risks ahead, my aggravation builds, not toward Dr. Lowell, but at myself. After my childhood experience with the broken leg, how could I, of all people, have swallowed those pills without first doing my homework? I take out my reporter's pad and make note of several resources Donna has found useful.

"Don't hesitate to call if you have any questions," she says. "Whatever happens, it's going to be alright. Really. It is."

When I glance at my watch, I'm surprised to see that it's almost midnight. Donna and I have been talking for close to ninety minutes. For the first time in weeks, the minutes have proceeded at a normal pace, rather than in tortoise time. When the hour tolls 1993, I'm gyrating and Joe is Freddying to Madonna. As we exchange a sweaty kiss, I feel better than I've felt since learning of Joe's lo-mo sperm.

Within days of that, I feel fine. Optimistic. Like me again.

Initially, I peer out at the world like a bear who has slumbered through winter and now emerges cautiously from her cave, distrustful that the snows have really gone. Hello? Am I really here? Will this last? As time gathers momentum and my thoughts expand to embrace my usual range of interests, I begin to forget about myself for minutes, then hours, then whole days at a time. By mid-January, the cloud of depression is completely dissipated.

At the office, the new year has ushered in our new managing editor, rekindling a magazine-wide feeling of anticipation and purpose. Coincidentally, my departmental transfer, engineered by the outgoing ME, has come through, putting me in place to write about the incoming Clinton administration from its first fitful days. The Zoe Baird debacle. The Kimba Wood debacle. The gays-in-the-military debacle. I even score a small reporting coup, tracking down an elusive fundamentalist preacher whose fiery Koranic teachings are exciting alarm in both Washington and Cairo. I feel like I've been recalled from the sidelines.

Though all of this helps, it's my rearranged thinking about infertility that has the greatest impact. Nothing about our still-undiagnosed circumstance has changed, yet I feel as if the prospect of having a baby is again open to Joe and me. Until the New Year's party, I'd been bumbling along in isolation and ignorance. That evening had suggested there were more effective ways to cope.

Following up on Donna's advice, I contacted Resolve, a national network of infertile people who share information through publications, seminars, and support groups. The first newsletter to arrive from my local chapter indicated that Resolve was equipped to handle almost any contingency imaginable. Support groups were customized to address the concerns special to Hasidic Jews or Catholics, women over forty or single women under thirty-five, couples interested in IVF or surrogacy, donor eggs or adoption. Have endometriosis? Call this number. Considering surgery to reverse a vasectomy? Call that one. On seemingly any subject, including the competence and bedside manner of specific doctors, you could get an earful from compassionate people who knew the problem from the inside out.

My concentration restored, I delved into the literature and learned that 5.3 million Americans are wrestling with infertility. That startling statistic, which embraces roughly 10 percent of the reproductive-age population, touches one of every seven couples who might reasonably hope to conceive. Thirty percent of the problems are attributable to the male; 30 percent to the female; the rest to both partners or unexplained factors. With everything in maximum working order, the odds of a woman conceiving in any given month are just one in four. Factor in any of the ugly-sounding problems that can arise—among them hostile mucus in the cervix, dilated veins in the scrotum, retrograde ejaculation or menstruation—and it begins to seem that the *real* freaks are the women who manage to get pregnant without benefit of needles, vials, or petri dishes.

I also began to collect personal stories. All I had to do was mention that Joe and I were facing fertility problems and— bam!—the horror stories rolled. The anecdotes told by men usually focused on careless treatment by callous doctors. One man was told by a specialist, "Don't bother to get undressed. You're clinically sterile." Another man spoke indignantly of a message left on their home answering machine: "Cathy. This is Dr. Cohen. You're barren. Don't try to have children." Click. My own favorite was the one about the guy who fled screaming from his doctor's office after seeing his defective sperm projected on a wall in living color.

The stories told by women focused more on the emotional toll, with words like "depressed," "obsessive," and "crazed" cropping up again and again. A friend confided that she'd attended a baby shower, only to spend the entire time in the bathroom sobbing. Another admitted that she couldn't bring herself to call her mom on Mother's Day. Repeatedly I was told, "If I heard 'Just relax and it will happen' one more time, I was going to—" What? They could imagine dropping bombs on the homes of insensitive relatives, killing pushy in-laws, ripping the wombs out of all-too-fertile friends. But never could any of them imagine the moment when they would just relax.

Invariably, the stories ended happily. "Barren" Cathy went on to bear two healthy children. Another woman had been in the delivery room for the birth of her adopted son and had even cut the umbilical cord. "You'll be a mother," I heard over and over. "You're just starting. Be patient. You'll see."

I had no way of gauging if all these happy endings accurately represented my odds of becoming a mother. Perhaps they reflected the tendency of people to share only good news, or the greater likelihood of satisfied customers to speak up, while those still choking on pain maintained their silence. What *was* clear was that as I inhaled these stories, what interested me most was the outcome, not the means.

Joe's February visit to the sperm specialist turns up two possibilities: a varicocele, which Dr. Edelson describes as a varicose vein inside the scrotum, or a semen blockage. Cautioning that corrective surgery may be required, Edelson schedules more tests.

A week later we cross town, almost to the East River, to have our first meeting with Dr. Feldman, Lynn's fertility specialist at New York Hospital/Cornell Medical Center. Lynn has cautioned that though Feldman is a knowledgeable doctor, she isn't one of the great communicators and can be quick to jump to alarmist conclusions. After an ambiguous ultrasound, she'd offered to abort the fetus Lynn was carrying, the one that eventually became Lynn's healthy son. On the other hand, Feldman is affiliated with one of Manhattan's finest fertility programs, according to a survey in *New York* magazine. And Lynn is now a mother, for me the strongest recommendation of all.

We wait. And wait. "God, I hate doctors," I mutter to Joe.

Finally, we're escorted into a tiny, cheerless consulting

room with an empty desk, three purple chairs, and some smudges on the mauve walls. After some more waiting, Dr. Feldman enters. She shakes hands with each of us, sits down behind the desk, then opens a manila folder, and begins silently to read the report from Edelson's office.

"Men with similar motility and volume problems have impregnated their wives," she begins. She tells us that among pregnant women, 70 percent conceived within the first six months of trying, and half of the remaining 30 percent within a year. "If you were a little younger, the nine months of trying would be no big deal," she says. "But given your age, you're right to begin getting diagnosed now."

Over the next hour as she takes our medical histories, I feel reassured by her throughness, her quiet, shy demeanor, her physical resemblance to a childhood friend of mine. When she observes that my menstrual cycles are erratic in length and frequency, I think she's a veritable Sherlock Holmes; none of my prior gynecologists had ever made that observation.

"Some of the shorter cycles may have involved no ovulation," she says. "Fertility drugs will help."

I tell her about my adverse reaction to the one cycle of Clomid. "I'm hoping to avoid any drugs."

"It could be a problem that you don't tolerate Clomid well," she answers.

I choose not to pursue the point. No longer depressed, I'm feeling less resistant to giving drugs another try. I'm also not concerned since I'm well aware that females are born with all their eggs and that as the supply shrinks with the passing of years, ovulation can become more sporadic.

Feldman prescribes a specific ovulation predictor kit and instructs me to begin testing on Day 8, two days earlier than is standard. She also wants me to return on Day 3 of my next cycle to draw blood in order to get a reading on the levels of my estrogen and FSH, or follicle stimulating hormone, which stimulates egg development.

I grunt, frustrated. I'm at Day 5, which means another month's delay. At least Feldman's heard of predictor kits.

She takes me to another room and, after a routine exam, instructs a nurse to draw blood. The nurse jabs my arm three times, and says irritably, "You have terrible veins," before getting the blood she needs.

As I leave, Feldman says, "You still might get pregnant on your own."

Three days later, I buy the predictor kit and read the instructions carefully. Unlike most kits, which offer results within a few minutes, this one requires an hour of vigilance as the urine specimen is shifted between three sets of vials. Although the instructions emphasize the need for to-the-minute precision, I get distracted and overshoot the last urine transfer by an hour.

I went for the Day 3 test today, I write in mid-March. *Once again, they had trouble drawing blood, turning my arm black and blue while they poked and prodded. This test should show if I'm ovulating . . . Joe, meanwhile, gave a semen specimen last week, only to be told his volume was too low and that he'd have to come back and give more. So he had an appointment this morning, too. He says part of his ejaculation got caught in toilet paper and that he may have to go back yet again. This can be incredibly time-consuming. With the subway delays and the [snow] drifts, it took me 90 minutes just to get to Feldman's office.*

Five days later, I begin a new predictor kit, vowing this time not to screw it up. When I hear nothing from Dr. Feldman, I assume my Day 3 test turned up no surprises. Then Joe and I leave for a two-week vacation in Guatemala, where I set aside all thoughts of babies and enjoy myself.

During Joe's second visit to the sperm specialist, Dr. Edelson expresses reluctance to proceed just yet with surgery that might augment volume and enhance motility. The long list of potential risks includes scar tissue, nerve injury, infection, bleeding, testicular atrophy. Before subjecting Joe to any of those possibilities, Edelson says, he wants to run one more test, a sperm penetration assay. The test, he explains, is designed to see if Joe's sperm can penetrate a hamster egg and, by inference, mine. If the results are positive, Edelson recommends that we try three intrauterine inseminations before putting Joe under the knife. When Joe concurs, Edelson picks up the phone and dials Feldman to run the plan by her.

Edelson consulted with Feldman, then told Joe I had "tubular problems, an inflamed disease history, ovulation problems." All of this throws and angers me. I never heard from Feldman after the Day 3 test, so I assumed all was normal. I don't know what that other stuff is; the fallopian test showed my tubes were open. I called Feldman's office and was told, "There's a death in her family. Call back the week after next." I'm pretty pissed. They take hundreds of dollars for the tests, then don't tell you what's going on. Does this mean that it's not just Joe with a problem but me as well? If so, does that mean I'll have to do Clomid again? Am I in a mental state to handle it? Can we get pregnant?

As I wait for Feldman to return and answer my questions, I become increasingly edgy. I worry that I may be slipping back into depression, and remind myself repeatedly that only now are we really beginning fertility procedures. If the hamster test is negative, there's corrective surgery. If it's positive, there's IUI. If that fails, there's IVF. If that doesn't work, then— I try to stop my speculating, knowing that if I race too far ahead of this slow process, I may lapse back into despair.

On April 28, the first national "Bring Your Daughter to Work Day," I awaken feeling nauseous. I dash to the bathroom and vomit. For the last three days, both Joe and I have been feeling queasy. We think it may be a touch of food poison.

At work, I'm paired with a junior from a local technical high school, my "daughter" for the day. This had seemed like a jolly idea when I'd volunteered for "mother" duty just a few weeks earlier. But with pregnancy concerns now rattling me again, the day seems interminable. Seeing so many of my colleagues with their daughters as I squire this pseudo-daughter from one planned event to the next leaves me fighting tears and the selfish question pounding in my head: Where's mine?

At a luncheon for all the participants, a colleague comes over to introduce her two daughters and asks if I'm going to address the group. When I say no, she says, "That's too bad. You're such a good role model. You handle it all so well." I look at her in amazement.

After the kids are taken to tour *Time*'s art department, I return to my office to work. My week's assignment deals with a newly released study of nine hundred and two female Harvard graduates who are wrestling with the "work/family dilemma." Though their hardships are real, I can think only that they at least have a family to juggle.

I hook up again with my "daughter," see her through a farewell serving of cookies and congratulations, then return to my office and burst into tears.

When I vomit the next morning for the fifth day straight, Joe convinces me to visit his internist, who tells me I have gastritis. I spend the next two days in bed, alternately vomiting and sleeping.

This is so unlike me to stay home from work that as I lay in bed, I wonder if I've unconsciously willed this upon myself to avoid the assignment about the Harvard women. I phone the colleague now handling the story and apologize for my absence. "Don't be ridiculous," she says. "Just get better." When I offer the same apology to an editor, he says, "You're the most professional person around here. No one would think for a minute you are anything but sick."

The unexpected praise from an unexpected quarter should

cheer me. When it doesn't, I call Miriam for the first time in months and tell her I fear I'm backsliding.

The next day, a Friday, I still feel weak and sweaty, but the symptoms seem insufficient to justify not showing up for work on *Time*'s busiest day. "Then take a mental health day," Joe presses. Plainly he, too, is concerned about the slippage in my mood.

That night as we turn out the light, Joe tries to kid me out of my descending bleakness by wondering aloud what it would take for a hamster to turn him on. It would help, he says, if the hamster were a little flirtatious. Maybe showed up in a negligee, a delicate strand of pearls at the neck. Perhaps a touch of lipstick. I start making squeaking sounds, and soon we're laughing.

The laughter helps. That night, I sleep.

Two days later, I'm back in the tunnel, my mind racing round and round in search of the escape hatch. I'm convinced that Dr. Feldman's undelivered news can only be bad, and I want a Plan B in place when she tells me Plan A has failed. I know what that plan should be; I've known for months. Without effort, without discussion, my mind and heart have easily embraced the idea of adoption. Without effort, without discussion, my mind and heart have also uneasily settled into certainty that Joe will never agree to such a plan. So I've said nothing.

"How can you handle all this so well?" I ask Joe. "Is it because you don't care if we have a child?"

Joe shrugs, nods. "A kid would just be a noisy pain in the neck." A moment passes, then perhaps reacting to my crestfallen expression, he adds, "Maybe I'll warm to a child."

"Would you be willing to consider adoption?"

"Why would I want to raise someone else's kid?" he snaps. Joe has been preternaturally patient with me these last six months. I back right off.

The next night Joe goes on the attack about Miriam. He insists that phone sessions aren't legitimate therapy and that I should be seeing someone in Manhattan.

"Don't you dare try to interfere in my relationship with Miriam," I tell him, furious. "Just butt out."

Miriam says this is a common thing by a loved one, wanting a "magical cure." She says parents will drag kids to twenty therapists to find the magical answer. For Joe, the local shrink is a magical solution.

I hear from Dr. Feldman the next day. She tells me that my ovulation results were in the "intermediate range, and is not a big concern." My estrogen is also a little high. If Joe's hamster test comes back positive, she suggests we proceed with an IUI this month. I'm to do the predictor kit twice a day. The insemination will be the day after my LH surges.

When I tell her about my depressed state of mind, she seems unsurprised. "This is an *extremely* stressful life experience," she says. "It can be more stressful even than losing a parent. You should get help with it." When I ask about antidepressants, an option that Miriam has again raised, Feldman warns that they can have an impact on the menstrual cycle. "Can you increase your therapy?" she asks. "This is a temporary event in your life."

She also asks that I come in for a Day 2 test. I say I'm on Day 3 of my period. "Then come in today," she says. At lunch I zoom across town. This time, I get a different nurse. She tells me that my veins are lovely and draws blood in a single prick.

Two days later, a colleague mentions that she's pregnant with her second child. "That's wonderful," I say, then feel embarrassed when my eyes start to water. "I'm having trouble getting pregnant myself," I explain.

"No wonder, given the hours we work," she laughs.

"It's not that," I say. "My husband and I are having problems."

"Are you seeing a specialist?" I nod. "God, I'm so stupid! That's the second time I've blurted out I'm pregnant, only to learn—"

"Don't be ridiculous," I interrupt. "It's wonderful that you're pregnant."

Though we smile at each other, we both feel like shit.

That night, I slowly fray Joe's nerves as I go over and over the timing of the days ahead. What if my LH surges before we get Joe's hamster test results? Will that mean missing the IUI and losing yet another month?

"So far, all we've done is be diagnosed," he finally cuts in. "What you've gone through so far is trivial."

"Not trivial," I lash back. "*You* are calm because you're indifferent about whether I get pregnant. Don't belittle or dismiss my emotions. We're in very different places on this."

He can hear that I'm working myself into a lather, and says in a more soothing tone, "I could understand if we'd tried everything and then you got upset, but we haven't tried *anything* yet."

I know he's right. We've tried nothing. If we miss this month, so what? We'll do it next month. Or the one after that. That's the reasonable position, the logical position. The healthy position. But after three months of restored normalcy, I'm no longer healthy and we both know it.

On Day 8, I begin the twice daily urine tests. When I have to conduct the evening tests at the office, I feel like I'm caught in a Monty Python sketch as I drape my minichemistry set under a towel, then escort my urine to and from the Ladies' Room with what I hope is a measure of dignity. During this hour, it is impossible to work efficiently, since I must keep a vigilant eye on the time.

On May 11, the day my LH surges, Joe's hamster test results

come back with encouraging news: there were 19.8 penetrations per hamster ovum; only 5 are required to satisfy the IUI gods.

The next morning, Joe leaves Hoboken near dawn to make the ninety-minute commute to the hospital lab. When I arrive hours later, I'm handed a test tube filled with an inch of magenta fluid. Joe's unrecognizable sperm. "Keep it warm," a lab technician instructs. Clutching the vial with supreme concentration, I escort Joe's sperm to the IVF clinic, then wait.

As the minutes tick by, the woman in the next chair strikes up a conversation. She tells me she's been doing fertility procedures for three years. She'd almost given up, she says, but her newest doctor, by reputation a divinity among infertility specialists, has given her new hope. Now, she travels from New Jersey to the IVF clinic several mornings a week for tests and sonograms. The time requirements are so strenuous that she's quit her job.

Three years? I marvel silently. Unimaginable.

An hour past my designated appointment, my name is called. The insemination, performed by a nurse, is swift and painless. "Have sex with your husband tonight and tomorrow night," she says.

That's sweet, I think as I follow her instructions and lie unmoving for the next twenty minutes. That way we'll never know if it was the IUI or us. Then again, I muse, what difference does it make? With doctors now telling us when we can have sex (to take best advantage of my cycle) and when we cannot (to maximize Joe's sperm volume), our couplings have become about as passionate and spontaneous as an IUI.

For days after the insemination, I feel a churning in my stomach. I wonder if the throbbing is a baby or an ulcer. Joe's internist had warned that the gastritis attack could give way to an ulcer. When my chin erupts in acne, I wonder if my hormones are acting up. Maybe I *am* pregnant. Just in case, I cut out all coffee and diet sodas, and though I have no appetite, force myself to eat lots of vegetables and fruits. But the depression doesn't ease. I don't believe I'm pregnant. Not really.

"You're controlling the grieving process, but you don't know it," Miriam says in reponse to my inability to feel any hope that I might be pregnant. "You're not a pessmistic person, but when something is important to you, you're so frightened of loss that you prepare, thinking that you'll suffer the loss less."

Ah, yes. Plan B.

When I get my period May 23, I'm surprised that I react so calmly to the disappointment. Maybe, I think, it's because after months of diagnostic tests and procedures, we're moving closer to identifying and correcting the problem.

May 25: *The ground has shifted again.*

Dr. Feldman, it turns out, hadn't yet read the results of my second Day 3 test at the time of the IUI. A normal FSH reading, she now explains, is 12; certainly, it needs to be under 25. The first test had come back 14. "Borderline. Not great, but not terrible." This time, however, the reading is 41. "That's markedly elevated and fairly serious. This kind of problem does not respond well to therapy. We need to do aggressive things."

"Do you mean in vitro fertilization?"

"Maybe," she says. "But it may not be worthwhile in your case."

What she's saying makes no sense. The information I've been gathering suggests that I still have many steps ahead in the infertility dance. Pergonal shots, egg extractions, sonograms. What about GIFT and ZIFT?

"What's going on?" I demand. Feldman is reluctant to answer my questions over the phone, but I'm persistent.

Finally, she allows, "The FSH and estrogen readings are surprising given your age. Your reading is more like that of a woman in her mid-forties. You're still ovulating, but your pituitary is working overtime." She pauses, then adds quietly,

"I'm sorry." She insists that Joe and I need to come in together for further discussion. And she wants me to come in today and tomorrow for Day 2 and Day 3 tests.

She transfers me to her secretary Elaine, who says the earliest available appointment is not for another two weeks. I take it, then call Joe, who works just eight floors above me in the Time & Life Building. "I just talked to Dr. Feldman, and—" I stop, unable to continue. Alarmed, Joe says he'll be right down.

I'm so distraught by the time he gets to my office that all Joe can do is rock me. When I regain my voice, I repeat my conversation with Dr. Feldman. "Maybe this is a blessing in its own weird way," I say. "Plainly, I'm not cut out for this infertility stuff."

"Maybe," Joe responds, "I should see a therapist to deal with my resistance toward adoption."

It is the first time he's brought up adoption by himself. I nod, only vaguely hopeful he means it.

V

"I'm sorry."

It is inconceivable that only twenty-four hours have passed since I last spoke by phone with Elaine.

"You must listen to hysterical women all day."

Only twenty-four hours since Dr. Feldman extinguished my last hope, then transferred me to this efficient scheduler for an appointment.

"But this is very hard."

It has felt like an eternity. During these twenty-four hours, friends have convinced me that two weeks is far too long to be left hanging about my diagnosis. They have persuaded me to call Feldman's secretary and demand that she move up my appointment. Now, I'm twenty-four hours more impatient. Twenty-four hours more agitated. Twenty-four hours more depressed.

"Have you gone through this, Elaine?"

"Yes."

"Then you understand."

"Yes."

For one brief moment we connect, this stern gatekeeper and I. She agrees that the discrepancy between my first two tests is large; that the results of this new set are important. She'll phone me as soon as they're in and, meanwhile, will put me on a waiting list.

"But," Elaine warns, "it's unlikely something will open before your next appointment."

"Dr. Feldman said I should come in as soon as possible," I persist.

"That *is* as soon as possible. Now, is there anything else? There are people standing here at my desk and—"

So forth. Forth, precisely as the dictionary defines it: forward in time, place, or order. Onward. Away from a specified place. Toward something else.

But in depression, there is no forward in time. No onward. No forth. There is only this moment, in this specified place. It has a single texture, a single color, a single tense. The texture is hazy. The color is gray. And the tense is precisely the one where I least want to be: Here. Now. Here. Now. That moment repeats itself endlessly, sixty seconds a minute, sixty minutes an hour, twenty-four hours a day. Day after day after day after day.

Two weeks, Elaine? Do you have any idea how long that is?

As my brain rages against its constant misery, it also battles a cloud. A murkiness. A mistiness that refuses to lift. This shroud has a physical weight that I try to slough off from time to time by rigorously shaking my head. But it has engulfed my mind as a body of water swallows a heavy object; the submersion is complete. This smothering miasma cloaks not only my mind, but my senses, diminishing eyesight and hearing, destroying any desire to taste, touch or smell. The remove I feel from the real world has such a density that I often feel like I'm walking through JELL-O.

Distinct from the heavy cloud is the constant yammering in my brain, a mental tape that cycles and recycles endlessly, monitoring my feelings, castigating me for inflicting such misery on myself, perpetually reminding me how helpless and trapped I feel. Every second of every hour of every day, this unforgiving tape calls attention to the misery I'm so desperate to escape. Like Brer Rabbit, the harder I struggle to pull free of my mental Tar Baby, the deeper I become mired.

Two weeks? You might as well be sentencing me to two years of hard time, Elaine.

Gone are the days when I could field a phone call, catch the top-of-the-hour headlines off the radio, and wash dishes at the same time. Bit by bit, the ordinary pleasures of the real world have faded to memory. First appetite, then sleep slipped away. Next, concentration, carving the most gaping black hole in my universe as it devoured my ability to immerse in a novel, then to read a magazine article, finally to digest even a single paragraph of a newspaper story. Gradually, I've lost the capacity to sustain a conversation. To follow the plotline of even the most banal half-hour sitcom. To forget myself as I gaze at forested landscapes from a moving car.

Nothing comes automatically any longer. Every task demands the same sort of painstaking effort required to navigate the snow and ice of an urban street after a heavy winter storm. When I brush my teeth, I must remind myself to unscrew the cap, squeeze the paste on the toothbrush, bring the brush to my mouth. Scrub. If I'm not mindful, I may gargle mouthwash before I apply the toothpaste, disremember to shut off the water tap, forget thirty seconds after spitting whether I brushed my teeth at all.

Life has lost all contrast. Nothing is easy, nothing is hard. The divide between exertion and distraction, enjoyment and discomfort, no longer exists. Whether I'm making the bed or making love to Joe, paying the dry cleaner or paying a visit to an editor's office, every minute of every waking hour is monotonously the same. I must marshal every remaining resource to write my stories for *Time*, but then, I must do the same to write a check. (What's the date? What check number was that, and to whom did I make it out? Did I enclose the bill in the envelope along with the check? I can't believe I just put the return-address label where the stamp should go. Wait, did I remember to sign the check?) Whether the effort falls into the category of work or leisure, I collide with the same frustrated question, Why must this be so hard?

Two weeks, Elaine?

Time is now moving so slowly that I can sink into reverie, plumb the depths of my soul, detail all that has gone wrong of late, search for explanations and solutions, strike upon one or two new ones, resurface—and discover only two minutes have passed. How then am I to spend all the two-minutes required to fill the two-hours that stretch into the two-days that will eventually add up to the two weeks?

"Is there anything else?"

I know, Elaine, I know. Everyone on your list is counting down the days to her next appointment, marking time until her next lab result, sonogram, insemination, egg retrieval. Is the waiting this cruel for each of them? For me, this impossible waiting involves acute awareness of the pain every minute of every day. It is a pain that attacks me the moment I awaken—if I have slept at all—and haunts me every second, minute, and hour until—*if*—I drop off to sleep.

"I said, Is there anything else?"

"What? Oh. Sorry, Elaine. No. Nothing else. Thanks for your help."

Even then, I get no relief. Want to hear what I dreamed last night, Elaine? I'm at a reunion of female friends, playing with my sister's new baby. (Actually, Ann's youngest is almost four, Elaine, but never mind.) When I turn my eyes away for a second, someone snatches the baby. Presents are then distributed to everyone. I sit, waiting for mine, thinking a gift will cheer me. But I never receive one. Instead, I'm left alone on a bed, wailing loudly. A distant voice asks, "Who's that?" As I awaken, I hear a voice answering, "It's Jill."

But who is this Jill? And how is she to make a sensible decision whether to discontinue fertility treatments or persist? The person who now inhabits my body and mind is eerily unfamiliar. Unreasonable. Unreliable. She's a woman who sees only the gallows, never the humor. She weeps for that monkey that fell out of the tree.

"Hey, Wease," Joe says, making yet another valiant attempt to distract me from my torpor. "Have I ever told you about Pat McDowell and anesthesia?" (Who? Oh, right. Friend of Joe's.) "The first time he went under, he discovered the meaning of the universe and wrote it down as soon as he woke up. But when he dug out the piece of paper a day later, it had just one word: Shoulders." (Joe's laughing. Why is Joe laughing?) "The second time Pat was put under, he again discovered the meaning of the universe. He was really determined to get it down this time. Guess what he'd written? 'Infinity has a shadow.'"

Huh? Wait, I get it! "Infinity's shadow," I say. "What a perfect metaphor for depression."

"No, Wease. That's not what I meant." (Joe's frowning. Why is Joe frowning?) "Look, forget I mentioned it."

I detest this fragile, morose person I've become. Even as I inhabit the skin of this humorless woman, I never lose sight of the fact that this is not a person I want to be around. I resent her unfailingly dark mood. Her brooding. Her tentativeness, indecisiveness, her lack of resilience. I not only find her self-absorption exhausting, but feel no sympathy for her, with her constant thoughts of me, me, me.

Even more intolerable than the presence of this loathsome stranger is the absence of the person who's always been my steadiest and most reliable companion.

"I don't know this person I've become," I say to Joe repeatedly. "She's not the real me."

Or is she? Now in the third consecutive month of unrelieved depression, an eternity, how can I be certain that the she I miss will ever return? Even a concerted effort can no longer break up the haze, as it could back before the new year when, if I tried, tried hard enough, the cloud might lift for a few hours. Now, I look back with envy to such moments of respite, particularly to an evening Joe and I had shared over Christmas in Pasadena.

I'd had to battle with myself to overcome my resistance to that night out with two strangers, one a television producer, the other a TV writer. As a consultant on the script that would turn one of his *People* stories into a made-for-TV movie, Joe regarded this dinner as essential. Until now, Joe had endured the isolation I'd imposed on us without complaint. I didn't see how I could say no to his request that I attend.

As I stood in front of the mirror in my sister-in-law's guest bathroom, applying make-up and inserting the contact lenses that I hadn't worn in months, I practiced smiling. The reflected image showed white teeth, dull and lifeless eyes. What if these two strangers thought Joe was married to a zombie? What if they judged him by the company he keeps?

Stop, I silently scolded my reflection. If you maintain a pleasant expression and don't zone out, they won't know you're part of the zombie underworld. You think your turmoil is on constant display. But it's not.

At the Belair Hotel in Beverly Hills, a blur of valets, maitre d's and waitresses saw us safely to the reserved table where our hosts waited. After brief introductions, Joe and our dinner companions launched into TV talk. Unable to follow the conversation's rapid shifts, I pretended to study the menu. Eventually, we ordered cocktails, then drank. Ordered appetizers, salads, entrees, then ate. Ordered dessert and coffee, then relaxed. All the while, the conversation continued at a Manhattan pace, several people talking at once, their voices and ideas overlapping and colliding.

As the excellent food came and went, and the quaintly outfitted Christmas carolers entered and departed, and the chatter rose and fell, rose and fell, something miraculous happened. The depressed me moved aside, and she suddenly appeared. The woman I count on. The woman who, until this depression, had always been me.

She entered tentatively, offering a comment here, a wry look there. Then, finding her footing, she began to get caught up in the conversation. She listened with interest and intensity, commented on subjects ranging from the state of democratization in Russia to the state of the arts in Hollywood. As she gained momentum, coming up to normal speed, she lobbied confidently against a particular actor for Joe's movie, argued with the producer about the merits of a particular politician, laughed delightedly at her husband's Middle East war stories.

This she whom I'd always taken most for granted bore no resemblance to the frightened, scattered person who'd entered the dining room a short while ago, the one who'd had to feign engagement in the conversation by matching her facial expressions to those of her dinner companions. When this she smiled, it was because she found her husband amusing. When she furrowed her brow, it was because she was trying to summon the precise comment by Yitzhak Shamir that had pissed her off. She didn't have to struggle either to connect one thought to the next or to interconnect with the others at the table.

As the depressed me observed this vital she, I appreciated her as I never had before, or since. I admired her wit, her intelligence, her versatility. I envied her confidence and the ease with which she navigated the world. She seemed damn good company, this woman. More than anything I've wanted before or since, I wanted once again to *be* her.

Joe's pleasure at her return was apparent, too, as we returned to Esme's apartment. We talked late into the night, rehashing the dinner, sharing our perceptions. It had been so long since I'd held up my side of our mutual interrogation.

Then, blissfully, I slept. But when I awoke the next morning, she was gone. I could neither summon her back, nor consult her. For the first time, I understood all the psychoblather about self-love. With a stinging loneliness bordering on grief, I grasped that I'd lost my best friend.

Now, I worry she may be gone forever.

Certainly, I can't await her return to make the next decision. I'm heading back into the part of the month where I have to monitor my urine for an LH surge. Even as Dr. Feldman nuked my hopes, she instructed me to use an ovulation predictor kit twice daily to make sure that we catch the surge. That means two hours a day of training my attention on urine samples. Two hours during which I can think of nothing but pregnancy and nonpregnancy, vague hope and certain despair. Two hours of disruption from my work at the office, where concentration is already battle enough. I don't know if I can, or want, to do this again.

The decision whether to continue is mine alone. Joe's unwavering ambivalence about children ensures he will not press me to persist with fertility treatments. That both lightens my load and deepens my loneliness. Maybe Joe's friend Pat had it right the first time. Maybe the meaning of life is a pair of shoulders, freighted with a load that cannot be shrugged off, yet cannot be borne.

I do not trust myself to make a lucid decision in such a fuzzy state. Yet I know that women who struggle with infertility do it all the time. Through the months when I'd gathered information on infertility, I'd heard enough horror stories to know that my depressed state was hardly uncommon. Indeed, during those months of listening and reading up on both infertility and depression, I'd begun to detect many fascinating and chilling parallels between the two conditions.

Demographically, both infertility and depression are taking a harsh toll on female Baby Boomers. While 10 percent of men under age forty have suffered depression, the toll is twice that among women of the same age group. Moreover, female Boomers have a 65 percent greater chance than prior generations of becoming clinically depressed. Those two sets of statistics made me wonder. Did many, maybe even most, of those one in five women suffer their depression after learning they were among the one in seven couples with fertility troubles? Was the greater incidence of severe depression linked to the higher incidence of conception and pregnancy problems? Nowhere could I find a study that traced the overlap between those two spiraling curves.

Medically, treatment for both disorders is often trial-and-error, and when the two hit at once, treatment for one can work against treatment for the other. While the assorted hormonal drugs used to stimulate ovulation risk stimulating depression as well, the various antidepressants may put a fetus at risk.

Economically, both can drain savings since health insurers often refuse to cover long-term treatment of either condition.

Psychologically, both depression and infertility beget profound feelings of helplessness, hopelessness, and loss. They can leave you feeling out of control of the present and pessimistic about the future. Both require tremendous patience and perseverence at a moment when time feels like your worst enemy. Worse still, both can rob you of your greatest ally—yourself—as they hack away at reason and reasonableness.

Socially, both are prolonged shrieks of pain that make no

sound. Since neither condition bears external traces of injury, each tends to be dismissed, minimized, or misunderstood. "Snap out of it!" is to depressives what "Just relax!" is to infertile couples. A sense of shame pervades both populations.

Sexually, both go a long way toward curbing any appetite.

Maritally, both conditions strain and test the bond. Couples tend to emerge either strengthened or broken; rarely is the union ever the same again.

And cruelly, infertility and depression often go hand-in-hand.

For godsakes, Jill, get a grip.

I'm standing at the pharmacy counter, trying to talk myself out of my absurd resistance to buying two predictor kits. It's not as if I'm being asked to swallow Clomid or to jab myself in the thigh with oily Pergonal injections. All I have to do is plunk down sixty-three dollars for each kit, pee into a cup, then play with a bunch of vials. This is not a tragedy.

Yet everything within me opposes this purchase. I can't tell if I've come to my senses or lost them. I just know that I have a keen, agitated desire to be done with the fertility voodoo. Now that Dr. Feldman is holding out about as much promise of results as the African fertility totem one of Joe's college buddies gave us for a wedding gift, I want no part of this exercise.

It's not as if fertility treatment is the norm, I remind myself. Only 2 percent of the country's 2.3 million infertile couples seek high-tech assistance, and among that elite, the claims of success are questionable. Many fertility programs cloak the high rate of disappointment among women in their late thirties and forties by scrambling the results from all age groups. No less misleading, a pregnancy is often tallied as a success even if the woman subsequently miscarries.

This is bullshit, my brain rants as I pay for the kits. Complete and utter bullshit.

Or is it? Unwilling to trust my own judgment, I've turned to others, hoping for affirmation that it's alright to end the fertility dance and get on with my life. But my admission that I want no more going month to month, hoping, despairing, making myself crazy with the endless uncertainty that attends these procedures, has produced advice as sharply divided as the debate raging inside my head.

"You've been grieving since November," Miriam responded. "Hear your feelings. Accept them."

"Nothing matters but you," my mother concurred. "Enough is enough. It's your body. It was your decision to try, and it's your decision to stop. You've given it a terrific shot. Let it go. Give your mind, your heart, and your body a rest."

My friends, however, insisted that I needed to learn more. "Dr. Feldman can be alarmist," Lynn reminded. "You might want to get a second opinion."

"Maybe," Jan suggested, "the lab inverted the numbers on the second test. Maybe the FSH reading was 14, not 41. Either way, you need to know more about FSH."

When a trip to the library turned up nothing on FSH, I left a message with the Resolve hotline. The woman who returned my call told me that the nurse who handles medical questions wouldn't be available until the following week. Could she be of help in the meantime? I'd shared with this discarnate voice the terms of my limbo and turmoil.

"I can't believe they're leaving you hanging for two weeks," she said indignantly. "These doctors are the pits."

Encouraged by her empathy, I told her how depressed I was, how much I feared taking more fertility drugs. "My year on Clomid was emotionally and physically hell," she responded. "But I had no problems with the Pergonal."

Did she think I should see another doctor? "It's always good to get a second opinion on existing lab results. But if that opens the door to more tests, you may want to stop there. That's what I did after three years. I just couldn't face any more tests."

I didn't ask the obvious question. If this anonymous ally had a child, I couldn't bear to know it at this moment. Instead, I asked, "Is it ridiculous to be thinking of cutting off fertility treatment after just seven months?"

"Not at all," she assured. "In the support group I was in, we discussed when to halt treatment all the time."

"What did your group decide?"

"The group was divided."

My last call was to Donna, now in roughly her seventh year of fertility treatment. "To stick with these fertility procedures," she said, "you need the back-up of a superspouse—"

I have such a spouse. Joe is proving a true partner, a steadfast mate. His patience with my self-absorption is heroic. He listens, consoles, humors, tries to reassure that the depression will lift. He does not complain when I'm unable to follow his conversation. He does not balk when I resist his suggestions that we see a movie or have dinner with friends. I have reduced us to watching reruns of *Bewitched* on Nick at Nite, and even then, I can't follow why Samantha and Darrin are mad at Endorra. Though I'm too depressed to take comfort from our relationship, I'm keenly aware, more than ever before, that our marriage is a blessing.

"—a superspouse," Donna said, "who wants this as badly as you do."

I don't have such a spouse. I cannot, do not, expect that Joe will ever want a baby as much as I do. As it is, he's given more than I'd anticipated. He's still maintaining his sense of the absurd as he trudges across town time after time to take a *Playboy* and himself in hand. He's still willing to consider varicocele surgery, if that's required. He's still accommodating each passing whim that seizes me after I hear of some new home remedy. (Pulling out as he ejaculates. Pressing the points on my feet that, according to a reflexology text, correspond to my ovaries. Not laughing when I leap out of bed after coitus to stand on my hands. Yes, quite the visual.)

It's impossible to hope that Joe will ever want a child as badly as I do. But it's no more possible to hope that my depression will lift if I don't become a mother. I can imagine letting go of my desire to bear a child. But relinquishing my desire to nurture, raise, and love a child? That is one possibility I cannot imagine.

Another hour. Another day. Another lifetime.

I try to leaven my misery with work on a cover story. The topic, assigned by editors at *Time* who know nothing of my infertility problems, is RU-486, the controversial abortion pill, as-yet unapproved by the Food and Drug Administration. Though I've always been a strong proponent of choice, I'm having a hard time mustering any compassion for all those girls and women whose greatest trauma in life is an unwanted pregnancy.

Where the hell is *my* choice? my inner voice remonstrates as I write. Have the baby. Give it to me.

Though I'd initially heard Joe's vague mention of adoption for what it was—an attempt to comfort—I've since replayed his words over and over until I hear in them the remote possibility of a reprieve from a childless future. So, when I pose my question, there is no way Joe can grasp how much darker my mental prison is becoming, how much narrower and more constricting the cell seems as the walls thicken with glutinous thoughts of never having the chance to nurture, to cuddle, to love a child. There is no way he can intuit how unsteadily I'm floating on the hope that somewhere deep within him, Joe is capable of making a choice that may give me the hope I need to emerge from this pain.

"Were you serious about seeing someone to talk about adoption?" I ask.

"It's more important that you see someone to talk about your depression," he answers.

"I do talk to someone."

"Phone calls are not real therapy."

He still won't acknowledge that this is about babies, babies, and only babies, I think angrily.

"I didn't bring up adoption, Joe. You did. Will you see someone?"

"It will be at least a year before I can even begin to consider adoption," he answers.

Another year? Doesn't he see I won't last that long? "How long are you willing to see me suffer?"

I want to pull the words back even as I speak them. But it's too late, and he responds in kind. "You're so impatient," he flares. "You're a quitter."

Until this moment, accusation and recrimination have not been a part of our repertoire. I understand that Joe can no more place this idea of children at the center of his life than I can place it at the periphery of mine. For either of us to blame the other for our impasse is as purposeless as me making Joe accountable for his immotile sperm or him holding me responsible for my prematurely aging ovaries. What is, is. Either of us, I know, would gladly shift position if there were some compromise that didn't scream: This isn't for a day, a year, a decade; this is for the rest of your life!

I retreat quickly, wondering if maybe Joe is right. I've never been a quitter before. Am I a quitter now?

Day gives way to night gives way to day gives way to night. Forty-eight more hours pass. An eternity.

As we set out on our three-hour drive to the country, I tell myself, Don't bring it up. We clear the Delaware Water Gap, the first hour behind. Good girl. You didn't do it. We clear Scranton. The second hour passes. Maybe, I wonder, there's a more indirect approach? You'll be sorry. It's too soon. Yes, but if he goes for it, we could skip the next IUI. I'm warning you, it's too soon. Don't do it. Don't do it.

I do it.

"Maybe we should see Grace again," I say.

"Sure," Joe says agreeably. "About what?"

"This adoption stuff. Maybe she could help us sort out where your resistance is."

Stupid, stupid. I get the angry response I deserve. What he offers about adoption this time has something I don't quite grasp, something about dog breeding and bloodlines. "It's not going to happen," he concludes. That part I get loud and clear.

Through the weekend, as I run urine test after urine test, I think and overthink my options. Drop it all now and start taking an antidepressant, as Miriam is encouraging? I don't see how this will help. No pill is going to produce the baby that precipitated and is fueling this depression. Put fertility treatments aside for the moment, get my head back on straight, then give it another try when I feel more calm, as Lynn has suggested? Not a chance. Once I get off the fertility treadmill, I know I'll never step back on. Do the IUI, as Dr. Feldman assumes I will? How can I not. If pregnancy is my only hope of becoming a mother, then I've got to keep trying.

On June 2, I dial the Resolve hotline and ask the nurse who fields medical questions to decipher the results of my FSH tests. FSH, she explains, is one of two hormones that stimulate the ovaries' production of eggs. She knows of no woman with a reading over 24 who's gotten pregnant. I ask if the numbers on the 41 reading may have been inverted and should have been 14 instead. She allows that there may have been a lab error. Perhaps, I suggest alternately, the high FSH reading was just a one-time phenomenon, a quirk.

"Maybe," she says. "But a one-time elevation has ramifications for the future."

The most common treatment, she says, is Pergonal, followed by IUI. Usually, the injections begin Day 3, with one to two shots daily for the next nine days. Every few days, the doctor would draw blood and do an ultrasound to see how the follicles are developing.

"That's the method of treatment," she says, "but your problem does not do well with Pergonal."

I tell her about my one ugly experience with Clomid and admit that I'm scared of trying Pergonal. She responds that most women have an easier time on Pergonal. "No black cloud," she says. "But it's a stressful regimen and the stakes are high."

"What about antidepressants? Do you think I should try one?"

"You have to think of the whole unit," she says gently. "You have to tend to your emotional state."

As we conclude our lengthy conversation, I feel that I've gotten the second opinion my friends have been urging on me. This nurse bears the imprimatur of Resolve. Unlike my doctors, she has no financial stake in stoking my hopes. She's not only responded to my diagnosis; she's responded to me. I hang up feeling there's no doctor I would trust more.

That night, I tell Joe what I've learned, but don't press the point. Better he should hear it from Dr. Feldman. He trusts doctors more than I do. Her words will have more weight.

When my luteinizing hormone surges the next day, I cross town and do the IUI, not because I hope, not because I believe, but because I don't want Joe to think I'm a quitter.

On June 8, a nurse escorts Joe and me to the same airless office where we'd had our first consultation with Dr. Feldman four months earlier. The small desk is still empty, save a box of Kleenex, and the walls are still bare, though someone has disturbed the sea of mauve with a black, smudged handprint. After Dr. Feldman enters, she opens a folder, reads briefly, then looks up at us.

"This is pretty serious," she begins. "Jill's four test results range. Some are worse than others. None are in a normal range." She reminds us that the optimal FSH reading ranges between 0 and 12. "Anything above 25 carries a poor prognosis for fertility." My four test results read 14, 41, 22, 21. "But the FSH can be false. In the last decade a woman's ovaries tend to sputter. They function, quiet, function, quiet."

As a backstop, she explains, she's also been tracking my estrogen level. The optimal target is 70 or less. My four tests have come back 96, 83, 72 and 35. "These are very significant numbers. Your ovaries are behaving like a woman in her mid-forties. On a bell curve with the lowest point being premature ovarian failure, you're the next point up."

"I'm in menopause?"

"No. Peri-menopause," she says. "But if you get hot flashes or a dry vagina, you should call me."

Dr. Feldman explains that while very few medical tests indicate conclusively how receptive a woman will be to in vitro fertilization, she feels my prospects are unpromising. When a woman signs onto IVF, doctors want a one-in-four chance that the procedure will take. Women with FSH levels over 25 have just a 1 percent chance of success. "Given Jill's age and the relatively short time the two of you have been trying to get pregnant, I'm putting you in the 10 percent category."

She suggests we put our names on the IVF waiting list, which is backed up for eight months, then let her know by September if we want to proceed. If we choose to go ahead, she reiterates, "You're looking at a low prognosis."

She then outlines three options. We can "relax" and see what happens. We can "get aggressive," either pursuing IVF or locating an egg donor, fertilizing the eggs with Joe's sperm, then implanting the embryo in my uterus, a procedure for which the waiting time is even longer. Or we can pursue a "child-free life." Looking a bit embarrassed, she adds, "That's the positive way to put it."

"Does any of this factor in the problems with Joe's sperm?"

"No. But I'd want him in optimal shape before we proceed."

"What are the risks with Pergonal?" Joe asks. "I've read that Gilda Radner died of ovarian cancer linked to Pergonal."

"There is only a single study that has linked ovarian cancer to Pergonal, and it was not a good study," she answers. "But that does not prove there is not a link."

"What does an IVF entail?" I ask.

"It's very strenuous. There would be daily Pergonal injections, possibly mixed with Clomid. Then there would be daily blood tests and ultrasound." Usually, the procedures last between seven and ten days, but in my case, she says, the drug dosages might have to be raised, and I might have to come in more often.

As Dr. Feldman patiently answers our questions, neither Joe nor I think to ask what might have caused my "peri-menopause." Pinpointing the reason isn't going to change anything.

Joe and I will also not think to ask, What if? What if we'd started sooner? Opted for procreation instead of procrastination? Tried to make a baby when both of us were younger and presumably more fertile? Joe and I had done the best we could, by and for each other. Neither of us is inclined to statements that begin, If I had it to do over—

There is, however, one point I want clarified. So often, too often, I've heard that my chances of getting pregnant would improve if I could just relax. "As you know," I say, "I've been very depressed. Is it possible that the stress is affecting my FSH readings?"

"Stress doesn't affect FSH," Dr. Feldman answers. "It could affect the pituitary by shutting it down, but your pituitary is functioning as would be expected in this sort of situation. That is to say, it is pumping out more FSH."

So.

"This is a personal decision," she says, then stands up. As she gathers the papers of our file, Joe and I exchange a look that tells me there is nothing left to decide; our decision is already made. "Let me know what you decide," she concludes, then leaves the room.

On the sidewalk outside the hospital, Joe places an arm around my shoulder and says, "I feel guilty that I couldn't give you what you wanted."

"It's my physical problems, not yours, that are the bigger obstacle."

"I feel guilty that you suffered all this pain, and I didn't," he persists. "I feel guilty that while all you got was pain, in the end, I pretty much got what I wanted all along."

Joe's admission is, for me, bittersweet. Though he has done his best to console and cajole me through these long months, Joe hasn't been able to mask his impatience with what he's regarded as mine. I hear in this statement a sympathy for my pain and an acknowledgment of its legitimacy. Finally, I see, I'm going to be allowed my grief.

But that's all I'm going to be allowed. During the last ten days, I've silently visited and revisited Joe's four inconsistent comments about adoption, each of them squeezed from him under the strain of my anguish and anxiety, sometimes to soothe, sometimes to get me off his back. "Why would I want to raise someone else's kid?" "Maybe I should see a therapist to deal with my resistance." "It will be at least a year before I can even begin to consider adoption." "It's not going to happen."

Now, the words that this grim, chastened Joe uses to soothe—"I pretty much got what I wanted all along"—affirm what my gut has been telling me. There is no hope, no hope at all, that Joe will agree to an adoption.

Years later, Joe will tell me, "I don't remember any of that." Time, for him, will have washed away any mention or discussion of adoption until after our final appointment with Dr. Feldman. What will surprise me is not that different moments stuck in our respective memories, but that even when I supply the detail of those moments, which were so key to my unrelenting despair—the setting, the circumstance, the tone of his voice—Joe still can't summon even a fuzzy recollection.

It will sadden me anew to think how alone I was, how far apart two people who love each other can be. How at the very moment when I was clutching at adoption as the only remaining line that could reel me back to shore, my only potential rescuer wasn't even aware that I was drowning.

VI

WHERE DOES ONE GO TO GRIEVE THE LOSS OF hope? The loss of a life's plan? The loss of a child who never existed? There are no ceremonies to legitimate such grief. No traditions to honor the pain of the living. No coffins to bury the remains of the unconceived.

I do not know that I've come to mourn when I enter Central Park at Fifty-ninth Street on this cool, sunny afternoon in early June. Rather, I assume that I've come to resume the walking and brooding that for months have been my daily habit. This act of putting one foot in front of the other, of moving from place to place, affords no pleasure. Wherever I go, I'm accompanied by the same tedious thoughts, the same monochromatic me. But at least I'm in motion. As I pass various landmarks, I feel that I'm traversing the hours that will help me put another day behind. By now, I've circled Central Park so many times that every path, every tree, every rock seems familiar. I'm grateful to have this urban sanctuary where I can tread undisturbed by vigorous joggers, sweating bikers, fellow zombies.

As I climb the steep path that leads up and away from the noise and traffic of Central Park West, I'm surprised to discover that I feel none of the restlessness that for months has propelled my incessant walking. Rather, what I feel is a great hollowness. What I crave is solitude. I search for a secluded perch and find a large, shaded rock overlooking a baseball diamond.

For the next several hours, I do not move. I just sit. And think. And cry.

In the coming days, I return again and again to this same rock to continue my solitary vigil. I do not resent the absence of someone with whom to share this intense grief. Though I'm alone, for the first time in a long time I don't feel lonely. There are too many thoughts for that. After the long months of berating myself for the irrational certainty that I would never get pregnant, I feel entitled finally to my grief. And I'm ready, so very ready, to let go.

Without resistance, I summon the myriad fantasies and discussions about children, both real and imagined, that I've entertained over the years. Sometimes dry-eyed, sometimes with tears flowing, I compel myself to confront them, listen to them, then bid them good-bye.

Though there's never been a face, a shape, a size, a weight, there has been a name. Will most probably for a boy; Becky almost certainly for a girl. Joe and I had discussed whom we might name as godparents and whom we would designate as guardian. We'd debated whether a boy should be allowed to play football. (Me: "Well, if it's what he wants—" Joe: "No way, Wease.") And wrangled over what age a girl should be allowed to pierce her ears. (Me: "Fourteen." Joe: "Forty." Me: "Get out!" Joe: "Okay, thirty-nine.") We'd settled on Christmas with Joe's family, Passover with mine, and agreed to punt on the rest. We'd even cased a few suburbs where we'd heard the public schools were good.

For all Joe's resistance, I now see, there had been a life that we'd imagined together, a life involving more than two.

I think of the excited visit to Joe's office, the one where I close the door and say, "Wease! I'm pregnant!" So often I have imagined the expression on his face, a mix of joy, dread, confusion. Sort of the stunned look he'd worn throughout his fiftieth birthday party.

And I think of the phone call to my parents. Once upon a time, back when they were waiting for the first of their four children to honor the covenant, "Get married, have babies," I'd thought I had the perfect opener. "Hi, Grandma." That line had lost its capacity to surprise after the birth of my first nephew in 1986. (Had I really been thinking about babies that far back?) Five grandchildren later, Joe and my efforts no longer private, the call that I now lay to rest opens, "Mom? You're not going to believe this."

Mentally, I hang up the phone on the other calls I'd imagined, the ones to friends that began, "Sorry, didn't mean to be so secretive but we wanted to clear the three-month hurdle . . . Amnio? Yeah, we want to check on the health of the baby. Huh? . . . No, we don't want to know the sex. We want to be surprised."

I retrieve from a great distance the thoughts that predated the start of our infertility troubles. Me delightedly watching my body swell and change. (How many years ago was it that I'd first read Nora Ephron's essay on the raptures of milk-filled breasts for the modestly endowed?) Me worrying that Joe and I, given our conflicting work schedules, wouldn't be able to attend Lamaze classes together. Me sitting on a couch in a *Time* story conference when my water burst. Um, sorry, Mr. Editor.

I revisit the debates I'd entertained during our fifteen months of trying to get pregnant, debates conducted interiorly so as not to overload Joe. Fashioning plans to make a baby's disruptive presence easier on Joe. Searching for strategies to coax him into doing his fair share without my becoming a shrew. Considering how to rearrange the furniture in the spare bedroom, the one that serves as Joe's office, to make way for Junior without totally squeezing Joe out of a work space. Wondering if Joe and I will sell our country retreat when Junior's weekend schedule becomes packed with sports events, music lessons, sleepover dates, or if we will rent it out until Junior is off to college. Off to his or her own future. Off to the day when Junior phones and says, "Hi, Grandma."

As I resurrect these fantasies, I see anew how extensively my thinking and planning about marriage, home, career, in essence my life, have been arranged around this never-to-be-born child. I see, too, that through the many years of deliberation, debate, and delay, my fantasies have gradually changed. Excited, unknowing expectations about pregnancy have been tempered by the horror stories of friends. Mental arguments with my parents about Jewish rituals have faded, their intensity ameliorated by the battles already waged by my siblings. Certainties about how I would raise a child have softened into uncertainties as I've watched friends and siblings fight the battles of the ages with their own tots. Once-rigid assumptions about an equal division of chores with Joe have been replaced by formulations that favor harmony over parity.

As I sit on this shaded rock, I see not only that I have grown up with these fantasies, but that these fantasies have matured as I have aged. I see that the mother I would be as I approach my forties is a more patient, accepting parent than the one in her late twenties or early thirties who unwittingly would have tried to force her own agenda on both husband and child.

For the first time, I realize that I would have made a good mother. A damn good mother.

And that makes me weep.

* * *

Lynn, my memory and mirror for almost three decades, marvels at the spontaneity of my sorrow. The clinical psychologist in her expects a more gradual trajectory of pain, and worries that I'm rushing my grief. But the friend who's listened all these months with an ear sensitively attuned to the calibrations of my emotional register, understands the outpouring. "It's as if somewhere within you," she says, "you knew all along."

"You've been grieving since November," Miriam says flatly.

Yet, oddly, now that people are no longer telling me that I've lapsed too quickly into pessimism, I no longer feel a hunger for their understanding. Though this grief wets my eyes, fills my throat, hollows my stomach, I find it neither frightening nor intolerable. My loss is sad, yes. Terribly, terribly sad. But unlike the inchoate suffering of depression, this is an ache that makes sense to me. It's a pure grief, a cleansing grief, a hard-earned and uncluttered grief. Though the pain is sharp, it has a clarity that is refreshing and a calm center that is less cumbersome than the diffuse agitation of depression. I soak myself in this pain, embracing it as not only permissible, but essential.

Even as I mourn, I see hope of restoring sanity, order, and a measure of control to my life. If Dr. Feldman's words have provided the final tug on the noose that has been strangling my hopes, they've also provided the means to cut me free. Despite the bad diagnosis, I recognize that I'm relatively fortunate. I've been spared so much. The ugly morning jab of Pergonal by a husband who looks as if he will heave as he plunges the needle into his wife's black and blue thigh. The high-cost, labor-intensive procedures that produce a multiple miracle, only to have each fetus miscarry, one by one. The bed-ridden, high-risk pregnancy that goes to term, only to end in heartbreak.

Or what if I'd been one of those women tethered with a diagnosis of "Don't Know," left to dangle in that cruel limbo where neither hope nor grief is possible? I've been fortunate to have a doctor who leveled honestly and didn't try to string me along for reasons having to do more with her own purse or pride than my prognosis. I can abandon my fertility quest without guilt or remorse. No longer must I struggle with the nagging question, If I want a child so desperately, how can I even think of abandoning fertility treatment? No longer must I face the unspoken opprobrium of those, Joe among them, who have faith that modern medicine can conquer all. No doctor or high-tech trick can counter the caprice of Nature that has sent my ovaries prematurely into decline.

A skeptical and impatient patient, I've been constitutionally unable to revere these physicians as fertility gods. From the start, I've put the doctors in an impossible position, paradoxically inviting and resenting their intrusion into so private an act. I'm relieved to be done with the syringes and stirrups, vials and rubber gloves. I lack the fortitude of those women— women whom I once dismissed as foolish, but now know to be remarkable—who are able to maintain their balance on the fertility treadmill month after month, year after year, their hopes cresting and falling with each new test result or word from a doctor. Through the months of testing, probing, and inseminating, the well-intended attentions of my doctors have served mostly to heighten my anxiety and exacerbate my depression.

I've resented being at the mercy of a growing roster of doctors and nurses, with their overbooked schedules and neverending succession of diagnostic tests, their pat expressions of sympathy and basic incomprehension of what I'm going through. For me, each office visit has been less a celebration of potential life than a small death.

I'm also fortunate to be walking away with no apparent damage to my self-image. When Lynn asked recently, "Is this a blow to your sense of yourself as a woman?" I understood that the answer lay in the fact that I'd never thought to pose the question myself. For all the pain I'd inflicted on myself during these long months, I'd never once tortured myself with punishing thoughts that a failure to conceive would signify some larger failure as a woman. Unlike the depression, for which I continue to blame myself mercilessly, I regard my malfunctioning ovaries the same way I view Joe's dog-paddling sperm: a biological anomaly, beyond human power to change, unconnected to one's worth.

No less important, Joe, too, regards these problems as quirks that require no adjustment in his perception of either his masculinity or my femaleness. Since he hasn't staked his self-esteem on the propagation of an heir, there will be no pressure from Joe to hang in for further medical treatment against improbable odds. Nor will there be any of the recriminations and regrets that can, and do, bust up marriages.

As I sit on my rock in Central Park, weighing what I've lost against what I'm now gaining, the cloud of depression begins to break up. At times, a Stephen Sondheim lyric plays in my head. "Bit by bit, putting it together."

Heavy as the day is, I keep thinking, This will break. I can see in hours of clear-headedness, sometimes even euphoria, that I can feel whole again . . . Time is flowing again. I can immerse in things: books, movies, TV shows. It is truly a joy.

On the seventh night of these daily vigils, as I lay in bed awaiting sleep, a luxury that is gradually being restored to my schedule, my attention is caught by the words running, unbidden, through my head. *"Yitgadahl v'yitkahdash sh'may rabah—"* It's the liturgy of *Yizkor*, the Jewish prayer for the dead.

On the morning of the eighth day, a Sunday, the intensity of my grief begins to subside. I step outside our home in the Endless Mountains to attend to some spring planting. Though it is already June, only now do I observe the buds on the trees, the lengthening blades of grass, the limegreen shimmer of the new foliage. As I inspect the juniper, rhododendron and holly bushes that had been stripped bare by deer during the heavy snows of winter, I feel heartened. In recent weeks as I've tended to these shrubs, watering, pruning, fertilizing, I've identified keenly with their naked, lifeless state. Now, as I notice the first hints of new growth, I feel a gratifying kinship.

I feel like we're in a battle together to rejuvenate, to survive, to live.

In the afternoon, I take out the brightly colored cloths and pillowcases that Joe and I had purchased in Guatemala back in March. Since our trip, they've remained zipped and forgotten in a bag. Now, I become absorbed by where to hang the fabrics and place the pillows. Ordinarily, my room by room, couch by couch deliberations would drive Joe crazy. But we both recognize what is happening and savor the task.

"Pillows, Wease!" I say. "I'm thinking about pillows!"

"Pillows!" he laughs. "She's back—and obsessing about pillows!"

At eleven o'clock on June 21, two weeks after our final consultation with Dr. Feldman, I cross town to New York Hospital. Eighteen days have passed since the second intrauterine insemination, thirty-one since the start of my last period, for me an unusually long cycle. I've come for my first pregnancy test.

It will be my last.

At four o'clock, Elaine delivers the results by phone. "Negative."

Was I floating on some unconscious hope that the second IUI would take when I seemed to let go of the "baby idea"?

I'm unprepared for the black cloud that rolls back in with the speed and force of a midwestern twister. Stupid, stupid, stupid, I berate myself. What made you think you could face and dispense with your grief so tidily in seven days? (Later, I will learn that shivah, the most intense period of Jewish mourning, lasts just that: seven days.)

Now, however, my depression is no longer tempered by baby love, baby loss, baby longing. The undistractable issue is me. It's about losing once again the woman whose gradual reemergence I have savored, and being trapped once again in a mental cage with the ghoul whose company I cannot abide.

I reenter the world of the walking dead. Again, I stop eating and sleeping. I resume smoking.

Joe notices the change immediately. Distressed, he snaps, "You're not the woman I married. You're indulging yourself in misery and it's got to stop."

Though I know he's right, despair and illogic are rapidly crafting a dangerous syllogism: this depression will not lift until I have a child; I cannot conceive a baby and Joe will not adopt one; ergo, I will never escape from this mental cage. Forget the past. This is your present. This is your future.

On a morning in late June after a long, sleepless night, I'm sitting at my smoking window in Hoboken, staring dazedly across the street at a clock tower, when my exhausted brain confronts me with a breakout plan. It's presented in the form of a question: Is that tower high enough to do the job? As if I were looking through a zoom lens, the face of the clock suddenly looms at me, close, closer, until the hands and Roman numerals are right in my face. Then I see a body, presumably me, plunging from the tower in a free fall.

I back away from the window, startled. It isn't the idea of suicide I find jolting. During the months of unrelieved depression, I'd occasionally conjured dark fantasies of death, knowing them to be no more than brief distraction from my pain. Always, they'd been comfortably distant. Always, they'd been offset by mental reminders about responsibilities and consequences. But this is very different. I'm a word person; ideas rarely present themselves to me in visual fashion. More disturbing, the terms have changed. I'm no longer playing with thoughts of suicide; thoughts of suicide are playing with me.

I slam the window shut and flee upstairs. "Wease. Wease," I whisper, shaking Joe awake. "I've been thinking about suicide."

There is alarm on Joe's face as he gathers me in his arms and cradles me. Then he escorts me into the shower and bathes me.

A half hour passes. "Go to work," I tell Joe. "I'll follow a little later."

"Are you alright, Wease?" he asks, reluctant to leave.

"I'm fine. Go. Really. I'm alright."

But I'm not. Now that the idea of an escape from my pain has insinuated itself so vividly into my mind, I cannot shake it. As I walk north along Eighth Avenue from Port Authority, my eyes case rooftops. My thinking is rapid, cool, methodical. The buildings that I could enter easily, I see, are too low. The roofs that guarantee getting the job done are all atop high rises patrolled by doormen. Even if I could talk my way past the uniforms, could I get onto the roof undetected?

I stop at one building and test it out. I want a panoramic view of the city, I explain to the guard at the elevator bank. Is it possible to get onto the roof?

"No, honey. The roof is locked." Yet another obstacle.

As I walk away with an oh-well shrug, I hear the guard joke to one of his colleagues, "Someone might jump."

Ha-ha-ha-ha.

I reach my office frightened, but determined. I'm serious about this. Serious enough to be considering and weighing options without regard to anyone but myself. Serious enough to know that I want to complete the job, not risk a bollixed attempt that might leave me physically or mentally impaired. Serious enough to know that the only barrier standing between me and death is a secure and painless means.

Do you have any idea how frightening it is to be afraid to be left alone with your own thoughts?

I call Lynn and ask her to meet me for lunch. Then I return my powers of concentration, undivided, undistracted, to identifying a fail-safe means.

When Lynn and six-month-old Max meet me in Riverside Park a few hours later, she sees that something has changed. My complexion is pale, my tone monotonous. As I tell her about my dark fantasies, I'm aware that I should modulate my voice, give it some cadence, some inflection, some rhythm. But I can't make the effort. Or won't. I don't know which. It no longer matters.

"Would you really do something?" she asks, gripping my hand, her eyes probing my face.

I know I should reassure her. But I can't. Or won't. I prefer not to.

As that long-forgotten phrase from a Herman Melville story flitters across my brain, I fleetingly envision its speaker seated at his wooden desk, fountain pen listlessly in hand. Bartleby, I think. I finally understand Bartleby the Scrivener.

"I don't know," I answer.

Lynn's professional judgment takes over. She insists I need to see a therapist here in town, someone who can prescribe and monitor an antidepressant. I no longer care whether it is Miriam or not Miriam. I don't know whether I'll make the appointment. But I nod when Lynn offers to consult a trusted colleague and get a referral.

At the end of lunch, a picnic that Lynn has thoughtfully prepared and I've barely touched, Lynn walks me down Broadway toward the subway station. She stops in a health-food store and buys three high-energy candy bars.

"You're too skinny," she says. "Eat these."

When we part at the subway steps, I look at Lynn and Max,

napping contentedly in his stroller, and wonder if I will ever see them again. That I cannot answer the question fascinates more than it frightens.

The next afternoon, I trudge up Central Park West to honor the appointment I've made with the psychiatrist Lynn has located for me, a Dr. Gooden. During the forty-five minute session, my tone is monotonous, my expression unanimated. I'm aware of both discomfiting aspects of my behavior and suspect that if I tried really hard, I could don the same mask I've been wearing for months at the office. But I do not. Or cannot. I prefer not to.

I don't remember all the particulars of that discussion with Dr. Gooden. My journal notes only: *Saw him. He prescribed Paxil.* I know, though, that after I shared my suicidal fantasies, he talked about something called serotonin, explained how an antidepressant works, and said he was specifically prescribing Paxil because he heard some "obsessiveness" in my thinking. He also said that the drug would take three to four weeks to kick in if it was the right one for me.

More waiting. More trial-and-error medicine. More painful outcomes. Thank you, doctor. But I prefer not to.

Even so, after the session I fill the prescription. I start to take out a credit card, then decide instead to pay for the pills in cash. By the time the Visa bill comes, I'll be gone. I don't want to saddle Joe with my bills.

I return to the office, sit for a few minutes, then for the first time in my long career know that I cannot, will not, work. I tell an editor I don't feel well, then go home. En route I get up onto two rooftops, peer over the ledge. Too low.

In my apartment, I look at the pink egg-shaped pills, each one tinier than my smallest fingernail. I break a tablet in half and swallow. Three days at a half dose, he'd said. After that, one whole twenty milligram tablet a day.

The ease with which the pill slides down my throat affirms

what I've been thinking all day. Pills. Clean. Painless. Fall asleep, stay asleep, never wake back up. I need more pills. But how to get them? And where? What kind? And how much? Who would have thought this business of killing yourself could be so complicated.

Hang on, a dimming voice cries wanly.

I prefer not to, comes the answer.

When I walk into the kitchen of my parents' home for the start of our annual reunion, my mother takes one look at me and whispers, "Oh, sweetheart," then hugs me hard.

I'm hoping that the combination of family chatter and the break from work, where it is becoming increasingly difficult to maintain a poised front, will disrupt my unrelieved thoughts of death. For several days now, I have been carefully plotting an escape that will be physically painless and final.

The visit does, in fact, prove distracting, though not in any way I'd anticipated. Back here on my parents' mountaintop, I'm reminded that the last time we'd parted, I'd taken some consolation from the thought that I'd be pregnant the next time we gathered. Back then, I'd been able to break up the depressional cloud by immersing myself in activity with my nephews and nieces. Now, as thoughts of babies come surging back, I cannot bear to look at them, talk with them, be with them.

Everyone tries to help. My siblings keep their children away from the room where I spend most days on the bed, hiding out. My father tries to distract me by taking me birthday shopping for clothes, but everything hangs, nothing feels right. I buy nothing. My mother tries to bolster me with talk of adoption, telling me that she has already begun to turn up possibilities in her rural county. But I am certain that Joe, for all his vigilance and concern, will never agree to such a plan.

As I lie on the bed hour after hour, surrendering to the peculiar grogginess induced by the medication, I wonder what

I can do to drain this reservoir of love reserved for a baby. How can I redirect this need to nurture a child? How can I sate this hunger to be a parent? I imagine snatching a child from a subway car. Finding a baby in a trash can. Quitting my job to become a live-in nanny. Adopting a child clandestinely, then dropping the news on Joe. Getting an old boyfriend to impregnate me, then hiding the biological parentage from Joe.

An ancient bit of Smolowe lore surfaces from memory. When I was a child, a woman with a reputation for being a talented psychic had visited my parents' home in Westport. While inspecting the oil portraits of me and my three siblings, she'd pointed to mine and said, "That one was a nun in a prior life." Is this my karma? I now wonder. If I was a nun in some prior incarnation, I would have been childless then, too. Is this torture payback for some terrible misdeed, if not in this lifetime then perhaps in a prior one?

"What did I do?" I plead silently to whom or what I no longer pretend to have a clue. "For what am I paying? Whatever it is, I am sorry, so very sorry."

Near the end of the vacation week, the grogginess fades and another feeling begins to stir. Anger. Specifically, anger at Joe. *I can just start to touch the anger at Joe. A feeling of desolation and frustration that he can't or won't accommodate me on this baby, on an adoption.*

This is new. As wounded and frustrated as I've felt by our impasse, anger at Joe hasn't been a conscious part of the mix. How could I even think to be angry with a man who's stood by this ghostly and ghastly anti-me, his support and love unwavering? A man who, despite his consistent preference not to have children, has gone through fertility treatments without a tussle. A man who, to every appearance, has done everything within his power to accommodate me. As Miriam used to say, "A person can't jump over his own shadow."

But that includes me. As I begin to emerge from the stultifying haze, my desire reasserts itself. I want a child, damn it. I want to be a mother.

Over the next few weeks as the depression continues slowly to lift, reality proves more amazing than anything my imagination has conjured. On a night when I'm trying to wrap my mind around the idea of a puppy to salve my spirit, I lie on the couch in my friend Valerie's Manhattan apartment, telling her about Dr. Feldman's diagnosis. I am talking about me, me, me, unable to distract my thoughts long enough to acknowledge the other in the room.

"I'd donate an egg," Valerie says. "I've never confused an egg and sperm with a child."

"I could never ask you to do that," I respond.

"No, Smo. I mean it. I'd be happy to."

The extraordinary offer startles and moves me. But on the subway home to Hoboken, I realize that no matter how much Valerie may mean it, I could never accept. Like so many of my friends, she is colliding against midlife pressures and stresses. She hardly needs the complication of my own crisis.

A few days later, I receive a letter from my sister Ann.

". . . It is difficult to see you in such pain," it reads. "I want so much to help. I have an offer. It's from the heart. It's genuine. And it's with a great deal of thought and full support from Jim. I hope you won't be offended or feel this is an intrusion, for this certainly is not my intent. I don't know all of the medical variables or possibilities for you and Joe to have a baby. I just know I want you to have what you want more than anything. If it is at all a viable and desirable option, nothing would mean more to me than to have a baby for you . . ."

At the bottom of the letter, my brother-in-law Jim has added, "I *do* fully support Ann's offer. Please consider it seriously. I realize it would be a difficult decision on many fronts, but consider it carefully."

I call Ann, overwhelmed. "I couldn't possibly ask you to do this," I say.

"You didn't ask," she replies. "I offered."

Ann's heartfelt offer gets me through the next few weeks. As Joe and I try to sort through the potential obstacles and consequences, it's evident that this prospect is more appealing to him than adoption. The child would be biologically his, and my sister and I so resemble each other physically that questions of the child's parentage would arise only when we chose to raise them ourselves.

When Joe and I talk with Jim and Ann by phone, they make only two requests. They want the four of us to see a counselor together. And they want me to come out to Oregon during the last month of Ann's pregnancy to help out with their two kids.

Though we all speak as if this might really happen, I know it won't. If an IUI doesn't take, Ann has offered to go the distance with in vitro fertilization. But how can I let Ann undergo the very regimen of hormone injections that I'm unwilling to try myself? Impossible. As for Ann's persistent refrain that she'll have no trouble separating from the child, I know that, too, is impossible. Every time our families would get together, she'd look at this child and wonder, second-guess herself, perhaps regret. The damage to our own relationship would be painful and irreversible.

Most compelling is the concern raised by my mother: What would this mean for Ann's children, Emily, now four, and Jeremy, three? How are they to understand that the baby in Mommy's stomach is not their brother or sister? If that baby can be given to Aunt Jill, what's to ensure that Mommy and Daddy won't give *them* away?

No. It's impossible.

July 19: *I'm reading better. The Paxil is helping I guess.*

July 21: *I noticed yesterday for the first time—hopeful sign—that I'm not telling myself so often "I'm depressed." I'm not monitoring how I feel every second.*

July 22: *Two nights ago, I detected the first REAL give in Joe, a willingness to yield to my need. Perhaps that's what accounts for my feeling better. ("He loves you so much," Ann and Lynn tell me.) Then last night we're back to his anger, his demand we not have a baby. We're just beginning. But I'm ready to fight now. To avoid confrontation, I've capitulated too often . . . He MUST face my pain.*

July 25: *The depression has lifted in recent days. I delight in reading, writing, playing the piano. This morning I put on Handel harpsicord sonatas and read the* Week in Review *and the book review. Normal Sunday pleasures. I even burst into laughter at a cartoon.*

July 26, my thirty-eighth birthday: *I feel better. It is such a relief to be thinking of something other than me.*

As Joe and I head north in the car, listening to the news, I pepper Joe with questions. What's this about an Israeli attack on Lebanon? When was it? The Senate is doing *what* to Clinton's budget?

Slowly, a look of pleasure spreads across Joe's face. "I haven't seen this Jill in a year," he says.

Despite the continuing absence of a child in my life. Despite my disbelief that Joe will ever agree to an adoption. Despite my distrust of doctors and their prescribed remedies. Despite my conviction that the depression has been all parts psychology and no parts biochemistry. Despite my fear that the antidepressant will suddenly fail. Despite all that, the Paxil, miraculously, has dispersed the cloud.

As I reforge connections with the world outside my head, the thrum of Here. Now. Here. Now. subsides, and time resumes its normal course. There is a past. A present. A future.

I look backward with bewilderment. *How could one so loved sink so low? How could I have become so detached from the life I've built?*

I experience the present with an acute sense of gratitude. I feel grateful to Dr. Gooden for his swift response, effective intervention, and formidable analytic talents. Grateful to Miriam, family, and close friends for their steady flow of compassion, advice and support. Grateful, above all, to Joe for having stuck close, in sickness as in health, through the tedious, enervating months of my depression.

And I look forward with renewed determination. Though I have laid to rest my longing to conceive a child, I now know that I cannot lay to rest my desire to be a mother. That attempt came too close to burying me. Firmly, without apology, I tell Joe that we need to see Grace to discuss adoption.

Reluctantly, he agrees.

VII

RULE NO. 1: EXPECT THE UNEXPECTED. EVERY adoption story is unique.

The first time we'd visited Grace in 1984, Joe had arrived in a crouch, ready to bolt our relationship. During our second brief series of sessions in 1991, my own commitment was showing signs of wear. Now, as we settle once again into the black leather chairs in late July 1993, neither of us is thinking of flight. We want to work this out, we tell her. But how?

"I can't give up on a child," I say. "Joe can't give in."

"This issue is as hard as it gets between two people," she responds. "What could be more difficult?"

I don't know if it's the message, at once soothing and subtly galvanizing, or the messenger, who over the years has earned the respect and trust of each of us. But Grace's words apply a brake to my churning to resolve this baby business once and for all. I, and Joe, too, I think, find it reassuring that the hell we've unwittingly inflicted on each other over the last year as we've drifted apart from a middle ground of malleable ambivalence to polar extremes, me desperately determined, Joe vehemently opposed, has at least been in the interest of a worthy cause.

"I want each of you to tell me your fantasy about children."

We look at each other. When Joe shrugs, I begin. "My fantasy is that we adopt a baby."

"Which sex?" Grace asks.

"Initially, I wanted a girl. Now, the gender no longer matters. I just want a child. We move to a house in the suburbs. Someplace where a child can go out the front door to play without our having to worry constantly about safety issues. I take a six-month leave from *Time*. Find reliable child care. I used to think Joe and I had to divide the responsibility fifty-fifty," I conclude. "Now, I'm willing to assume more of the child-care burdens. Seventy-thirty, eighty-twenty." One hundred percent, I think. "Whatever it takes. I just want a baby."

Grace's gaze shifts to Joe. "I'm more comfortable with Jill getting pregnant or carrying her sister's egg," he says. "The idea of her sister carrying our baby, or adopting, doesn't sit well with me."

Joe and I look at each other. Raise our eyebrows, as if to say, Anything you want to add? Shrug. Then we look back at Grace. So.

At first, the ground is old. Familiar. Frustrating. Joe speaks of my impatience. I bridle at his suggestion that my desire for a child is sudden and precipitous.

"You're talking about this as if it dates from our last consultation with Dr. Feldman two months ago," I say. "The way I see it, I've been waiting to have a child since 1990."

"Given his response," Grace intervenes, "do you trust Joe on the baby issue?"

"This isn't about trust," I answer. "Joe never indicated that he'd go for adoption. But this makes me angry. I don't feel he's responding to my needs."

"That's trust," she says.

Perhaps it is. Yet during our talks over the next four months, I'll continue to regard this concession I seek from Joe as so large that, if achieved, it will forever skew our vague quid-pro-quo ledger. By the crudest calculation, it's possible for Joe to reimburse me for the four years of financial support I'd provided while he wrote his novel. It's even possible for Joe to repay me for career opportunities sacrificed to support his own. If he could not give me Miami or Johannesburg then, perhaps he would give me London or Timbuktu or an extended leave to write another novel. But there's no recompense for a baby. No refund. No return policy.

As we begin to probe our respective attitudes about adoption, it quickly becomes apparent why I've shifted so easily away from childbirth toward adoption. My mother, who was raised under the inflexible laws of Orthodox Judaism, never knew her biological father. Her parents divorced right after her birth. Five years later her mother married a lawyer named David. Though David adored his new stepdaughter, he declined to adopt her. Why? The court proceeding that attended an adoption would be recorded in the newspaper. Such publicity was unthinkable. In those days, in those Orthodox circles, divorce was shameful, something to be hidden, not advertised. David preferred to keep his wife's divorce quiet. So quiet, in fact, that my mother's four younger brothers didn't learn until they were adults that their sister was, by blood, a half-sister.

The next generation was also kept in the dark. I was well into my teens before I learned about my mother's parentage, and even then, only because I chanced to overhear a conversation not intended for my ears. After her family secret was out in the open, my mother spoke often about the feelings of rejection that she'd suffered throughout her childhood, feelings that continued to haunt her adult life. Though David, who died in

1981, had been a loving father, my mother never forgot that he failed to claim her as his own. My siblings and I couldn't understand David's small-mindedness. To us, adoption seemed the obvious and healing choice for my mother.

And so it seemed for me now. My view of adoption as a happy solution, rather than a second-choice alternative, was reinforced by my parents and siblings. My mother was already scouring her rural county, talking with social workers, school principals, and doctors, in hopes of locating a baby for us. She was undeterred by Joe's reservations. Joe, she was certain, would "come around and be a wonderful father as soon as he held a baby of his own in his arms."

"My parents are more than behind me on the idea of an adoption," I tell Joe and Grace. "I think, in a way, this would close a painful circle for my mother."

Joe's family situation is markedly different. When Joe was three, he'd been bitten by a cocker spaniel, an attack that had scarred his face and left him terrified of dogs. Determined to ease that fear, Joe's parents had bought a dalmatian. That one pup changed the Treen household forever. Soon Joe's parents were showing dalmatians. Then breeding them. Writing about dalmatians. Then judging them. In time, Joe's father ascended to the board of the American Kennel Club. To this day, both his parents spend most weekends of the year judging dog shows, either in this country or abroad.

Although none of this enhanced Joe's love of canines, he did learn a lot about decoupling dogs from fights and recoupling them for breeding. When it comes to the latter, the guiding principle is purity of bloodlines. So, though Joe's parents have never spoken about adoption, pro or con, Joe is certain they'll be even less enthusiastic about the idea than he is.

As for his own reservations, Joe reminds me that the brief, tense period when he'd played stepfather to preadolescent twins had hardly been an endorsement for fatherhood. There are his growing doubts about starting a family so late in life. "I should be saving for retirement, not for a kid's college fund." And then, there are his doubts about me.

"I'm worried that you'll try to micromanage every detail of life with baby," he says. "That you won't let me be the father I want to be."

"I find this ironic, Wease," I answer. "Here, you're worrying I won't let you be a father, and I'm worrying that you won't choose to participate."

I tell him about an afternoon I'd spent years earlier with my friend Beth, when her daughter Molly was still a toddler. Beth is my model of an outstanding parent: attentive, relaxed, adoring, above all, accepting. The joy she gives and takes as a mother is apparent in her every interaction with Molly. As we chatted and watched her daughter that afternoon, Beth mentioned how creative her husband John was at playing with Molly.

"He's much more imaginative than I am," she said. "He'll do things like get under that glass table and make funny faces up at Molly."

Until that moment, it had seemed to me that Beth was doing most of the heavy-lifting in the raising of their daughter. But that comment, so generous and appreciative of John's contribution, had subtly shifted my perception. If we ever have a child, I'd thought, Joe, like John, would be the playful one.

"I'm assuming that you'll be the parent who provides most of the fun," I say to Joe. "You're so natural at it. Certainly much better than I am. This is the part of parenthood we keep forgetting about. The fun stuff. Your mother once said that to us. 'Kids are really funny. Being a parent can be fun.'"

I can't tell if the look of doubt on Joe's face is about me and my ability to flex, or about him and his ability or desire to parent a child. I plow on, repeating arguments that I've made before. I tell him that I know the depth of his love and the strength of his commitment as a mate. That I've seen his loyalty and responsibility to friends and family. That I've witnessed his capacity to delight small children.

"You'll be a terrific father," I say, "if only you'll give it a chance."

I mean every word. For all Joe's expressed reservations, I remain convinced that as with marriage, so with parenting: once we have a child, his ambivalence will be replaced by determination, and his commitment and love will follow. The Joe I know is far too caring, responsible, and relentlessly self-improving to allow himself to fail at something as important as fatherhood.

If anybody else is harboring doubts about Joe, they don't raise them with me. Not any of our friends. Not any of our relatives. Not Grace. I push ahead with my campaign, never pausing to consider what might happen—to him, to us, most importantly to our child—if I'm wrong.

In early September, Grace calls a halt to our circling. Perhaps she's remembering Joe's tendency to avoid major commitments. Or maybe she just feels we're ready to move on.

"Jill is being Patient Griselda," she says to Joe. "How long do you need to make up your mind about adoption?" Our next session is three weeks away. Grace suggests Joe give his answer then.

As with the marriage deadline I'd set a decade earlier, I have a feeling of finality about this schedule. Now, as then, I mute my musings, wanting Joe to decide for himself. But unlike the weeks that preceded Joe's marriage decision, this waiting stirs neither anxiety nor excited anticipation. Now that I'm out of the tunnel, my vision is clear. Even if Joe agrees to pursue an adoption, that's only a beginning.

At our next counseling session, Grace turns an inquiring gaze to Joe and he says, "Alright. Let's do it."

I nod and accept his statement without question or comment. I know that Joe is still reluctant, still ambivalent. I know that won't change until we have a child. And I know, unspoken, that the effort to locate a child will be all mine. Joe will just come along for the ride.

Fine.

Still, there are decisions we must make together.

Rule No. 2: If you thought the journey of a million miles from "Let's have a baby" to "Let's adopt" was convoluted, you ain't seen nothing yet.

Where to look? What to look for? What sex? What age? What health condition? What ethnicity? What information do we feel we must have about the child's origins? What information can we make do without? How much contact do we want with the biological parents? How much control are we willing to surrender? How long are we willing to wait? How much can we afford to spend? Which adoption lawyer or agency to pick? Which social worker?

For all our differences about whether or not to adopt, Joe and I are remarkably in sync about the child and situation we want. First, foremost, we agree, we want a healthy baby. Neither of us feels equipped to take on the challenges of a special-needs child. We agree that while we would have learned to adjust our lives around any such need had such a child been born to us, one advantage of adoption is that we do not now have to risk such a situation.

To my surprise, Joe shares my preference for a girl.

"Really? How come, Wease?" He shrugs.

Less surprising, Joe, too, wants a newborn. Both of us have read that a child's development is most critical during the first three years of life. The more time a child has spent in an unloving environment, we reason, the more likely we are to confront problems not of our own making.

We also agree that neither of us feels up to the emotional rigors of an open adoption. We will place no ads in newspapers, establish no special phone line into our apartment to handle the responses. Neither of us wants close, personal contact with potential birth mothers. Like many adoptive couples, Joe and I have been made uneasy by the sensational stories played up in the media about the Baby Jessicas and Baby Richards who become human footballs between biological and adoptive parents. Though we assume such cases are aberrations—Why else would they make headlines?—we don't want to chance becoming that one unfortunate couple in a million. Our mutual preference is to keep the birth parents as distant as possible. We acknowledge that we want our love and our claim to be exclusive, unrivaled, unchallenged.

Given that need, we agree, an international adoption might be the most comfortable. It's an option that makes sense for us. We met as foreign affairs writers, we've traveled extensively together, we continue to share an interest in international affairs. For me, there's the additional hope that an overseas adoption will move more swiftly. In the U.S., where an estimated twenty-five to forty couples are queued up for every available infant, the waiting time for a newborn can be up to three years.

A white newborn, that is. The preponderance of waiting parents, I've learned, are Caucasian, and want a white baby. Black newborns and babies of mixed race are more readily available. Whether we look abroad or domestically, race will be a consideration. What *are* we willing to consider?

Again, Joe and I are largely of one mind. Caucasian, yes. Latino, yes. African-American, no. My research has familiarized me with the heated debate in parts of the black community about white adoptions of black children. The National Association of Black Social Workers, which in the early seventies branded transracial adoptions "cultural genocide," has eased its position only somewhat in recent years. Joe and I agree that adoption issues confronted within the privacy of our home may prove dicey enough in the years ahead; we don't need the Politically Correct forces breathing down our necks as well. Native American? Yes. Asian? Me, yes. Joe, maybe. He's hesitant, though he's not sure why. Mixed race? We agree to remain flexible.

We're dimly aware that our grab bag of choices will incur certain risks. By opting out of situations that will bring us into contact with birth parents, we increase the likelihood that the child will be orphaned or abandoned. What effect will such conditions have on the child's development? Also, absent contact with birth parents, we may have to forego such critical information as the medical history on both sides of the child's biological family. Without that information, how will we or our child know what to look out for in the years ahead? And what emotional risks do we court by opting for a child whose inevitable questions—Why didn't my mother keep me? Who was my father?—may have no convincing answers?

Even so, I feel we're making progress. We've agreed, finally, to move ahead on an adoption. We've made some tough choices about whom we are seeking. We're a healthy, comfortably situated, loving couple. There are countless infants around the world as in need of parents as we are in need of a child. The hardest part, I think, is behind us. Finding our child should be a relative snap.

Hah.

It's not coincidental that books on infertility and adoption tend to use the same pat phrase to describe each of those bumpy experiences: "emotional rollercoaster."

During my months of infertility anguish, some people had facilely suggested, "Why don't you just adopt?" I'd bridled at the implication that it's so simple a matter to shift a couple's focus from conception to adoption. Now, as I enter the adoption labryinth, I begin to understand that such well-intended comments are not only ill-advised, but ill-informed.

Rule No. 3: There is nothing straightforward or obvious about adoption. It's a complicated, high-risk process that, like fertility treatment, requires determination, tenacity, and patience.

From the outset of our adoption hunt, I enjoy a wealth of resources unavailable to most potential parents. Down the corridor from me at *Time* is Lois Gilman, an adoptive mother of two children born overseas, and author of *The Adoption Resource Book*, a popular text on the ins and outs of the adoption process. Though Lois and I don't know each other well, from my first tentative inquiry forward, Lois offers the support of an old friend. Through her, I gain access to an adoption elite who can answer my questions quickly and authoritatively.

Even so.

Rule No. 4: Though there is an answer for every question, answers only tend to beget more questions.

Our adoption options are at once ridiculously unlimited and annoyingly tight. I learn early on in my research, for instance, that at fifty-one and thirty-eight, respectively, Joe and I are too old to be matched with a newborn by a public agency.

Fine. Scratch public agencies.

I also discover that the current practice favored by both lawyers and private agencies is to offer birth mothers a choice from among several potential parents. No matter what the race, younger birth mothers, which is to say most of the pregnant women who are willing to consider adoption, tend to prefer younger couples. Joe and I are likely to be bypassed as too wrinkly.

Fine. Scratch a domestic adoption.

That still leaves the rest of the world to choose from. But which country? And should we pursue more than one avenue at a time?

The map of the world, at first so daunting, shrinks rapidly. Just as laws, regulations, and requirements vary state to state in the U.S., overseas they vary country to country. Nothing is fixed; rules are constantly in flux. At this hour in 1993, Western Europe, Canada, and Australia are out. There, middle-aged couples are queued up in lines as long or longer than in America. We can also eliminate some of the countries that at other moments have proved a great source. Romania, for instance, had opened the doors of its orphanages and permitted a large number of adoptions after the bloody fall of the Ceaucescu regime. Now, those doors are again shut indefinitely.

Rule No. 5: Stay informed. Adoption is a fluid process. Rules change. Information that was good yesterday may not be good today. Doors that are open today may be closed tomorrow.

At present, most of the foreign governments permitting placement of children in U.S. homes are in Latin America, Eastern Europe, and Asia. Again, though, our ages are prohibitive. South Korea, which has supplied more children to U.S. couples than any other country in recent years, refuses to consider those couples where either partner is older than thirty-nine. Ditto, Bolivia. For couples seeking healthy infants, Russia prefers parents under age forty-two. Ecuador and El Salvador won't consider anyone over fifty. Moreover, religion is an unexpected potential obstacle. Some agencies in Mexico, I'm informed, will reject us because neither Joe nor I is Catholic. Some of the former Soviet republics and satellites, we're warned (incorrectly), may balk because I'm Jewish.

Here, then, is the startling picture that I piece together. In a world where children go wanting for food, shelter, and love every day, the combination of our ages and religions leaves Joe and me with essentially two countries to choose between: China and Paraguay.

"I want a girl, Wease," I say. "I can't help it. If we have a choice, I want a girl."

I'm pressing for China. The country's one-child-per-family

policy, in place since the 1970s to curb a population explosion, has produced an abundance of abandoned girls, the "lesser sex" in a culture that has traditionally favored sons.

Though Joe also favors a girl, he's tilting toward Paraguay. Since he offers no reason, I assume it has something to do with his Native American heritage. His mother's grandfather had been a principal chief of the Cherokees. When I'd looked into the possibility of adopting a Native American infant in the U.S., I'd discovered that the 1978 Indian Child Welfare Act, which recognizes the sovereignty of Native American nations, gives tribes the authority to make all decisions about adoption. Like the Association of Black Social Workers, tribal leaders rank broad ethnic considerations above the interests of specific children, and are even more militant in their objections to transracial adoptions. Our chances of such an adoption are about zero.

"Is it your Cherokee heritage?" I ask Joe. "The possibility of a child who might look a bit like you."

"Maybe," he answers. "I'd prefer a baby that I didn't have to explain all the time."

I have little problem yielding on this. Anything to ease Joe's discomfort with the idea of adoption. But his answer isn't entirely convincing. Latin America is awash with drugs and HIV; China remains largely untouched by either problem. Our chance of getting a child who is both healthy and female is better in China.

Finally, Joe admits there is more behind his preference for Paraguay. "I was born during World War II when we were at war with Japan; the movies I was raised on were anti-Japanese. Next came the Korean conflict. I came of age during Vietnam. All my life, it seems, the U.S. has been at war with Asia." The expression on his face is one of embarrassment. "I can't explain it. Though I have friends who are Asian-American, and I've never thought anything of it one way or the other, I'm uncomfortable with the idea of an Asian child."

He looks at me with a humiliated expression that telegraphs how hard this has been for him, discovering an unsuspected prejudice within himself. Instead of being repulsed, I feel grateful for his honesty. Bonding with a child, any child, is a chancy enough proposition. I see little point in upping the risk by pursuing a child who, instinctively, makes him uncomfortable.

"Okay, Wease," I say. "Paraguay, it is."

Rule No. 6: Honesty with yourself and your spouse is not only the best policy; it's the only policy.

Infant. Healthy. Paraguayan.

Those decisions behind, we still have to choose our route. Lawyer? Who? Private adoption agency? Which one? Given that adoptees represent only about 2 percent of America's juvenile population, the number of services that are scattered throughout the fifty states is really mind-boggling.

From Lois, I learn about Spence Chapin, one of the country's oldest adoption agencies, located right in Manhattan. Lois puts me in touch with a woman who, courtesy of Spence, had recently returned from Paraguay with a healthy infant. The woman has only positive things to report about the agency. I call Spence and learn that the next orientation meeting for people interested in overseas programs is a few weeks away. I add our names to the list.

On November 15 at six o'clock, Joe and I are running late and have to rush from the office to Spence's headquarters on the Upper East Side. A receptionist directs us to a room off the waiting area where we encounter a dense crowd of well-dressed people who look much like us. White. Middle-aged. Tired after a day's work.

I give the Spence people a lot of credit for their display of enthusiasm that evening, given the wall of impatience and skepticism they encounter in that room. It's obvious that these people have been through the emotional wringer and want to skip the happy talk about the joys of adoption. They want just the facts. Availability of children. Length of wait. Length of stay in the host country. Cost.

During the Spence presentation, we learn there are six countries where prospects are most promising as of this hour. Peru is scheduled to open its door December 1; adoptions are expected to move quickly after that. El Salvador and Ecuador are slowly starting to move. Paraguay is moving, but there is a waiting line. Russia is processing only special-needs and "ethnically different" children. China remains closed indefinitely while Beijing and the provinces wrangle over the restructuring of adoption regulations. This last update eliminates any remaining doubts I have about our choice of Paraguay.

While I take notes, Joe stands grim-faced, plainly wanting to leave. On the way out the door, I drop a check for one hundred dollars in the in-basket on the receptionist's desk, the price to take the next step.

That check is a drop in the ocean we are about to traverse. According to the literature distributed during the meeting, the cost of this adoption will run in excess of twenty thousand dollars, an estimate that includes neither the expense of our airfare to Paraguay nor the anticipated two-week stay required to complete the adoption. We—I—have to hope that this Cadillac of agencies will live up to its reputation for excellence. Given the estimated expense, it's now clear that we won't be double-timing with another agency or lawyer.

Then we wait. After several weeks, we receive a call from Spence informing us that our next appointment, a private interview, is set for early February.

Fine.

I know. I'm sounding rather bloodless about all this. But that's the way I felt. Calm. Practical. Undeluded. After the long

months of passion and depression over infertility, I was determined not to ride the sine wave of emotions that the adoption
process threatened.

When I look at all the things that could block our being an
acceptable couple, let alone finding a child, I don't feel my hopes
rising to expectation. There's my depression, Joe's two marriages,
our ages. What if we get a child, and the child is taken away? . . .
None of this seems quite real. I don't think about it much, except
when I'm doing research.

Instead, I throw myself into work with renewed vigor,
enlivened by a banquet of perverse stories with a high giggle
factor. Skater Tonya Harding's attack on rival Nancy Kerrigan.
Bob Packwood's alleged sex peccadilloes.

My restored enthusiasm for the weekly grind, so depleted
through the months of fertility treatment, is reinforced by a
promotion. The promotion itself, from Associate Editor to
Senior Writer, changes nothing in my life; just a snazzier title
for a job I've been doing for years. What does provide a brief,
fuzzy feeling of warmth, however, is the announcement that
attends the new title. Not the nice stuff about my writing, but
this: "[Jill is] also just a wonderful colleague to have around.
Eminently sensible, smart, broadly informed, Jill displays an
intellectual rigor, a dedication to the profession and" so forth.
After so many months of struggling to keep my mental disintegration hidden behind my office door, I feel like running up
and down the corridors, doing a Sally Field: You think I'm
sane! You really think I'm sane!

The bit about being a "wonderful colleague" also has
special meaning, reinforcing my efforts to find outlets for
the frustrated energy that wants to settle into motherhood.
I've recently begun tutoring a Hoboken teenager in math
and reading. A letter from a media-struck high school student in the midwest has resulted in a correspondence that
makes me feel that I have something to offer this girl. A

mentoring relationship with a younger colleague is proving gratifying.

I also reconnect with people from whom I've deliberately or inadvertently carved a distance in recent months. After Lynn gently chides, "I hope maybe now you'll get to know Max," I make greater efforts to get to her apartment on the Upper West Side. Max is already nine months old. Where the hell have I been? After I learn that Donna is at long last a mother, I'm able to revel in her joy without envy. And when during a visit with my sister's family, Emily murmurs several times, "I'm so glad you're here, Aunt Jill," I'm able to embrace my niece without protectively holding a piece of myself apart.

This is not to suggest that I'm completely divorced from my pain about children. When the stomach of a pregnant colleague begins to swell, the only way I can deal with her is by partitioning her off from the neck down and keeping my eyes fixed on her face.

As for what might yet be, I begin to look with new interest at Latino children in the subways and on the streets. Though I've never tried to imagine what a child, conceived by Joe and me, might look like, I now stare with fascination at the cherubic faces of these children and wonder, Will my child look like that? Or that? Maybe that?

Mostly, though, my attitude toward our potential adoption is that of the detached reporter. While eager to gather as much information as I can, I manage, without much effort, to let little of what I learn touch me. That cool detachment proves a benefit in dealing with others. While Joe and I had confined discussion of our fertility problems to family and a small circle of friends, we initially share an impulse to put the word out that we're trying to adopt. Given our far-flung network of journalist friends and acquaintances, who knows what opportunity might arise if people are aware we're looking? There is, however, a cost to going public.

Rule No. 7: People say stupid things.

Though people mean well, the folk wisdom about adoption can be as insensitive and misguided as it is about infertility. The adoption equivalent of "Just relax" is "You'll probably get pregnant after you adopt." Never mind the offensive implication that adoption is a distant second choice, pursued mainly to ensure an eventual pregnancy. The probability that a couple will fluke into a postadoption pregnancy is equal to the odds that a couple will achieve a pregnancy after halting fertility treatment: just one in twenty.

Another irritating bit of popular lore is that though there are no guarantees of success with fertility treatment, in adoption you *will* get a baby if you "just hang in there." Although probably true, that message presupposes that financial or emotional resources won't run dry first. It also implies that control resides with the waiting parents. Hardly. The unsettling fact is that any prospective adoption is a crap shoot. The best any waiting parent can do is throw the dice and hope that a birth parent or distant relative, court judge or social worker, state law or foreign government, won't suddenly abort the effort.

Rule No. 8: Until the adoption papers are signed, do not settle your heart on any particular child. Anywhere. Anytime.

As we wait the three months until our next appointment at Spence, I keep my research efforts to myself. Though I'm learning a lot about adoption and the challenges ahead, Joe, I understand, pretty much just wants to be told when and where to show up next.

In early January, my computer screen blinks "You have a message," and I find a note from Lois about a lawyer who might be able to push through a Latin American adoption more speedily than Spence. I forward the note to Joe, thinking this will require a decision involving the two of us. When a day or two passes without comment, I ask Joe whether I should check the guy out.

After a horrible explosion that left us not talking to one another
for several weeks, we sorted out that Joe is settling into the idea of
a baby, but wants a nine-month gestation period. The Spence
route gives him that. So we've agreed to follow up any leads that
result from my parents' efforts, but to pursue nothing new.

Fine.

My mother's ceaseless efforts have put me in touch with an
Ecuadoran woman living in North Carolina, who has a lawyer
cousin in Quito who's trying to track down an adoption
attorney who—. You get the idea. Though I've followed
through by writing a letter to the cousin, I don't regard this as a
likely channel. A Filipino friend of my parents provided a
number that proved to be an agency that, like all agencies, has
a queue. Moreover, Joe and I are not eligible for the Philip-
pines: we're too old. Another phone call from my mother, one
that began with a tearful, "I think we've found a baby,"
momentarily made my pulse race. When I followed up on the
lead, the contact proved to be a Pennsylvania agency that deals
only with Catholic couples.

Rule No. 9: If it sounds too good to be true, it probably is.

After that, I entreat my mother to tell me nothing further of
her efforts. "I appreciate what you're doing more than you can
know, Mom. But unless something demands my personal
attention, I don't want to know about it."

I really, really don't.

Joe's parents, in their own understated way, also signal
unexpected support. Over Thanksgiving, during a father-son
trip to buy shoes, Joe's father asks several thoughtful questions
about adoption. Though Joe hears mostly the drumbeat of
"bloodlines" in his father's questions, I sense a genuine
expression of interest and an attempt to begin grappling with,
what for them, must be a very difficult subject.

A month later when we gather in Pasadena for Christmas,
Joe's mother informs us of changes recently made in the

Treens' will. She mentions that there's an alternate plan "if there are any issue." My initial reaction is to recoil. Issue? But when I rerun her words in my head, I feel encouraged.

"That's the first acknowledgment of this child we might adopt," I say to Joe. "It's an indication that your parents are mentally preparing to embrace this baby as their grandchild." For a brief moment, Joe's lips form the crooked smile that indicates he is pleased.

On February 3, Joe and I return to Spence for our intake interview. We've devised a strategy. Keep the conversation trained on Joe, and away from me. The last thing I want is a social worker probing into the recent state of my mental health. If asked directly, we've decided, I'll do something that is neither my habit nor my inclination: I'll lie.

Looking back, I realize this was silly. Who *wouldn't* get depressed by the ups and downs of fertility treatment? But at the time, I feared that if Spence workers knew I was taking an antidepressant, they might reject our application. So, when I'm asked if I've ever consulted a psychiatrist or been on medication, I smile and say, "No."

Heroically, Joe makes himself the focus of the conversation by speaking of his reservations about children. We talk about the marital counseling we've been through to reconcile our differences about adoption. Here, we've reasoned, candor can only benefit us. Various books I've scanned stress that adoption is a big step; that spouses are often of different minds on whether to proceed; that counseling may be useful. Moreover, we're in Manhattan, therapy capital of the world. As we suspected, our mention of counseling draws knowing nods of approval.

During the meeting, we're asked if we have a preference for a boy or a girl. Joe and I look at each other, then I say, "Well, if we were really pressed, I'd say a girl. But it's not a strong preference."

"That's good," the worker says. "It will go much faster if you're open to a boy."

"Really? Why?"

"Because most adoptive couples want girls."

"You're kidding," I say. "That's totally counterintuitive. I thought most couples prefer boys, at least for a first child."

"Not adoptive couples."

"Why's that?"

"I don't know," she answers. "There haven't been any studies."

Briefly we detour into a discussion of possibilities, and come up with two theories. By tradition, sons carry the family name forward to the next generation; if a couple adopts a girl, there's less risk of flack from relatives who regard "pure" bloodlines as the sap that runs through their geneological tree. Or perhaps adoptive couples, men especially (Joe, in particular? I wonder silently), are less wed to the idea of producing a daughter in their "image."

Then, back to the business at hand. Joe and I coast through the rest of the meeting, coming off as the couple we are most of the time. Affectionate. Committed. Well adjusted. Well settled. Healthy. The Spence worker says she'll recommend us for the program.

Smiles. Handshakes. We're in the loop.

I leave feeling confident we've selected a prudent path. We won't have to deal with prospective birth mothers and their own difficult drama. We won't risk bonding with a swelling stomach, only to have our hopes dashed by a postbirth change of mind. Instead, we'll be able to keep the process at a comfortable distance, limiting our participation to supplying the proper documentation and letting Spence's experts do the rest. By going overseas, we face a shorter waiting time. And of the international options available to us, we have chosen the route that in recent years has proved fastest and smoothest for older couples.

After the interview, I say to Joe, "All we have to do now, is sit back and let the agency do its job."

Fine.

Rule No. 10: Rules are easily broken. So are hearts.

VIII

TWO WEEKS LATER AS I CROSS THE LOBBY OF THE
Time & Life Building, I spot Eric, a colleague I haven't seen in
months. Eric is the classic year-of-living-dangerously journalist, always parachuting into trouble spots. Though we don't
know each other well, we have a warm relationship. I love to
hear about his adventures; he loves to recount them.

"Hey, Eric," I call. "Long time, no see. What's up?"

His vivid blue eyes have a wild, excited look. "I'm leaving for
Sarajevo in a couple of hours."

The question comes out of my mouth before I'm aware it's
formed in my head. "Could you do me a favor if you get a
chance?" Impulsively, I tell him that Joe and I are trying to
adopt, and that we've heard conflicting reports about the
situation in Sarajevo. "Could you try to find out if there are
infants available for adoption?"

"Sure."

I walk away, embarrassed by my rudeness. Here, this guy is
going off to trench hop, and I'm bugging him about babies.

Despite our resolve to confine our efforts to Spence, in January Joe had asked a *People* correspondent to check into the situation while on assignment in Bosnia. He'd also phoned a former *Newsweek* colleague in London, who'd recently visited Sarajevo for the United Nations. Their conflicting replies had left us wondering what *was* happening to all those babies we'd read about in the newspapers, the unwanted children born of the rape of Muslim women by Serbian troops.

A week later on February 17, my office phone rings, jarring my concentration. What the hell? I think. Friends and family know better than to call on a writing day.

"Jill?" The line is crackling, the voice barely audible. "It's Eric. Are you serious about adopting a baby?" His voice is so distant that I have to shut off my office fan. "I've been to a hospital in Sarajevo. There are six babies there, two and three days old. The director of the hospital is determined to get these babies to safety."

"Are you serious? Do you think it's really possible?"

"Yeah, I do. A *New York Times* reporter recently took a baby out of here for an Italian couple."

"Are these babies the children of rape?"

"I don't think so. Their mothers are dead." Eric isn't sure if the infants are Muslims, Serbs, or Croats. "The babies are all healthy. Do you want a boy or a girl?"

This conversation is beginning to feel surreal. "If it were just me, I'd say, yes, do it. I'm ready to hijack babies off subways. But I have to check with my husband." We agree that I'll leave Eric a message on his office answering machine. That way, we won't have to try to coordinate phone calls between two continents, two time zones, and two unpredictable work schedules.

I grab the next elevator to the *People* floor, then sit in Joe's office, nervously waiting for him to return from a meeting.

"Wease?" His tone is surprised as I gesture for him to close the door. We rarely visit each other during the workday.

"I'm sorry for intruding, but there's something that can't wait."

After I tell him about Eric's call, Joe responds without hesitating. "Let's do it." I pitch forward off the couch and throw my arms around his neck. "You know," he laughs, "you'll have to quit smoking now, Wease." The ultimate seal of approval.

Back in my office, I call Eric's machine. "Yes, yes, please, please, please, go ahead. We are so very grateful." I'm so excited that as I leave Eric our assorted phone numbers so that he can reach us any hour of the day or night, I forget our Hoboken number halfway through.

A little later, Joe appears at my office door. "We should bring in our passports," he says. Joe, who used to parachute into Middle East wars for *Newsday*, is mentally preparing to be able to take off at a moment's notice.

"Maybe you should leave a message for Eric, too," I say.

As Joe jokes into the receiver, "Maybe we'll name the kid Erica," I can't tell which excites me more: those Bosnian babies or Joe's enthusiasm.

Late that afternoon, Joe and I kick instinctively into a mode we both know well, that of journalists reporting against a tight deadline. As we both work the phones, letting each conversation point the way to the next, we understand that our window of opportunity is narrow. Eric might have to make a hasty exit from Sarajevo; a grenade or artillery fire might destroy that hospital, those babies, our hopes, in an instant.

For the first time since our baby odyssey stalled on infertility, I feel that Joe and I are traveling in tandem. It's a great relief to have him to brace against. Unlike fertility procedures, slow but steady and predictable, this rollercoaster moves at a fitful clip, the zigs and zags sharp, fast, and disorienting.

Neophytes that we are, Joe and I assume the trickiest part will be getting into war-torn Sarajevo, then getting the baby back out safely. Flights aren't exactly running on schedule. Joe is optimistic we can work our journalism contacts to get onto a relief flight. We don't think to question Eric's assurance that the infants are available for adoption. The hospital chief, he's told me, is only too happy to cooperate with us to get these kids to safety. Bosnian authorities, we assume, will feel the same way.

Down. My first call is to Lois, who asks if our documents are in order for an international adoption. From November until now, I've held fast to my determination not to get out ahead of the Spence process, so I haven't yet looked into the required paperwork. "We just got the letter from Spence yesterday saying we've been accepted into the Paraguay program," I answer. "Why? What do we need?"

"A home study." I've heard of that; something that involves social workers writing up a report attesting to our fitness to be parents. "An I-600." That form, she explains, petitions the Immigration and Naturalization Service for a visa that will enable the baby to enter the country. The clearance process, she warns, can take months while the INS runs a check on our fingerprints.

Huh? "Fingerprints?"

Though Lois loads me down with contacts who might be useful, she sounds wary.

The immigration lawyer I call next sounds even more skeptical. "To adopt a baby overseas, you have to prove that one or both parents are dead or uninvolved," he explains. "How are you going to do that in a war situation? You could land up getting stuck in Europe for four to six months, and then have the U.S. consulate in Vienna turn you down. I suggest that you proceed with your agency adoption."

Up. When I phone Joe to tell him about the document problem, he's way ahead of me, having consulted a colleague whose daughter was adopted from Bulgaria. He's already ordered the blue I-600 forms from the INS office in Newark.

"You're the best, Wease."

"You know two people at the State Department," he answers, referring to an old college pal and a former colleague. "Maybe one of them could help."

"I don't know," I say, surprised. Neither Joe nor I am inclined to lean on friends' professional resources for personal favors. If anything, we share a disregard for people who confuse friends with contacts. "Let me think about it."

I then call Francine, one of Lois' contacts at Adoptive Families of America in Minneapolis. Francine, who is involved in an ongoing effort by the Hague to develop international standards for adoption, is well versed in international protocols.

"The issue is not whether or not you can adopt one of these babies," she says. "It's whether you can get an orphan visa." She warns that Eric's example of the Italian couple is not useful because Italy doesn't have visa requirements. "The United States has the toughest visa laws in the world. You have to prove the baby is orphaned or abandoned."

"What if a doctor at the Sarajevo hospital attests that the baby's mother is dead?"

"Then it sure sounds possible." She says we'll need to obtain the baby's birth certificate, the mother's death certificate, and information about the father. "You've got your home study and I-600 in order, right?"

"No. Not yet," I say, feeling like a complete idiot.

"There's no getting around that. You'll need them for—"

"I know two people high up in the State Department," I blurt. "Do you think either of them could help me bend the rules?"

"There's something called a humanitarian parole visa," Francine answers, enthusiasm returning to her voice. "That would enable you to get the baby out of Bosnia, then to complete the paperwork here." She suggests that I contact the State Department's liaison to the INS.

Down. "My experience with Bosnia is that it will not fly," the liaison says. "The Bosnians don't want their kids leaving the country. This could mean only heartbreak for you."

Up. If Sam, my college friend at State, is as uncomfortable with my request as I am making it, he's deft at masking it. "A humanitarian parole might be possible," he says energetically. "I'll look into it." He tells me that the State Department recently had success with one such case, an eleven-year-old boy who'd been taken out of Bosnia by an American couple after the boy's parents were killed. "The U.S. consulate in Vienna was obstreperous," Sam says, "but it all worked out."

When Sam starts to commend me for my "great humanitarian gesture," I cut him off. "This is filling *my* need, Sam."

When I try to thank Sam for his help, he cuts me off. "This is one of the great pleasures of my job."

Down. "In my twenty years of adoption practice," says a Brooklyn attorney who specializes in international adoption, "I know of only one humanitarian parole that worked." When I tell him about my friend at State, he chuckles. "If you've got him, you don't need me." As further ammunition, he suggests, "Try to enlist a senator in the effort."

Up. This time, I don't even hesitate. I dial another old college friend, one well connected in New Jersey political circles.

"No problem. I know people in Frank Lautenberg's office," he says, referring to one of the state's two senators.

My final call of the day is to Children of the World, a New Jersey adoption agency. If we can assemble the required documents, the woman tells me, the agency can crash a home study in as little as a week.

Amazing, I think, as I take notes on what documents we will need. This agency can accomplish in one week what Spence, after three months, hasn't even begun.

The next morning I travel to lower Manhattan so early that I'm first in line when the marriage bureau opens. Fifteen minutes later, I emerge with a certified copy of our marriage license in hand. On the way to the subway, I spot a shop that advertises fingerprinting services. This is feasible, I think, as I jot down the address.

Down. "This effort will probably be illegal, inadvisable, and very expensive." The woman at the other end of the phone line is with the State Department's Overseas Citizens' Services Department, an office that State's liaison to the INS has told me will best be able to answer my questions. "Even if you are able to get the baby as far as Vienna, the U.S. consul will need certification that the child is an orphan."

"The hospital director in Sarajevo is willing to certify that the mother is dead," I explain.

"That's very noble of the hospital director," the woman answers, with a hint of sarcasm, "but his word would not be considered sufficient. The INS still requires a field study, which would have to be conducted by the U.S. consul in Zagreb. Obviously, we have no consul in Sarajevo at this time. The problem is that the staff in Croatia can't get into Bosnia to conduct the study, given the war conditions."

"These kids need homes. Their mothers are dead," I plead. "A doctor is willing to say so."

"He's going to say anything to get those kids to safety, but think about it," she counters. "You say there are six newborns. How did so many mothers suddenly die? It seems unlikely they all died in childbirth." That point has crossed my mind, too. "There's a good reason why the consul proceeds cautiously," she continues. "Suppose, when the war ends, the children's fathers turn up at the hospital, wondering where their kids are. For them, it would be adding insult to injury to find that their children have been taken away from them."

I hear not only the political implications for the Clinton Administration, but the personal ones for Joe and me. Do we want to spend the rest of our lives wondering if we broke up a family and, in essence, stole a child from a parent?

More gently, the woman says, "Go with Spence Chapin, as you planned. It takes longer, but it's by the book and you'll know the child is really an orphan."

"I think it's over, Wease," I tell Joe.

"State Department people were never a help when I was in the Middle East," he responds, unimpressed by the woman's warning.

"Well, even if we can get State to flex, there's still this business with the consulate in Vienna. Everybody says the guy there is a pain in the ass, and won't let us through."

"Why do we have to go through Vienna? Why not London?"

Why *not* London? "I knew there was a reason I married you, Wease."

Up. I leave a lengthy phone message for Eric detailing everything I've learned. That night as I'm closing a story, the secretary in *Time*'s New York bureau calls. "Eric says to tell you he got your message. He says, " 'I have two people working on it.' "

Ten days pass. I don't hear from Eric. *I am not thinking about it. What's to think about.* Then three more. *I haven't wondered when Eric will call. Part of me hopes he doesn't. What he's offering includes the potential for heartbreak.*

Down. On the morning of March 7, Joe and I are awakened at five-thirty with a call from Eric.

"Is that gunfire I'm hearing?" I ask.

"Yeah," he says, unperturbed.

Eric has learned of an eleven-month-old girl, currently residing in an orphanage. "Her mother is out cavorting and might be interested in signing off on an adoption." Father: unknown. "I've also found a lawyer who can handle the paperwork, but I've got to warn you, this is a country of screwups. I'm sure something will happen." According to the lawyer, we would need to make two trips to Sarajevo, one to file papers, another two months later to pick up the child.

"Who in the government would sign off on this adoption?" I ask.

"I'll find out."

Shamelessly, I make another request. "Could you find out how much experience the lawyer has dealing with the U.S.? We're apparently stricter about these things than other countries."

Four hours later, Eric calls back to tell me that the lawyer has done several international adoptions, none of them involving Americans. "The lawyer will handle everything. The child's name will be changed on the birth certificate." That way, the lawyer has indicated, we can take the baby out of Sarajevo, no questions asked.

Joe and I are both uncomfortable with this plan. Even if the birth mother is in earnest about the adoption, couldn't lying on a birth certificate pose problems down the road? We also question the wisdom of relying on a lawyer who's never tangled with the U.S. bureaucracy. By now, Sam has affirmed that the best authority on this situation is the woman I spoke to in State's Overseas Citizens' Services Department. Given her blunt warning, it's easy to imagine getting into Sarajevo, holding a baby, then having it taken away from us at the border or in Vienna—my worst nightmare.

Even if all that went smoothly, what about the rest of our lives? Though we're both reluctant to leave this child in an orphanage in a war zone where the latest tentative cease-fire is already shattering, the baby will be more than a year old by the time we get her home. That seems a long distance from the newborn we'd agreed to pursue. Between Bosnia's war situation and the baby's orphanage experience, there's no telling what behavioral or developmental problems we might encounter.

Too risky, we agree.

That afternoon, I leave Eric a final phone message. "We're

going to have to pass. I can't thank you enough for everything.
It's been a learn-as-you-go process."

End of ride.

I let go quickly and without regret. The emotional investment has seemed relatively small for so large a return. Together, Joe and I have gained a better understanding of the politics,
procedures, and ethics of international adoption. In my rolo-
dex, I have the names and numbers of new adoption contacts
whose generosity and support have melted my resistance to
asking for help. Adoption, I'm beginning to understand, is a
person-to-person business, and people are willing, even eager,
to assist.

But I've also learned that a not-what-you-know-but-who-you-
know attitude can take us only so far. There are rules that
cannot be infringed, and frustrating as they might be, they are
good rules, important rules, rules that make sense.

Of Joe, I've been reminded not only that this man with such
keen reporting instincts is a resourceful ally but that he deals
far better with specifics than abstractions. Resistant as he may
be to the idea of change—marriage, relocation, children—
when confronted with a concrete challenge, he moves aggres-
sively and tends not to look back. His being there beside me,
taking an interest and helping make key decisions, had been
worth the price of admission.

As for me, I'd seen that unlike the infertility rollercoaster,
this is a ride I can handle. I'd held steady through the
careening, neither letting go nor trying to steer. This ride, it
seemed to me, was a lot like a hot stock tip: Act now. Regret
later. Cut your losses quickly.

On March 23, four months after our getting-to-know-you
meeting with Spence officials, we have our getting-to-know-you
meeting with the three other couples and two single women

who are to be our eventual traveling companions in Paraguay. After formal introductions, we all are handed thick packets of information.

I'd thought I'd gotten a feel for the procedural aspects of an adoption during the Bosnia cyclone. Only now do I learn that Mother Nature has no less a hand in the creation of an adoptive family than she does a blood-related one. If the biological family, conceived from microscopic drops of bodily fluids, is born of water, the adoptive family is sewn from earth elements. Trees, to be more precise. Best as I can tell, Joe and I will have to fell whole forests to lay a paper trail from Hoboken to Asunción. The Spence list includes:

- 3 certified copies of birth certificates, each parent
- 3 certified copies of marriage certificate
- 3 certified copies of divorce decrees
- 1 notarized medical report, each parent
- 1 notarized psychologist report, each parent
- 2 notarized financial statements, copies in both English and Spanish
- 3 copies of most recent 1040 income tax form
- 1 notarized affidavit, verifying 1040
- 3 copies of most recent W-2 forms
- 1 Child Abuse Clearance form, each parent
- 1 notarized Police Good Conduct letter, each parent
- 3 copies of business references, all originals, two of them notarized
- 3 personal references
- 1 autobiography, each parent
- 1 I-600A form (preadoption clearance by the INS)
- 1 I-600 form (postadoption clearance by the INS)
- 2 fingerprint cards, each parent
- Photocopy of picture page of U.S. passport, each parent
- 1 power of attorney form

• Color photos of self, relatives, house, neighborhood, and so on.

Wait. There's more. All those notarized documents? Each must be forwarded either to the county clerk of the county where the notary is registered or the secretary of state for the state where the notary resides (stick with me here) for validation of the notary's seal and signature. These "notarized" and "verified" documents must then be delivered, along with the "certified" ones, to the Paraguayan consulate for, yes, "authentication." And while all of this is going on, you must also obtain the all-important "home study," a profile written by a social worker after this person conducts a "home visit" to inspect our house, hearts, and heads. And after you bring baby home, there are more papers to file, papers for citizenship, papers for a U.S. adoption, papers for a U.S. passport—

Like I said, whole forests.

Many infertile couples look at all of this—police references? fingerprints? child-abuse clearances?—and get very, very angry. How is it, they want to know, that any unmarried, drug-addicted, alcohol-swilling, shoplifting, truant, teenage girl who gets knocked up by mistake can raise that baby, no questions asked? Yet, when a mature adult whose only crime is an inability to reproduce wants to adopt a child, the operating assumption is that he or she is a child abuser, baby killer, or vendor of infant body parts?

I understand such indignation. Really I do. But Joe and I had a different reaction to the absurdity of this paper chase. For me, who was no doubt checked off a to-do list before my mother raced to the hospital to give birth, the process was familiar and reassuring. As I made lists of letters still to be written and documents still to be obtained, then methodically checked off each item, I found the exercise gratifying. After months of only setbacks and disappointments, here finally was progress I could chart. With each newly obtained document, I felt like we were drawing one step closer to our baby.

For a while, Joe could forget the child for the trees. His many years as an investigative reporter for *Newsday* had left a warm spot in his heart for tracking down and sifting through documents. Though I, as anticipated, made most of the effort, Joe pitched in without complaint to gather those items that only he could obtain. He became particularly galvanized by his pursuit of the divorce decree from his first marriage. Though Joe had the original decree in his possession, Spence's triplicate requirement set him on a months-long paper chase through El Paso and Chihuahua, where neither his American attorney nor the Mexican court that had granted the divorce were listed any longer.

During these months, I felt that Joe and I were in this venture together, a satisfying development after feeling for so long that the grief and turmoil were mine and mine alone. Now, as Joe reported back to me on his efforts to track down his divorce decree, showing the edgy excitement of a journalist closing in on an elusive prey, I began to think that his resistance to adoption was easing.

That feeling was reinforced by a house search we'd launched at the beginning of the year. We'd started in Hoboken with plans to buy a townhouse, but after finding nothing we liked in our price range, we'd moved our search to the suburbs. I had my eye on Montclair, a New Jersey town in Essex County which enjoyed a reputation for diversity and might make a comfortable home for a multiracial family. Joe had been pointed by a colleague toward a suburb in New York's Westchester County, one that promised a shorter commute. Eager to offer any concession that might make Joe more comfortable with the dual prospect of a house and baby, I deferred.

As we explained our particular needs to real estate agents, talk of adoption became casual and comfortable. Each of them

knew someone who had adopted, was adopting, or was thinking of adopting. As with the infertility stories I'd collected, this
accumulating bank of tales made adoption seem almost as
common as pregnancy.

Albeit with one pronounced difference. While the standard
pregnancy is a modest, intimate drama with two players and a
single set, our own production was now coming to resemble a
Broadway musical extravaganza. The cast of characters, which
had once seemed overcrowded with doctors and nurses, now
expanded exponentially. Local police. State bureaucrats. Federal bureaucrats. Fingerprint technicians. Clerks. Secretaries.
Notaries. Translators. Employers. Social workers. Lawyers.
Friends. Acquaintances. Friends of friends. As we had to
approach friends and colleagues for the required letters of
recommendation, it was no longer possible to think of our
effort as a private, exclusive engagement.

To my surprise, I found it a relief to have my inner and outer
worlds more closely aligned, no longer having to pretend day
in and day out that everything was fine. When the aggravations
of the process left me short-tempered or remote, I could say, "I
got some frustrating news about our adoption," and trust that
people wouldn't take my mood personally. For Joe, the univer-
sal response to any mention of adoption—"God, it's so great
you're doing that!"—was reinforcing. Although I never lost
sight for even a second of what was motivating our adoption
search, Joe, I think, was briefly seduced by a vision of himself
as Great Humanitarian, rescuing some poor child from a
horrible fate.

We never called a formal halt to our plan to confine our
efforts exclusively to Paraguay. After Bosnia, it just happened.
Joe asked a journalist friend based in Moscow to keep an eye
out for an adoptable baby; I asked a friend in Mexico City. Like
a patched tire, our flattened map of the world rounded back
out into a globe.

* * *

Within weeks of the blowout in Bosnia, our search detoured unexpectedly into Ecuador. Until very recently, Ecuador had required couples to live in-country for at least five years prior to an adoption. We knew from Spence Chapin that Ecuador was a long shot. Spence, which had been among the first U.S. agencies to sign an agreement with the government in Quito, had yet to place a single child with a waiting family.

Moreover, our Ecuador connection had seemed flimsy at best. Months earlier, Lydia, an Ecuadoran friend of my parents, or more accurately, the daughter-in-law of friends of my parents, had requested a letter expressing our interest in adoption. Lydia had translated that letter into Spanish, then forwarded it to Quito, where it had gone astray. When Lydia had phoned fourteen days earlier to say that her cousin, a lawyer, had finally received the letter and was now trying to locate an adoption attorney, I'd been profuse in my thanks but reserved in my expectation.

Now, Lydia is on the phone with promising news. Her cousin has found a prospective adoption situation: an unmarried nineteen-year-old, three months shy of her due date. The girl, who months earlier had resisted her parents' demand that she abort, had recently run away from home.

"The girl has passed word through an intermediary that she wants to leave Ecuador, have the baby, and give it up for adoption, then return home," says Lydia. "My cousin is going to try to locate her within the next ten days."

"Do you know anything else about her?"

"The family is middle class. The girl is healthy. No drugs. No alcohol."

By now, I've learned that the field study that had nuked our hopes in Sarajevo is a standard procedure, required by both the INS and the country of origin. Because this search for birth parents typically takes several months, adoption of an overseas newborn is virtually an oxymoron. Hence, this prospect is tantalizing. But we must decide quickly. With the girl's delivery date just three months away, time is running out on how long she'll be permitted to make a transcontinental flight.

Up. "Sounds doable," says Francine at Adoptive Families of America. "The main hitch will be obtaining a visa to get the girl out of Ecuador. The State Department balks at bringing foreigners over to deliver babies, but doesn't exactly stop it. It becomes more complicated if there's an identified father. State doesn't like to deal with two-parent situations, even if the father is willing to sign off."

Back to Lydia, who phones her cousin, then calls me back. "The father is the girl's boyfriend, but it's not clear if he knows she's pregnant. I wouldn't worry about him. He won't be a problem."

"Is this kosher?" I ask an adoption attorney.

"If she's here legally on a visa of any kind, you can adopt the baby legally," he answers. "As long as the birth is in our territory, that's all that matters."

Down. Every night for the next week, Joe and I sit on the living room couch, turning the prospect over and over, trying to see it through the eyes of one, two, and three people.

Our concerns for this faceless stranger are many. We figure she must be strong, first to go forward with a pregnancy supported by neither her boyfriend nor her parents, then to run away from home. Even so, she's got to be running scared. What effect would a sudden and dramatic displacement have on her? In Hoboken, she would have neither friends nor relatives to lean on; just two wary adults who don't speak her language. Even if Joe and I could succeed in making her feel welcome, we both work. She would be alone most mornings and afternoons, right at a time when this unmarried pregnant teen might feel most in need of attention, pampering, and support.

"It would be cruel," says Joe.

For the two of us, the concern is financial. Say, we fly the girl over. Put her up. Pay her delivery and postpartum costs. Then, she decides to keep the baby. It would eat up the money we need to complete the Paraguay adoption, the one gamble that seems closest to a sure thing.

"Money pit," we agree.

And what of the three of us? Joe and I have known from the start that we want no part of an open adoption and the inevitable relationship with a birth mother. It's hard to imagine that during three months of shared living arrangements, we wouldn't grow fond of this vulnerable girl as she lives in our home and carries to term the baby we hope will be our child. It's even more inconceivable that we—or at least I—won't attach to the unborn infant, whose future may yet be in Quito.

"I don't want to have to find out how I would handle it if the girl changes her mind," I say.

Up. When I call Lydia to express our reservations, she counters with an astonishing offer. "I'll take the girl in myself, talk sense to her through her last months of the pregnancy." Lydia has three children of her own. She figures that seeing the effort that goes into raising small children will keep the teenager's eyes wide open. If Lydia's life doesn't sound complicated enough already, what makes this heartfelt offer all the more astounding is that she and I have met just once, and only briefly at that. Yet Lydia is insistent she wants to do this for me and Joe, whom she's never met at all.

Down. Reminded by my adoption gurus that the laws for independent adoption are as different from state to state as they are from country to country, I order a state-by-state breakdown of regulations from the National Adoption Information Clearinghouse in Rockville, Maryland. North Carolina, I learn by return mail, is one of only two states that permits no "attack on a final adoption decree." In other words, once it's done, it can't be undone.

That, to me, sounds promising. But when I check back with the adoption lawyer, he warns, "North Carolina is a hard state. It's not going to give you permission to take that baby out of state."

This can't be right, I think. Surely, it's not possible that I can move a baby from Ecuador to the United States, but not be able to transport that same baby from North Carolina to New Jersey. I phone another adoption attorney. "North Carolina's a bad state," he confirms.

When I phone Lydia, embarrassed that she's expended so much effort for nothing, she still refuses to give up. "I'll tell my cousin to keep looking," she tells me.

End of ride.

So many people are now helping us in our search: friends, acquaintances, total strangers, most particularly my mother, whose response to the Ecuador disappointment is to redouble her unflagging efforts. Each person brings to the effort the same naive assumption Joe and I started out with: if a child is in need of a home and a home is in need of a child, it shouldn't be hard to solder a link. Each person eventually phones me back, bewildered and frustrated by the many complicating layers that separate two such acute and answerable needs. As the months pass, I find myself in the improbable role of consolation counselor, allaying others' disappointment with assurances that they've done everything humanly possible. Thank you so much, you've been wonderful. Not to worry. I'm sure something will work out.

In truth, I neither count blessings nor discount possibilities, believe nor disbelieve. With Ecuador, as with Bosnia, I've navigated the twists and turns in a state of suspended expectation, then let go without regrets. Maybe that's because I feel I have a safety net: Spence Chapin's pipeline to Paraguay.

Methodical and laborious as the Spence route seems, Joe

and I are slowly making progress. On the day we mail our completed paperwork to Spence for forwarding to Washington and Asunción, we also call off our Westchester house hunt. Spence has warned that while our papers are going through the INS hoops, we must maintain residence in a single state.

During the same period that the two adoption prospects have fizzled, so have two house deals. In one instance, the sellers backed out, uncertain that they really wanted to move; in the other, Joe and I took a hike after receiving a poor inspection report about the roof. A house, a baby. Even with good faith on all sides, how easy it is for a deal to fall through.

Actually, I'm glad to be done with the Westchester suburb. Though it's a town of great beauty and seeming serenity, it's come to feel too small, too quiet. Too white. Despite our chatty realtor's assurances that there are other mixed-race adoptive families in town, in all the weeks of walking and driving the streets, I've yet to spot a single non-Caucasian face.

Because Joe and I are finally in serious pursuit of both baby and house, my mood is resilient and basically optimistic. Joe's mood is harder to read. With seeming interest and composure, he's helped scope out the Bosnia and Ecuador opportunities. With seeming amiability, he's suggested that we now take a look at Montclair, the New Jersey town I've favored all along. With seeming ease, in recent weeks he's erected an invisible wall between us that effectively bars touching—sexual, affectionate, playful—of any kind.

One week before our ninth wedding anniversary, he says almost casually, "I'll help you get a house and a kid, then I'm going to move out."

I don't know if things are alright or not. I can't tell what's going on with him and with us. It's like when I first met him, constantly blaming me for everything, continually angry, moody, unpredictable.

Yet, when a Spence social worker calls on us for the home visit, Joe seems as determined as I to convince her that we're eager and fit to be parents.

Though Joe and I are mutually tiring of the Spence process, with its emphasis on group meetings headed by buoyant staffers, we both like the social worker assigned to us. Laid back, unboosterish, and a newcomer to Spence herself, Hannah conveys both professional detachment and a modicum of embarrassment that she has to conduct this survey. She makes the mandatory inspection of our rooms and intentions quickly. We spend the rest of the time talking about the frustrations of the adoption process. Hannah tells us that the Paraguay pipeline has been temporarily suspended since the appointment of two new judges in Asunción who want to review the country's adoption laws. Nothing to worry about, she says. She also mentions that Moldova is opening and China is moving again.

Joe comments that he could get interested in China, a pleasant news bulletin for me. He's charming, relaxed. After Hannah leaves, he seems pleased that the meeting went so well.

On the night of our ninth wedding anniversary, we drive to Montclair. This is our third trip in five days. Unlike the leisurely Westchester hunt, this one is frenetic. Houses in our price range are moving so rapidly that many are being listed and sold the same day. We've already seen two houses we'd feel comfortable bidding on, but I've been holding out to see the inside of a roomy-looking colonial that only now is coming on the market.

As we step into the center hallway and I see the high ceiling and large windows of the living room, I have the same certain feeling I had when we first saw our house in the Endless Mountains: I want it. Behind the agent's back, Joe's nose wrinkles at the gold wallpaper and wall-to-wall gold carpeting.

Though I have no talent for interior design, after tromping through so many houses, I can see with X-ray vision to the white walls and wood floors beneath.

"It's just cosmetics, Wease," I whisper. "Trust me. Refinish the floors, strip the walls, this place will look great."

As we move from floor to floor, I see potential everywhere. The semifinished basement screams, Playroom. The three large bedrooms on the second floor telegraph: master, Joe's office, nursery. The smaller third-floor bedroom could be my office.

While Joe and Mr. Wayne, the seller, do manly things in the basement, I make strained conversation with Mrs. Wayne, a soft-spoken homemaker who's poured a lot of love into this house and is plainly finding the thought of leaving difficult. "We raised our three boys here," she says, scrubbing too furiously at a fingerprint on the dishwasher's chrome handle. "The boy across the street, he was like a son, too."

The neighborhood, as she describes it, is what I've been hoping for: a constant traffic of kids between houses; adults who keep an eye out for other people's children; neighbors who are only too happy to provide an egg or cup of milk in a pinch.

When we step outside in the dark to try to survey the mature shrubs and ground cover she's cultivated through three decades, I ask, "What about cars?" Though the house is well distanced from any heavily trafficked roads, it sits on the corner of two residential streets. I can envision a stray ball rolling into one of those streets, with my child mindlessly chasing after it. "We're in the process of adopting," I explain. "Once we have a child, cars are going to be a concern."

At the mention of children, Mrs. Wayne's reserve melts. "The heaviest traffic around here is the police car that comes around every night," she laughs. "My boys used to play their soccer games in the street."

By the time Joe and I bid the Waynes goodnight, Mrs. Wayne

and I are on hugging terms and I feel comfortable enough to say, "I have a good feeling about all of this. It seems appropriate. This is our ninth wedding anniversary." The Waynes gush appropriately.

"I really want it, Wease," I say on the car ride home. "It's a lot more house than anything we saw in Westchester, and it's twenty thousand dollars less. You can have whichever room you want for your office."

Joe's still having trouble seeing past the gold carpeting, so I don't know what tips the balance in favor of the house. The warm feelings attending our anniversary? A desire to be done with the time-consuming house search? The appeal of a large office?

"Okay," he says. "Call tomorrow and make a bid."

Just one other couple will get to see the Waynes' house. The realtor tells us that though that couple is ready to start a bidding war, the Waynes have decided to accept our bid. "It's important to them who gets this house," she says. "They really liked the two of you."

Two weeks later, the requisite inspections underway, Joe and I leave for St. Bart for a much-needed vacation. Away from housing, adoption, and office pressures and surrounded by exquisite views that look vaguely familiar, probably because they've served as the backdrop to countless ads, Joe begins to relax, though not entirely. As the days pass, I notice that no matter where our conversation begins, it eventually wends back to the same issue: Joe's agitation about a particular editor who's making his work life hell. I try to convey sympathy, but as I listen what I feel is relieved glee: It's not the adoption. It's not the house. It's not me. It's the job! It's the job! It's the job!

We resume our sex life, though admittedly that's not saying much. Our efforts to conceive have pretty much zapped the allure out of sex for both of us. That Joe and I have yet to recover our spontaneity and pleasure doesn't worry me. Most infertile couples, I assume, have a lousy sex life for a while after so much intercourse-on-command and so many unappetizing fertility procedures. But this business of not touching at all, that's bothered me a lot. I feel encouraged when we now resume our habit of holding hands.

I return home feeling relaxed, renewed, optimistic. Joe and I have reached the end of our house hunt; we are about to move to a place with trees. We have reached the end of the paper trail; our documents will soon be in Asunción. And we have reached the end of our brief physical estrangement; we've found our way back to each other.

That night, I call my mother to wish her a Happy Mother's Day. "I've been thinking about you all day," she says. "Thinking that maybe this time next year, it's you we'll be celebrating."

I absorb this without comment. Like I said, I neither count blessings nor discount possibilities, believe nor disbelieve. So why, I wonder as I hang up, am I crying?

IX

I'M AT MY OFFICE DESK READING THE MORNING papers when Arthur phones two days later. Though we live in neighboring New Jersey towns and both work in New York City, we mostly see each other up in the country. There had been a rainy afternoon during fertility treatment when Arthur had patiently walked me round and round a stretch of woods, listening to me cry.

"Eileen called," Arthur says, referring to another friend who divides her time between Manhattan and the Endless Mountains. "She knows a pregnant girl who's looking for adoptive parents, and thought of you. But she doesn't feel she knows you well enough to call." Arthur pauses, as if catching himself. "I mentioned to her that you and Joe were looking. I hope that was alright."

"Of course it's alright." How Arthur, I think, smiling. Always sensitive to others' feelings.

"Anyway, she wants to know if you're interested in talking to this girl."

"Sure," I say. "Tell Eileen to feel free to give me a call."

"Her name is Debra," Eileen tells me by phone the next day. "She's a receptionist at my office. She's Catholic, which is why she didn't abort." Eileen is a former actress with a natural exuberance and a mile-a-minute patter. As the details whiz by—white, twenty-six, a college graduate, due in July—I try to steel myself against Eileen's contagious enthusiasm, searching for the flaw in the design beneath this too-pretty a picture.

"If she's already seven months pregnant," I ask, "how come she hasn't already looked into adoption?"

"She talked to a state agency and didn't like what she heard. She wants a 'good home' for the baby, and is fighting guilt that she wants something traditional."

"What does that mean?"

"You know, not a single parent or a gay couple. Wait! I forgot to tell you the best part. Guess where she lives? Hoboken! Isn't that incredible?"

This is exactly the sort of arrangement Joe and I vowed we would never explore. An open adoption. A young birth mother who might have a change of heart. Worse still, a birth mother right in our backyard. Even when we move, she'd still be far too close.

And yet.

It all sounds frankly too good to be true . . . Eileen says she thinks Debra took a degree in journalism . . . I don't want to talk with her, put a face on her, unless I know she's clear about wanting to give up the baby . . . It seems awfully late in her pregnancy to be starting to look into this. It raises questions about her commitment . . . Eileen says Debra eats health food, doesn't smoke or drink. All that sounds wonderful. Joe's reaction was to want to know everything about the father.

By the time I phone Debra that evening at the appointed hour of seven, our social worker at Spence has primed me how to handle this initial interview. Be friendly, natural. Leave questions about the father or any other subject that might make Debra uncomfortable to Spence. Ditto, any discussion of financial arrangements for medical care, since direct payment of money to a birth mother is illegal.

"Mostly," Hannah has explained, "you just want her to like you."

As I dial, I feel like an adolescent on my first date, nervous and excited, determined neither to talk too much nor too little, uncertain how to be myself when I don't know which part of me she might like. Debra picks up on the first ring.

"Hi, Debra. This is Jill. Eileen's friend? Is this a good time to talk?"

"Yes, fine."

"How are you feeling? Eileen told me you've been having some problems with poison ivy and anemia."

It proves a good opener. Debra has been to her doctor that day and is eager to talk about her lab results, all positive. She's been well primed by Eileen and seems as eager to like me as I am to like her. As we both begin to relax, I slip comfortably into the role of big sister, supportive, capable, as ready to laugh as I am to commiserate. She, in turn, seems happy, even relieved, to have someone in whom to confide her worries and concerns. When I pose questions, I find her answers level-headed, thoughtful. Believable. As we get deeper into conversation, the picture that emerges gets prettier and prettier.

Debra grew up in Nebraska, an only child of a couple who, like Joe and I, were a bit older than most new parents. After taking a journalism degree at the state university, she'd spent a few years as an accountant, then moved to Manhattan to pursue a career in publishing. She was "paying dues" now as a receptionist at a book house and was certain she would move up the ladder. She was also certain she would have no trouble letting go of her child.

"I'm adopted," she explains. "I have only good feelings about adoption."

"Your parents must have done it very right," I say levelly. "How did they handle it?"

"They always said, 'We wanted you, we didn't just have you.' As a result, I always felt special."

"How smart of them. Did you ever search for your biological mother?"

"No. I never had the desire."

"Do you think your parents might want to raise this baby?"

"No," she says firmly. Debra hasn't told her parents she's pregnant and doesn't intend to. Her father, now in his sixties, has a heart condition. She fears what the stress might do to him.

"Anyone else?"

"No. The father was my boyfriend. I thought we'd get married and have the baby. But we broke up. Now, he's engaged to someone else and has bowed out altogether. I've been sorting this through by myself. I decided on adoption about three months ago. I've been really anxious, worrying about where the child will be placed." She'd talked with a few state agencies. "I hated the anonymity. I feel adamant about meeting the parents. I need to know this baby will be in a good home."

"What do you think of when you say a good home?"

"I want this child to have what I had. A nice, stable home, wonderful parents. Financial stability."

Hearing this as an invitation to talk about Joe and me, I briefly describe our efforts to conceive a child, our strong relationships with our families, our desire to have a family of our own. I tell her about our house in the Endless Mountains and the house we are about to buy in Montclair. I speak of our journalism careers, but deliberately omit where we work.

"Yes, Eileen told me you were journalists," she says. "I love the idea of this baby being raised by journalists."

I ask if she's been getting good care prenatal care. "Yes,

wonderful." She's been seeing a doctor at St. Mary's Hospital, one block from our apartment.

By now, the conversation has gotten so cozy that we're both leaping on any coincidence as if it were a happy portent. Her baby is due July 23, but could be a few days late. "She might be born on my birthday, the 26th!" I say. I tell her that the baby will have five young cousins. "I grew up with cousins!" she exclaims. "My mother was one of six children." The hardest part of pregnancy, she confides, has been giving up jogging. "Joe jogs!" I announce triumphantly. When I tell her that I'd written an unpublished novel in which the character based on me was named Debra, she marvels, "That's amazing!" We both squeal with delight at the book's title: *Goodly Prospects*.

After we arrange to have dinner Sunday night, Debra says she's going to bring Rick.

"Who's Rick?"

"My best friend. He's been my support through the pregnancy." Recently, she says, the relationship has taken a romantic turn. "We're planning to get married, but I don't know when."

Shit. "Have you and Rick thought about raising the baby together?" I ask, working to keep my tone cheerful, inquisitive, nonjudgmental.

"Yeah. We feel we're not ready. This may sound selfish, but when my friends call wanting to do things, I want to be able to go. That's what I want at this point in my life."

"That's not selfish," I answer in my best big sister tone. "That's generous, knowing that there are things you want for the child, knowing that you don't feel ready yet to give them, finding people who can."

As the conversation winds down, Debra says, "My health insurance from work has covered all the doctor bills, but if I have to stop work because of the pregnancy, I may have trouble meeting my rent."

I murmur sympathetically, but heed the advice from Spence and let the mention of money pass. "As you probably know," I say, changing the topic, "adoptions happen all sorts of ways these days. Do you have an inclination how you'd like to handle this?"

"My inclination is just to want to know you guys, and to know this child is yours," she answers without hesitation. "I want to wish you the best. It might hurt more to know where the child is all the time, wondering what he's doing. I just want to know in my heart the child's okay. It's too confusing for a child to be introduced to a biological mother."

As we end our forty-minute conversation, Debra says, "My doctor has told me that I need to stop being so anxious. Just talking to you and knowing there may be a good home makes me feel less stressed."

Can it be this easy? It's too good to believe. Debra sounds like the dream biological mother.

I call Joe at the office, and read back her comments. "So, we've bought a house. Got a baby," I say giddily. "Anything else we need to do today?"

"Yeah. Close a *People* cover," he laughs. "Hey, Wease, let's not tell anyone about this. We don't want to jinx it."

Like I said, Can this all be true? It seems so perfect.

We rush back from the country Sunday night, only to have Debra cancel dinner on us. "Rick and I just got back from the beach and I'm really tired. Can we do this tomorrow night?"

"No problem," I say. "It's more important that you take care of yourself."

"This isn't going to happen," Joe says, irritated that we cut our weekend short for nothing. "She's backing out."

When I defend Debra, reminding him that she's seven months pregnant and probably *is* tired, the conversation takes a nasty turn. Soon, we're fighting about nothing.

"I could strangle you when you talk to me that way," I snap.

The next morning, I throw myself into any task that will take my mind off Debra. I complete the paperwork for the mortgage, walk it over to our broker. I finish the last paperwork for the Paraguay adoption, mail it to Spence. At one-thirty, Joe and I meet at Grace's. I have come to regard these counseling sessions as maintenance work, more for Joe than for me since they focus on his feelings about our adoption efforts. Mostly I sit back and let Grace do the heavy lifting.

After I tell her about Debra, Joe says heatedly, "It's too fast. I don't want it." He says his main fear is that a child will break us up. "Jill threatened to kill me last night."

Startled, I think, You son of a bitch. You're not going to let me get any joy out of this.

"Jill's way of coping with the stress is to keep busy doing things," Grace observes. "Joe's way is to reflect." She cautions that with both a house and a baby in the works, "You'll have to plan. You can't let a baby land out of nowhere."

It was a relief to have her say that so Joe could hear it. Any conversation I want to have about the house or baby he categorizes as "obsessive."

On Monday night, I arrive at Lady Jane's, a local restaurant, a few minutes late from my weekly session with the Hoboken teenager I tutor in reading and math. When I see Joe already seated at a table with Debra and Rick, my first thought is a relieved *He came.* My next is, *She looks like Woody's girlfriend.* Like the character on *Cheers,* Debra has long, straight blond hair and is pretty in a sweet, bland sort of way.

The two-hour dinner is remarkably unstrained, given the circumstance. As Debra repeats to Joe what she's already told me, I'm heartened by her consistency. When she and Joe compare their midwestern upbringings, they discover they both have Cherokee ancestors. Debra seems particularly interested in the pictures I've brought of our families, carefully selected to emphasize my nieces and nephews. For several minutes, she gazes at their young faces, and is delighted when she spots my parents' cat.

"I have a cat, too," she says.

Though Debra is chatty, she defers to Rick on most questions concerning their plans for the baby and themselves. It's Rick who says they're planning to marry.

"But not soon," Debra interjects, looking pointedly at Rick.

As Rick talks about his own father, who is also his employer, it becomes clear that Rick's dad is acting as a surrogate parent to Debra during the pregnancy. "My father is supportive of adoption because this isn't my child," Rick says.

"We can't afford to take care of a baby," Debra adds. "I'm a receptionist, Rick's a bartender. We just can't."

Joe and I let the subject of money pass. Spence Chapin, I've told him, will deal with that if Debra agrees to see one of the agency's social workers. I wait until after Debra has downed her dessert of fresh mango ("I crave fresh fruit," she says, "especially mango") to raise that prospect.

"The idea is for each couple to have their own social worker, so that everybody's needs and concerns are considered," I explain. "The social worker is supposed to be your advocate, to make sure that you're making the best decision for you. I've been given the name of someone for you to contact if you're comfortable with this. Her name is Roberta. Joe and I have never met her." Debra writes down the information and says she'll call the next day.

"I won't be in touch again unless I hear from Eileen that you want me to call. I don't want to disturb you," I say to Debra. "But, please, feel free to call us. We are, of course, very eager to hear from you."

Debra and I hug good-bye. As she steps back, she looks at Joe and me and says, "I'm one hundred percent sure I want to do this."

After they're out of earshot, Joe says, "If we get the child, we'll either name it Lady Jane or Mangohead." Laughing, we pay the bill, then replay the dinner as we walk home hand in hand. "Debra said that she couldn't make out the sex of her baby on the sonogram," Joe tells me, "but she could see the child's eyes and lack of eyelashes. Amazing."

"Do you think she's for real?" I ask.

"This is as good a prospect as we could hope for," he answers.

I can't tell if it's the prospect of a newborn baby or a white baby or an American baby or the baby of a healthy jogger, but Joe's buoyant mood and the glow in his eyes make one thing clear: he's excited about this baby.

Eileen phones the next morning sounding excited. "I just saw Debra. She said, 'They're perfect.' She says she's going to call that social worker at Spence Chapin as soon as she can find a private place to make the call. Her cubicle is out in front where everyone can hear her."

"Did she say anything else?"

"Yes. She said she feels relieved."

It sounds so honest, so real. "I don't know how to thank you, Eileen." As I hang up the receiver, a female colleague enters my office. "I think we've found a baby," I blurt, then burst into tears.

I can't stop myself. "Mine," a refrain starts in my head. "I'm finally getting mine."

For the first time, I begin to think like an expectant mother. I call my sister and ask what child-care books I should read. She says she'll mail me a bunch of hers. When I call Lynn to ask where to shop for baby furniture, she offers to be my "slave" for a few days if we find ourselves with a newborn in the middle of our move to Montclair. I consult with my benefits counselor at *Time* and learn that adoptive mothers don't get the company's eight weeks of paid maternity leave since, technically, that's a medical leave; instead, adoptive moms get the same one-week "parental leave" as male employees. The counselor, who is due to deliver her first child around the same time as Debra and can barely fit behind her desk any longer, has been preparing methodically for her baby.

"Have you taken a child-care course yet?" she asks. I shake my head. "A baby CPR course? No? God, it's really important. Here, let me give you a number. And you should—"

I left feeling already like an inadequate mother. This is a bizarre twilight where I can't think about these things, but I can't not think about them. I want to scream. We're having a baby! On the other hand, maybe we're not.

I phone around and learn that St. Vincent's Hospital in Greenwich Village is offering its once-a-month, three-hour, infant-care course at the end of the week. After I sign us up, I call Joe, bracing for him to tell me that I should attend alone.

Instead, he says, "That's a good idea."

It's useless to try and do any work. I go to the gym and work out on a treadmill, trying to expend some nervous energy. "You're going to be a mother," I silently address my image in the mirror, then start to cry.

On the walk back to the office, I pass a store window featuring a display of children's books, and cry some more as I think of the wonderful characters I'll get to rediscover with this child. Winnie the Pooh. The Sneetches with no stars upon thars. Horton the Elephant. Hey, wait! That one about him hatching an egg? It's really an adoption story, isn't it? Wow. I never realized that before—

Later, I check the stock market listings, then phone my broker and sell off a block of stock to help cover the costs of the house closing and move. The downpayment on the house is going to gut our joint account. We've agreed that any adoption expenses will come out of the savings account I've been building for seventeen years, one that I've always thought of as for my children's college education. Joe's own savings are negligible after so many years of freelancing. Now, I see that some Pepsico stock he's owned for decades is surging and could net us forty-five hundred dollars. I send him a computer message saying this may be a good time to sell.

"That stock has sentimental value," he messages back. "It was a childhood gift from my godmother. I'll think about it."

He may come around. It just shocks me he could even think that way. Joe has no tolerance for me to be emotional about any of this. He expects me to focus when he's ready, not a second before, not a second after . . . I can imagine myself hating Joe. Here is just where Joe's fears are. That a child could break us up.

Three days later, Eileen calls, agitated. "Some incompetent from your agency called Debra last night and opened the conversation, 'I understand we're going to be working together.' Debra is completely freaked out."

When I phone Hannah, she explains that Roberta, another Spence social worker, had phoned Debra at home, thinking only to catch her someplace where their conversation couldn't be overheard. Roberta had gotten the sense the conversation went well. "Debra is scheduled to come in to talk with Roberta next Wednesday."

"Debra found the conversation invasive, inconsiderate, and frightening after a long day of work," Eileen counters. "She said something about needing to see a lawyer first."

Late that afternoon, Hannah tells me, "Debra's lawyer just called. She was rude and abrasive, demanding to know where we got Debra's number and how dare we call her. I think we calmed the lawyer down some." Still, Hannah is uneasy. "The lawyer may have clients of her own with whom she wants to place the baby."

Joe is more optimistic. "Maybe the fact that Debra is consulting a lawyer indicates that she's serious about going through with an adoption."

Eileen is encouraging, too. "Don't worry. It's just Spence Debra is mad at. She still feels good about you. She wants you to call her at home tonight at seven."

I dial St. Vincent's and withdraw from the infant-care class scheduled for that evening.

By seven, the lawyer has intervened again, this time instructing Debra not to talk with me. Instead, Rick takes my call. "We're not upset with you and Joe. Debra is one hundred percent sure she wants to do this," he says, echoing Debra's parting comment four nights earlier. "I know that you're excited and that you've waited a long time for this." Now, he sounds like he's regurgitating lines fed by the lawyer. "But the best thing would be restraint."

Rick's insta-wisdom infuriates me. Who the hell is this kid to suggest he has a clue what we've been through? "That's fine, Rick," I say pleasantly. "I'm glad you're taking your time, thinking it through. Joe and I will wait to hear from you."

Twice, before he hangs up, Rick says firmly, "You'll hear from us."

"This is about money," Joe surmises.

The lawyer, he hypothesizes, wants the bounty of this increasingly rare specimen: the newborn baby of a white, college-educated birth mother who's been vigilant about her diet and health during her pregnancy. Why should the attorney risk a potential windfall on two unknowns when she no doubt has a list of rich clients whom she knows will pay up and shut up? Joe thinks we might yet salvage the situation by telling Debra what her lawyer is up to.

In truth, though, we haven't a clue what the lawyer is up to. We also don't know where the divide lies between legitimate and illegal costs, or if we would cross it in pursuit of our own self-interest. But it's easier and safer to direct our anger at an anonymous attorney than at Spence, whom we still need, or at Rick and Debra, whom we could turn off if the tone of our voices isn't just right.

"I don't know, Wease," I say. "If Debra trusts the lawyer, we don't want to get in the way of that relationship."

By bedtime, I've convinced myself it's over.
There is no sound when the heart breaks. It just breaks.

Years later, Joe will maintain, "You were bouncing off the walls. I was afraid you were going to plunge back into depression." My own recollection and notes suggest a greater detachment.

I got through the weekend well, without dwelling on this Debra business. My gut instinct is to sit tight and wait . . . Debra is like a Rorschach blot. You can read her any way you want. Someone who won't be pushed around. Someone who is malleable. Someone slow-moving and tired. Someone who tells each person what she thinks they want to hear. Someone who is open and honest.

After two more weeks of silence from Debra, Joe presses me to call Rick and demand to know what's going on.

Joe said he just wanted to put an end to the uncertainty. Sort of ironic. Here's the guy who told me throughout the fertility stuff that I was impatient. And after two weeks, he's fed up. I talked him down, convinced him that the last thing we want to do is alienate Debra and Rick.

But after my brief interlude of resignation, I, too, am growing agitated. Debra or no, I've been counting on Spence to deliver a Paraguayan baby. Now, Spence is reporting what Hannah had told us during our home visit; the Paraguay pipeline is shut indefinitely. Also, Spence advises, China is moving very slowly.

My colleague Lois thinks I should learn more about China. She encourages me to call her friend Carla, one of the first Americans to complete an adoption after Beijing opened its orphanages to overseas agencies in 1991. Carla is founder of a growing organization called Families With Children From China, Lois tells me, and often has more timely information than many of the agencies.

"China's open and moving well," Carla says. "Right now, there is no risk of not getting a baby. On the other hand, these things can change quickly." When I tell her Spence's less optimistic prognosis, she responds, "Spence is slow. It has fifty-five couples backed up for China at the moment. I used a Seattle agency that moved a lot faster." I ask if working with an agency so far away complicates the process. The only difference Carla can think of is that we'll need to find a licensed agency in New Jersey to produce our home study.

When I relay this information to Joe, he responds, "Clinton recently renewed China's most favored nation status. The pipeline should remain open." I hear this as a green light to check out the Seattle agency. From our counseling sessions with Grace, I know that Joe's been wrestling hard with his resistance to an Asian child. Such prejudice is not in keeping with his values, his character, his self-image.

Even so, the prospect of changing agencies, changing countries—in short, starting over—is so unappealing that Joe and I resume our second-guessing of Debra. Was it the call from Spence? Wild sums of money offered by the lawyer? Our own failure at dinner to respond to Debra's concerns about money? Has she decided to keep the baby? Perhaps raise it with Rick? Or was it something about us? Joe thinks we erred by withholding our last names and not telling Debra that we work for *Time* and *People;* he's learned that a colleague's adoption went through largely because the birth mother was impressed by the *People* connection. I remain convinced that it's more important to safeguard our privacy and not run the risk of Debra someday showing up on our doorstep to demand her baby back.

In early June, Eileen reports, "Debra still wants to give you the baby."

Joe and I mull that over for several days, then I leave a friendly message on Debra's machine. "Haven't heard from you in a while. Hope you're well. Wondering what you're thinking." We hear nothing back, but after that, Debra, at the advice of her lawyer, stops talking to Eileen, and our last conduit closes.

A week later, I phone Francine at Adoptive Families of America to ask what she knows about the World Association for Children & Parents, the Seattle agency used by Carla. "WACAP," Francine says, "has done more China adoptions than any other agency."

Meanwhile, tensions between North Korea and China are suddenly heating up. As world leaders worry about the potential for a nuclear confrontation, I worry that our last chance for an overseas adoption will be nuked.

"This could strain relations between Beijing and Washington," I say to Joe. "We should get moving on a China adoption. The door could slam any day."

The timing couldn't be more inconvenient. We're scheduled to move July 12, and have a long-standing commitment to be at my family's annual reunion the first week of July. In addition, Joe wants to attend a two-week publishing course at Stanford University that begins two days after we move. Though the seminar makes a lot of sense in terms of his career, it makes no sense in terms of our lives.

"What if Debra decides at the last moment to give us the baby?" I demand. "What if we suddenly need a completed home study and you're off in California?"

What if. What if. The real what if, of course, is, What if Debra and Paraguay fall apart at the same time, and we're suddenly back to square one, with no prospects to buoy my hopes?

We agree to a quid pro quo: I'll shut up about the California trip if Joe will cooperate in my efforts to launch a new home study quickly. Children of the World, the agency I'd phoned during our Bosnia misadventure, has told me that it can handle any contingency—Debra. China. Whatever.—and for a fraction of the price Spence is asking for our home study, as-yet still unwritten. Within forty-eight hours, we're at the COTW office in Verona, inking our fingers for a new set of prints. New Jersey has just enforced a new law requiring a state, as well as a federal, check on fingerprints.

"Why the hell didn't Spence tell us about this?" I grumble to Joe.

I also phone WACAP in Seattle and request an application. The person who takes my call predicts we could be in China by the end of the year. That's only six months away. How can that be, when after seven months with Spence, our dossier is not yet in Asunción? When I run this by one of my adoption sources, she confirms that the WACAP projection is realistic. Spence, she says, has a built-in waiting period to make certain that families are in earnest about adoption.

The comment reminds me of something a Spence worker had said at one of the early group meetings. Asked why it had taken three months to process applications for the Paraguay program, she'd answered, "We want to make sure that you've thought it through and are serious about adoption." At the time Joe and I were new to the process and had assumed it was a routine delay.

"How dare they?" I now fume at Joe. "Don't they know that many of these couples have been trying for years to have a baby? Who the hell are *they* to make us wait longer?"

I'm not the only person unreasonably angry with Spence. When we attend a meeting on June 20 of all the groups awaiting word from Asunción, the questions are anxious, the mood edgy, even hostile. Paraguay isn't shut down, after all, we're informed. Rather, the price of an adoption has been raised another three thousand dollars. The processing in Asunción, Spence workers assure, will resume shortly.

Joe and I leave, our patience with Spence spent. After only brief discussion, we agree to move ahead with WACAP and China. We're luckier than many other prospective parents who, like us, pursue a passage in the adoption labyrinth to a dead-end. The cost to us has been mostly time; out-of-pocket, we're down only sixteen hundred dollars.

Over the next two weeks, Joe and I pack for the move, close on the Montclair house, and arrange for the floors to be refinished while we're in North Carolina. The deepening strains between us strike me as predictable as my need to approach the move methodically collides with his tendency to postpone until the last minute. Rather than fight about who's going to do what, I take it upon myself to pack up the entire apartment, save Joe's office with its mounds of clutter and vast collection of theater books.

It's sad we can't navigate changes better together. This move should have more joy, less strain. At times like this, I don't particularly like him and he doesn't like me. And we both miss each other acutely, feeling abandoned by the other . . . With COTW in the works, I've relaxed on the adoption front. I don't think of Debra too often. I don't hold my breath. On the other hand, I don't rule out the possibility she'll have the child, freak out, and call.

Once we get to my parents' house, the tension eases. Though it's yet another year that I arrive without a child, I'm okay. I play with my nieces and nephews and take heart as I listen to Joe spellbind the oldest among them with his Great Snake stories. At the moment, the slithery reptile is stirring mischief in the trenches of Bosnia and the subterranean pipes of Paraguay.

Michael, at eight, is more inclined to question, less inclined to believe. "How come I've never met the Great Snake?" he challenges Joe again and again. "I think you're making it all up."

Rather than lose patience, Joe steps up to the challenge, determined to win Michael over anew. He concocts more stories and discusses the Great Snake's history at length. Finally, one night, Joe leaves a message beneath Michael's pillow: "I was here. Where were you? Your pal, The Great Snake." That settles it. Michael pronounces the note "awesome," refuses to let younger brother Alex handle the sacred communication, and buys into the Great Snake for another year.

I'm not the only adult who watches these antics with more than amused interest. "There's no way Joe won't go gaga for a child," my father says when we slip off together to feed my parents' two llamas. "No mature, thinking man cannot love a child."

"He'll be a fabulous father," my mother predicts while we're off in the woods sneaking a cigarette together. "Wait. You'll see. The minute you have a baby, she's going to wrap him around her little finger."

Though I appreciate their attempts at encouragement, I hear less a reassuring truth than a dull cliché: every man comes around to fatherhood once a baby is placed in his arms. My parents know only the public Joe, the congenial, charming man who seems so easygoing and rarely lets his anger or indecisiveness show. His darker side he entrusts almost exclusively to me.

But that, too, I regard as a promising sign. For all Joe's vacillating about children in general and adoption in particular, the message he consistently puts forward to the world, one that I've by now heard over and over as he repeats his Frank Rogers story, is basically the same one as that of my parents: "I just assume when it's your own child, you feel differently."

One night as Joe spins yet another Great Snake saga, Michael removes a retainer from his mouth. As he plays with it between his fingers, I'm reminded of something Joe told me long ago, something he'd mentioned only once. During his second marriage, he'd offered to pay for the orthodontic work on one of his stepchildren. Though the marriage busted up within a year and though the twins had both a mother and father who could foot the bills, Joe insisted on honoring his commitment. (Years later, when I asked Joe how long he continued to pay the bills after the marriage broke up, he shrugged. "I don't know. A year? Two years? Whatever it took.")

Now as I remember that story, I'm reminded why, against all evidence, I remain convinced that even if Joe chooses to be a distracted and uninvolved father, he'll be a responsible one. Once Joe makes up his mind to do something, he throws himself into it and doesn't look back. If Joe's inability to make decisions is one of his more frustrating qualities, his stubborn tenacity is one of his habits I admire most.

Toward the end of our week in North Carolina, Joe and I pose for pictures for our China application. The resulting photos snapped by my sister suggest a happy, affectionate couple with no sign of strain between them.

The day before our move to Montclair, Joe and I decide to phone Debra one last time. After six weeks of silence, we want the courtesy of an explicit "no" from Debra and Rick. Both of us feel the need for some sort of closure.

Rick answers the phone and tells us to call their attorney. Though Joe and I have had the lawyer's name and number for some time (I've even checked with the New York Bar Association to make sure she's legit), only now do we phone her office for the first time. When her secretary refuses to put our call through, we phone Rick again. He assures us the lawyer will be in touch shortly.

An hour later her secretary calls and says, "I've been told to deliver the message that Debra will not be putting her baby up for adoption with Joe and Jill."

"Is Debra keeping the baby?" I ask.

"I have no idea," the secretary answers coldly.

Joe and I, who have become convinced that the lawyer is the most evil person on the face of the earth, don't trust the messenger. We call Rick to make sure this is the message he intended us to receive and are startled when an electronic voice informs that the phone number has been changed. "The new number is unlisted."

That is the last we hear of Debra and her baby.

The insensitivity of the final blow leaves me too angry to feel any pain. Then, I'm too busy. After our move, we race to get the house in order. By the time the social worker from COTW arrives for our home visit two days later, most of the packing boxes are gone. The floors, refinished while we were in North Carolina, look wonderful. So does the guest room, which we've had painted a pale yellow.

"This will be the baby's room," I explain. "We painted it a neutral color, since we don't know if the baby will be a boy or a girl." Or if there will ever be a baby, I think. Though I express enthusiasm about adoption, I'm too exhausted physically and emotionally to feel much of anything.

After Joe leaves for California, the numbness thaws into relief. With decisions about Debra, the move, and China behind, I feel lighter, less encumbered. Each night after work, I putter contentedly, exploring the house, arranging books, taking frequent breaks to sit on the screened back porch and smoke while I listen to the cicadas.

Over the weekend, a friend who lives a few streets north of us drops by with her two-year-old daughter to survey the new house. After schlepping up and down the three flights of stairs, the toddler turns to her mother and says, "But where are the toys?"

Exactly.

That night as I'm drifting off to sleep, a moment floats back from the family reunion. I'm on my parents' deck. Emily and Jeremy are tussling. I say something about an empty lap. There's a move toward my arms. A quick hug. An uneasy silence.

Suddenly, a loud, gut-wrenching wail fills the bedroom. The noise is unlike anything I've ever heard before, and even as I weep I listen with detached fascination. I was wrong, I think as I abandon myself to sobs so forceful that each one lifts my head, then hurls it back against the pillows. There *is* a sound when the heart breaks, and it's frightful.

X

"I KNEW THEY WERE LYING WHEN THEY SAID thirty minutes. It took me ninety minutes to get to work this morning." Joe's voice is loud, his expression angry. "If this commute doesn't get better, we're moving back to Manhattan."

"Aw, come on, Wease," I say. "Give it a chance."

Back from California just two days, Joe seems bent on hating everything about our new home. It's not just the traffic snarl on Route 3 that is, indeed, tripling the promised time of the rush-hour commute. It's the town. ("How can anybody get any sleep when those damn lawnmowers start so early in the morning?") It's the neighborhood. ("We live in a tacky house on a street with a bunch of tacky houses.") It's the din of the cicadas. ("I can't hear myself think.") And it's me. ("You reek of cigarettes. I don't want to come near you when you smell that way.")

In the three months since our return from St. Bart's, there's been an escalating edge to Joe's manner and tone when we're alone together. Some of this, I know, is the toll of the grinding demands that have kept him late at *People* night after night since the June arrest of O. J. Simpson on charges of murdering his ex-wife. Joe has overseen multiple cover stories.

But if Joe believes, as he maintains (both now and later), that his testiness is largely the expression of job stress, I (both now and later) do not. With Joe, there's always work, always office pressures. My beach chair analysis of "It's the job" has become successively, "It's Debra's silence"; "It's the purchase of a house"; "It's the move to the burbs." As his moodiness and rudeness now begin to remind me of our first year together, I decide, "It's us."

But after the tranquility of his two-week absence, I don't want to engage. "The commute will get better, Wease," I say. "Want to see what's on the tube?"

The next morning, the backup on Route 3 is just as bad. "If this doesn't straighten out by Thanksgiving, we're moving," he announces that evening. "That should give us enough time to get the house in shape to sell it."

"Oh, that's just perfect, Joe." So much for disengagement. "Perfect." I leave the room.

"How are you enjoying the house?" Lynn asks the next day.

"Joe's threatening to move. I think he means it."

Instead of her usual sympathy, Lynn bursts out laughing. "He's just not going to grow up during this lifetime." It strikes me as so apt that I can't help but laugh, too.

But only briefly.

If he truly insists on going back to New York, I can't say with certainty it will be with me. It seems so improbable, our splitting up. But this impatience of his, this refusal to give what I want a chance, is infuriating. I waited five fucking years for this house, since South Africa. And he's ready to quit after two days of commuting. I guess I can anticipate multiple threats of walkouts once a child arrives.

When Joe's friend Kathryn phones one night while he's still

at work, I tell her about his threats. Usually with Kathryn, I steer wide of any talk about Joe or our relationship, wanting neither to make her feel caught between us nor to interfere with her role as one of Joe's most trusted intimates. But I'm so irked with Joe that when she asks how we're liking Montclair, I answer honestly.

"Oh, Treen," she says, her tone dismissive but affectionate. "He's such a curmudgeon about change. The trick is to not think or react when he's going on."

I savor that rare perspective from someone who I feel knows Joe in all his complexity. Her response reminds me of something Grace had said two months earlier during our final counseling session, after Joe had announced, "I don't think we have much of a relationship anymore." He'd gone on to accuse me of "giving up too early" on trying to have a baby and to voice fresh doubts about pursuing a China adoption. Heatedly, I'd responded, "I'm ready to be a mother."

"Are you backing away from adoption?" Grace had intervened.

"No," he'd answered.

Turning to me, she'd said, "You take him too seriously."

I knew she was right, and let the crack about our relationship pass, reasoning it was one of those inflated statements that requires a twenty-four-hour cooling period. If he really believed we were on the rocks, we wouldn't be buying a house, would we?

I'd been unable, however, to let his other comment slip. *I feel guilt percolating, the sense or at least the question of "Am I giving up too easily?"* With Joe incapable of mustering enthusiasm for an adoption, I wanted him at least convinced that it was the only avenue open to us. I located a new gynecologist and underwent a new battery of tests, this time walking through the paces without anxiety or depression. While the new blood work suggested I wasn't in premature ovarian failure, a biopsy confirmed I wasn't ovulating. Diagnosis? The dreaded Don't

Know. Prescription? Trial injections of Pergonal, to be followed by IVF if eggs resulted.

To my relief, Joe hadn't been interested in any part of this. "I
don't want to come home to an obese, depressed wife," he'd
said. "I've just always thought you should get a second medical
opinion, and now you have."

Reasonable. Concerned. Loving.

Now, I want to heed the advice of Lynn, Kathryn, and Grace
and not take Joe's complaints about the house so seriously. But
I can't. There's something in his tone and persistence that
suggests I may not be taking him seriously enough. I can't tell
if we're reprising our decision to marry, fitful but final, or
heading for another South Africa debacle. The possibility it
may be the latter is slowly draining me of any pleasure in the
house.

For that, I resent him more each day.

As the dog days of August creep by, our every interaction
becomes drenched with bile. I do not yet perceive how quickly
our skein of trust and mutual forebearance is unraveling.
Instead, I attribute Joe's prickliness to the commute, the
suburbs, my own edgy impatience with adoption delays.

The layer of callous around my heart is growing so thick
from disappointment that I neither think about the children of
Bosnia, Ecuador, and Hoboken who might have been, nor
dwell on the fact that after eight months of wandering through
the adoption labyrinth, Joe and I are back where we started.
Instead, I throw myself into exploring new byways. I check out
leads in Philadelphia and Miami, Colombia and Mexico. I also
vet a well-established agency in Kansas and a lawyer in South
Carolina. Both come highly recommended for domestic adoptions. Both require a retainer of only three hundred dollars.
Both strike me as fool's missions. I sign us up, anyway, figuring
I can tolerate more disappointment without too much
damage.

But plainly I'm on adoption overload. When a friend offers to put me in touch with an adoption attorney in Bolivia, I respond with a curt "no," then spend the next fifteen minutes apologizing. When another friend, herself childless, says to me for the second time, "Are you sure you want to do this? Do you have any idea how much *work* children are?" I rudely answer, "I'd appreciate your not saying that again."

I'm just so damn sick of it all. Sick of talking about it. Sick of filling out papers about it. The only person I really want to talk to about any of this is Joe. But we're not talking. Only snarling. *The adoption stuff is out of control and Joe won't let me process it with him. It was easier when he was away. I hadn't realized until he was gone how much lighter I felt not having to shoulder his life. He's not willing to shoulder mine.*

The first time he says it with conviction, we're zooming along a deserted stretch of Interstate 80 toward the country, Joe driving as if he can't escape the suburbs fast enough. Our late-night travel is timed to avoid weekend traffic snarls and drunken drivers. But Joe, usually a careful driver, is in such a fury that I fear we'll land upside down in a ditch.

"I'll get you a child," he yells. "But then I'm leaving."

I say nothing. Stay calm, I tell myself. This is stress talking. The stress of his renewed battle with his editor from hell. The stress of our recent move. The stress of the tension between us. We've been through so much already, I tell myself. He'll cycle back around.

A few nights later he arrives home late from a dinner date and announces yet again that he wants to move back to the city.

"Okay, let's do it," I answer calmly. "It's not worth wrecking our marriage over a house."

Briefly, we talk about where we might move. The Village? The Upper West Side? Then, suddenly, we are two skaters goading each other toward a precipice that we both know is there, but neither of us can quite make out.

"You're always so crabby and unsupportive," he says. "I can't even discuss my work with you anymore. You don't listen."

"While you were in California, I saw for the first time how oppressed I feel by your constant criticism and chipping away at my competence," I answer. "It was easier without you."

"I don't know if I want to stay in this marriage," he says. "My leaving may be imminent."

"How easily you seem to breeze in and out of marriage," I reply coldly. "When did you plan to tell me that you're thinking of leaving?"

"I'm not leaving. Jesus, Jill, why can't you just let me be miserable and complain?"

"I'm agreeing without a fight to move again. I can let go of the house. It's a child I can't give up on."

"I'll go with you to China and help you get a kid," he answers. "But then I'll probably leave." This time when he says it, his tone is steady, almost glib. He reminds me that he's never wanted kids. Not when we married in 1985. Not when we started trying to conceive in 1992. Not when we consulted fertility specialists the year after that. Not during any part of the adoption search throughout this year. "I don't want a child," he repeats, "and I never did."

I nod curtly. "I'm going to take a shower."

When I get into bed, he's already beneath the blankets, reading. I open a book, then close it. "What the hell am I supposed to trust? First there's a house, then no house. A marriage, then no marriage." My tone is icy, unemotional. "Can I trust you to help me get a child?"

"Yes."

"I know that somewhere in me, I still love you, Joe," I say. "But I don't trust you. I don't trust you at all."

"You can trust me," he says firmly.

I look into his eyes, nod, reopen my book.

By the time we turn off the lights, Joe is already in retreat. "I don't make changes easily. I just need until Thanksgiving to settle in." Before his breathing turns to deep snores, he mutters, "You shouldn't take me so seriously."

By then, it's too late.

The next morning, I make a gesture of reconciliation. "We both need a hug," I say and reach my arms toward him. Even as he responds, I feel anger stirring that it was I, not he, who made the overture.

Divorce at this moment, I write later that morning, *is not unthinkable, and that is scary. Very scary. I know I've had quiet suspicions for a long time that it shouldn't be this hard. That a couple, married for nine years, shouldn't have to struggle so hard to make a home together, to raise a family. I expected him to be a pain in the ass through the move. I anticipate no help on a child. How can this be a marriage? . . . There was a blip of a moment when we thought we had a Caucasian infant and he seemed genuinely excited. I thought then it would be alright. Maybe that is something to hang onto. But I keep envisioning a Chinese baby. Him looking at the child and making no connection. Me resenting him. Resenting his assumption I'll attend to child, hearth, and him with no help coming back. There is no give in this scenario. I feel an acute need to start protecting myself, big time. To prepare myself for our splitting up.*

Joe and I both know that our fight crossed some unspoken boundary. Through the day, we reach out to one another in little ways, each of us in search of reassurance. I send him an E-mail asking how his commute went and get a friendly response. He calls to apologize for a dinner date the night before. In the late afternoon when I'm assigned a story about a child custody battle, I think to start my reporting with a call to a particular divorce attorney, a friend of a friend, but I can't recall her name. I dash off a message to Joe asking if he remembers.

A moment later, my phone rings. "Don't get a divorce lawyer!"

"What? Oh, no, no," I say, grasping the misunderstanding. "This is for a story, Wease. This has nothing to do with us."

"Okay," he says, still sounding upset. "But don't go getting a lawyer."

I hang up, now knowing that he has no intention of running. Yet, I don't feel reassured.

I keep thinking about the movie The Way We Were. *The way the couple agreed to stay together until the baby was born. That's what I see shaping up here. I don't mean to be melodramatic. It just feels real. I know marriages break up over children. [Two friends recently] split over kids. I read that a Hollywood couple is splitting up because she wants a baby and he doesn't. We're walking stereotypes, Joe and I.*

Joe comes home that night to find me sitting on the porch, my face splotchy from dried tears. "What's wrong?" His tone is casual, as if nothing has happened. When I shrug, he says, "Last night was good. We said some things that needed to be said."

He's chirpy, bent on pleasing. He grabs my foot playfully and says, "Shake a leg." When we move inside, he praises the progress on the sunroom renovations that I've been overseeing. Though I hear in this an attempt to say, Look, the house will work out, I'm unmoved. Ah, yes. Joe has vented and is feeling better. Now, I'm supposed to feel better, too.

While he showers, I sit outside on a lawn chair, smoking and pondering a future I haven't considered since our wedding day, a future without Joe. Is it easier to raise a child alone in the suburbs or in the city? If I move, would it be back to Hoboken or to Manhattan? And how soon? Can Joe and I split up without rancor? I see Joe through the bathroom window brushing his teeth and wonder what I'll tell my as-yet-nonexistent daughter about the nonexistent father whose name is on her adoption certificate. Is there a way to keep his name off that certificate to avert needless heartache? As these alien thoughts run through my head, I'm struck by the calm, angerless quality of my meditations.

I don't feel the panic I felt when I was bouncing between Joe and Marc and knew I could land up alone. Alone doesn't seem unmanageable; it just seems daunting.

We end August with a trip to a friend's house in the Berkshires. As we recline on the lawn at Tanglewood, our stomachs filled with wine, cheese, and pâté and our ears with Beethoven's *Ninth*, Joe and I hold hands. When the *Ode to Joy* commences, our fingers begin a playful game that makes us both giggle.

He's trying. He's got new bus schedules. He hasn't complained this week about the commute. Yet I remain wary and pissed. I am hardening, bracing myself. I know I should just let this all pass, not take Joe too seriously. He balks, he kicks, but he comes around. On marriage. On moving. On getting a job. Perhaps he'll ease into fatherhood. But all I foresee is a reaction, like his reaction to the house. Him making my life miserable, depriving me of the joy of having a baby. And me finally saying, Enough. Get out.

In the days ahead, I try for the first time to envision how my plan to shoulder 80, even 100 percent of the childcare duties would actually play out. I see only how tired I am, how resentful I feel trying to juggle baby, job, and household against Joe's needs and demands. The evening bath that should be a merry bubblefest appears instead as a power tussle, me vexed that after having made the baby's dinner, cleaned up after her, played with her, Joe still does not think to lift a finger, and Joe annoyed that I would even think to ask. I hear the baby's cry at three in the morning, then Joe's angry, "Can't you shut that kid up?" as I drag myself out of bed. The constant interrogation that has been our life together sputters, then stops, frustration and sadness choking me into embittered silence when Joe's embrace fails to enlarge to include this child.

The more he ignores the child, the more I'll resent him. In the end, it'll be sickening and a relief to leave. And there I'll be, on the cusp of forty, a single mother. A position I never envisioned myself in. I can see this with a dim clarity. I can't see him diapering a baby. Not at all.

On a hot evening as I gaze at the stars, I finally realize this is not about Joe. This is about me. Joe's never misled me, never pretended to an interest in this child and life I want so badly. It is I who have changed. Grace was right. This is about trust. But it's not Joe who can't be trusted. It's me. Though I love Joe now, I can't imagine loving a man who does not love the baby I love. It would be kinder to the child, easier on me, if I were a single parent.

As I continue in the weeks ahead to contemplate this un-wanted future, I see that the threat to our marriage is real, and that it comes not from Joe, but from me. Somewhere along the way, I have stopped putting our relationship first. I can no longer flex: a child is now my top priority.

September passes. Then, October.

Though I share none of my dark ruminations with Joe, he senses my withdrawal. More tactile, more affectionate, he stops complaining about the commute. He's also more inter-ested, suddenly, in Chinese children. One day as we ride the subway, he points to an Asian girl and says with obvious pleasure, "That little girl is looking at me," then mugs at her humorously, making her giggle.

Joe seems to be settling into the idea of a child from China. It's been growing on him. He makes cracks about China, points to Chinese kids. He has asked questions about adoption, supportive questions, not hostile. The situation seems to be that as long as we're getting along, he's willing to go for the ride. I'm trying.

During this period, WACAP, as promised, has bypassed all the how-do-you-feel-about-adoption-and-are-you-really-sure-you-want-to-do-this stuff and is moving swiftly to get our application off to Beijing. Unlike the triplicate demands of Spence, WACAP needs just one copy of our documents and is handling the procurement of the cumbersome state seals required on each piece of paper.

Yet I grow more leery of believing it will happen. Too many pieces of me are now strewn around the globe. Sarajevo. Quito. Asunción. Hoboken. Philadelphia and Miami have come and gone. So has Mexico City. We've heard nothing from the agency in Kansas, nothing from the lawyer in South Carolina.

Periodically, WACAP checks in with us, voices from afar about an adoption that seems even more remote. "Will you keep your minds open to a child as old as a year?" Will that enhance our chances? Fine. "You might want to check with the INS to make sure they still have your I-600A form." Fine. "Your papers have been sent to Beijing." Fine.

I report each development to Joe matter-of-factly, then wait for his response. What I get each time is a nod. So, we uncork no champagne when we receive word that our paperwork has cleared the INS hoops. We exchange no excited hug when documents stamped with Chinese characters arrive from the State Department. We dance no pas de deux when WACAP phones at the end of October to say that we could be on the road shortly after the new year. I celebrate each milestone alone, not disturbing Joe with my mounting excitement.

Then Joe throws me a curveball. *People*'s start-up sister publication in Australia, *Who*, wants Joe to come to Sydney for a ten-week stint beginning in March.

"But we might have a baby then," I protest.

"What's the big deal? You're planning to take a maternity leave anyway. So, you'll take it in Australia."

"You can't be serious, Joe. Neither of us knows anything about taking care of a baby. What if something goes wrong? We're going to want family and friends around."

I remind him there are follow-up procedures to an adoption, that we may not even be allowed to leave the country during that period. "Why don't you at least find out?" he says irritably.

"*You* call the agencies, if this is so damn important to you," I respond.

Within hours, the same Joe who's maintained all these months that he has no time for contact with adoption people phones me back to say that both WACAP and COTW see no problem with our going to Australia. He *is* serious.

For two days, I stew. Talk about classic baby denial! He might as well have gone out and bought a two-seat sports car!

Then, I calm down. When I dissect my objections to what is really no more than an extended vacation, I realize that though I thought I'd been floating without expectation, I have in fact fashioned a plan. I've been envisioning my maternity leave as an interlude when I not only revel in my child, but settle into Montclair. A time to get to know the other mothers in the neighborhood, make play dates, explore the local resources for kids. Also a time to hit the road and introduce our child to her grandparents, aunts and uncles, young cousins. I've been envisioning those three months as a warm soak in every parental cliché of the nineties: bonding, nesting, sandwiching cozily between generations.

At the same time, I resonate to Joe's insistent message that he "needs a change of scenery, a change of pace, a change of job." I've been there; still am, in fact. What he's proposing is not life altering; it's just a disruption, albeit a poorly timed one.

Not wanting to engage in another heated discussion, I write him a letter. "Because I DO empathize, I can't ask you not to go. But I also can't make a firm commitment that I'll join you for the entire ten weeks. . . . Once we get back from China, settling the baby and settling into parenthood are going to be my top priorities. If this is doable in conjunction with Australia, I'm open to going. But I can't see that far down the road . . . It could be that after a month, I'll have cabin fever and feel ready to hit the road . . . Would I prefer that you put baby and family first? Yes. But do I understand why you want to do this? Yes to that, too . . . I'll do my best to work around you if you decide to go."

Within a week, the minicrisis is resolved when *People*'s managing editor nixes the trip. Joe is too valuable in New York. The news extinguishes the glow in Joe's eyes, much as the Australia contretemps has quashed the excited flutter in my stomach. It's reminded me—as if I needed reminding—that Joe is unlikely ever to put baby and family first.

"No, I can't say for certain when the referral will come." The soothing voice at the other end of the line is Carey of WACAP's China program. "The way things are moving now, you'll probably have about two months after that before you travel."

Because there's no predicting either when our referral will arrive or how soon we'll be required to travel after that, I want to know if Carey thinks it's safe for Joe and me to purchase plane tickets for our annual trips to California for Christmas and South Carolina for New Year's. We're already in possession of tickets to Utah, purchased at a discount over the summer for a February ski trip with my father.

It's a small matter, stupid really. So we eat the price of some airline tickets. Big deal. We've squandered larger fees along the adoption path and survived. But now that our papers are in Beijing and we've received WACAP's "China Travel Packet," my need for reassurance and guidance is escalating. Carey, whom I've never met, is responding magnificently, her tone sweet and concerned, as if she hasn't answered similar questions a million times before.

"Whatever you decide," she says, "be prepared to travel."

We're not. In the days since WACAP's twenty-four-page travel packet arrived, Joe and I have inspected the lengthy list of supplies for every contingency—and done nothing. I know it's up to me to nudge the shopping along, but I don't want to look at diapers and pacifiers, bottles and Baby Tylenol, until I'm convinced there will be a baby to use them. Our only concession to the pending change is a weekend outing to look at baby furniture. We speed through the cramped aisles of a single store and agree that we like the look of natural maple.

"There, that one looks fine," Joe says, pointing to a crib.

"Looks fine to me, too." (Later, Joe will object, "There were a dozen Nina Kruschevs and one Cindy Crawford. What was there to decide?")

I jot down the order numbers for the crib plus a matching dresser, changing table, gliding rocker, and toy chest. Though I'd like to linger a bit longer over the fabric samples for the rocker, I choose quickly, not wanting to press my luck. To my mind, it's a small triumph that Joe has come on this errand at all.

There are perhaps a dozen Chinese-born children in the sprawling Upper West Side apartment, all of them girls, all of them adorable. I find an eight-month-old clad in a puffy party dress particularly mesmerizing. Something in her smile, the cock of her head, her alert expression.

"Did you see this one?" I whisper when Joe passes me in the hallway. "She's a heartbreaker."

"She has brown hair," he answers, without stopping.

"Your daughter is wonderful," I say when a woman appears with a bottle for the child. "When did you travel?"

As we talk, I notice that the woman has the same expression

as most of the other new parents in the apartment. Exuberant. Proud. A touch smug. I move on in search of Joe and find him in the kitchen with a knot of adults who telegraph that they, like we, are still awaiting a referral from Beijing. The women have a drawn, slightly desperate look; the men seem awkward and bored, as if they'd rather be anywhere but here.

The stated purpose of this gathering is to give waiting families an opportunity to meet members of WACAP's China program. But the real point, it seems to me, is to hearten us with a dazzling display of kids, proof that WACAP delivers. And I *am* feeling heartened. Not because the kids are cute. Not because we've been told by a WACAP staffer, "It's looking pretty solid for a January departure." But because Joe has come to this gathering without squawking.

We're doing better, Joe and I. He's no longer talking about leaving; I'm no longer debating whether he should move out before or after we bring the baby home. With our group now projected to travel in January, just two months off, the emotional distance between is again narrowing, he wary of a child, me wary of another "sure thing" adoption.

As we put on our coats to leave, Joe points to a little girl and says, "There's another one with brown hair. That's at least three I've seen. I thought all Chinese kids have black hair."

Until this afternoon, I'd thought so, too. I think to make a joke about our ignorance, but there's something in Joe's tone I don't understand, so I say neutrally, "Well, I guess some do and some don't."

Outside on the sidewalk, he says, "I want a kid with black hair."

"Oh, come on," I laugh. "You can't tell a bunch of Chinese officials, 'This child won't do. The hair color is all wrong.'"

"I want a kid with black hair," he repeats firmly.

As I search his face for some hint of irony, I no longer feel heartened. Instead, I feel that no matter how hard I try to protect myself, one way or another, my heart is going to be broken again.

"Look," I say, pointing across Broadway. "There's a lighting store. Want to get a lamp for the sunroom?"

With WACAP now urging us to prepare to travel, I phone the baby furniture store and place an order, requesting that delivery be held until after we return from China. There is no way I'm going to set up a nursery before I'm certain there's a baby. When the itemized receipt, noting our deposit, arrives by mail a few days later, I wince at the message penned at the bottom: "ADOPTION—Refund can be given." How appropriate. Furniture that may never arrive for a baby who, too, may never arrive.

The beautiful set is a gift from my parents. I know I should send them a thank-you note. But when I sit down the next day, Thanksgiving, to write, I can't do it. Not now. Not yet. Not when I don't quite believe there will ever be cause for thanks.

On Friday, December 9, Carey calls me at the office with news that our referral has arrived from Beijing for a child in Yangzhou. Instantly, I sense something is wrong. WACAP's usual practice is to mail the long-awaited referral to the prospective parents, sort of like a college acceptance letter. I ask Carey to hold and patch Joe into a conference call; we should hear this together.

"You've received a referral," Carey begins, "but the child is thirteen months old. I know you wanted an infant."

"That means she'll be at least fourteen, fifteen months before we pick her up," I say.

"Yes. And you stated very clearly on your application that you want a child twelve months or younger. If you're not comfortable with this, decline the referral. There's no risk of not getting another child."

"You mean from the same orphanage?" I ask.

"I don't know," she says. "That would be good. We know this orphanage. There are no neglected children. But the orphanage may not have younger babies."

There's a hesitation in Carey's voice I can't read. Wanting so badly to believe this is the one, I think, What's two more months? "Can you fax us the information on her?" I ask.

"Sure," she says. "What I have here is the results of her ten-month checkup."

When I compare the child's weight and height against the Chinese growth charts provided by WACAP, I understand. This baby is so small she's off the charts. How are we to divine if she's simply very diminutive, or if she's suffering from malnutrition, a temporary illness, or some chronic disease? It's been a stretch convincing first myself, then Joe, to remain open to a child as old as a year. There's no way he'll agree to a special-needs child. In a calmer state, there's no way I would either.

But I'm terrified this may be our last chance. In the weeks following the 1989 crackdown on student demonstrators in Tiananmen Square, I'd written some articles for *Time* sharply critical of the Beijing regime. What if this is Beijing's response? Improbable as that may sound, even Joe has been worried that Chinese authorities may signal their disregard for Western journalists by assigning us an unhealthy child.

"What if Beijing says, 'To hell with you,' and refuses to give us a new referral?" I ask Joe.

"Let's report it out," he answers.

For the first time since embarking on this journey more than a year earlier, Joe takes control. Over the weekend he makes several calls and asks most of the questions while I listen anxiously on another extension. All my China adoption gurus encourage us to decline the referral. Beijing officials, they maintain, are eager to match children with adoptive families. They'll come through with another baby. A WACAP client who'd returned from Yangzhou in November with a five-month-old daughter, tells us he toured the orphanage. "I know there are younger kids there."

Yet I'm incapable of being reassured. Only when Joe asks Carey, "What will happen to this child if we don't take her?" do I feel a flicker of hope. I've been such a wreck that I've not once thought of the child whose life will be so dramatically affected by our decision. Joe's question briefly revives my slumbering conviction that beneath his display of resistance to children, Joe harbors the capacity to be a responsible, concerned father.

By Sunday night, our decision is made. *Joe is clear; I am muddle-headed and know he is right.*

The next morning, I tell Carey—please, respectfully—to decline the referral. "How long do you think it will be before Beijing provides a new referral?"

"We have very good relationships," she says. "We should hear within thirty days. You may still be able to travel with this group. If not this one, certainly the next."

As I'm putting on my overcoat to make an appointment late Tuesday afternoon, my office phone rings. "I have good news," Carey says. "We have your new referral. She's—"

"Wait! Let me get Joe on the phone, too."

"Her name is Yang Saiming," Carey continues when we're all on the line. "She's six months old and weighs seventeen pounds. Her health stats are all well within the normal range." She ticks off the numbers. "I'll fax the information as soon as we hang up."

"Is there a picture?"

"Yes, but it was photocopied in Beijing, then faxed to us." She laughs. "The quality isn't very good." She explains that a photograph has not yet been mailed from China. Unlike the others in our group, who received photos with their mailed referrals, we may not see a picture of our daughter before we meet her.

Carey tells us our itinerary is now firm; we are to be in Nanjing on January 16. While she and Joe discuss where that is, and the best way to get there, I, the directional dyslexic, get out the Chinese growth charts and mark Saiming's weight, height, and head circumference along the curves. All my red dots fall between the fiftieth and ninety-fifth percentiles.

"Please, fax me that information," I say when Joe and Carey conclude. "I can't thank you enough."

I run down the corridor to the fax machine, grab the pages, dash back to my office and dial Joe. "She looks like a Martian with a mustache. She's gorgeous! I'm late, gotta run. I'll show you later."

That night, Joe and I study the "physical exam record" faxed by WACAP, with its thirty sets of numbers and comments from Saiming's checkups at age two and three months. It's obvious she's healthier than the other child. At three months, she weighed almost as much as the other child did at ten months, and her head circumference was already larger. Where the other child's nutrition status was listed as "above average," Saiming's reads "good." Muscular, mental, and nervous development are all "normal." Then again, so were the other girl's. Joe spots only one cause for concern. The recorded size of Saiming's liver has shrunk by a third between checkups.

The next morning, I phone doctors in Minnesota, Massachusetts, and Michigan. I've gotten the names and numbers from a recent Families With Children From China newsletter that identifies these physicians as "medical resources for international adopters . . . all three available for telephone consultation before you go (advice, to help evaluate referral information)." All three assure me that Saiming's checkup results suggest she's healthy.

One of the doctors even laughs when I raise our concern about the liver. Those readings, she explains, are only rough since it's difficult to feel the liver of so young a baby. What's important, she says, is that both readings indicate none of the inflammation that would suggest hepatitis B, a common problem in China. "You've got a good one," she says. "Take her."

Joe grounds my flight of exhilaration the next day with a single comment. I'm reading WACAP's travel packet with care, adding up the costs as I go. Our joint account, gutted to one hundred and seventy-seven dollars when we purchased the house, is not going to be much help during this cost-intensive period of the adoption.

When I again raise the possibility of Joe's selling his Pepsico stock, he erupts, "This is your baby. I thought you were paying for it."

Two days later, I leave for Oregon to visit my sister. As Ann digs out baby paraphernalia, long since outgrown by her own kids, to pack and ship to New Jersey—car seat, baby backpack and books, stuffed animals, clothes, high chair, crib sheets— I'm not at all the portrait of a happy, expectant mother.

I'm not "excited," as everyone keenly inquires. I'm more nervous, anxious than excited . . . I think of how our lives will be disrupted. I worry how Joe and I will get along.

When I'm not fretting about whether our marriage will survive, I'm worrying about my fitness to be a mother. Will I be patient enough? Attentive enough? At thirty-nine, energetic enough? Will I be able to put the child's needs before my own? Will I resent the intrusion on my reading hours, work life, brooding time? Do I really want a child? Ahhh! How do you change a diaper?

In all the years of wanting, trying, looking, I'd been too busily in pursuit of a baby to pose these obvious questions. Now, I'm getting a crash course in the sorts of concerns that attend the nine months of a first pregnancy—or so Ann and Lynn tell me.

"I was ambivalent right up to the moment of birth," Lynn reassures by phone.

When I meet up with Joe in Pasadena for his family's

Christmas celebration, he's feeling chastened about his hateful crack about money. *He apologized, said he'd been tired. To say he's enthusiastic would be stretching it.* Then again, to say I'm enthusiastic would be stretching it, too. *I have heard, I have read, that bonding is not necessarily instantaneous. That it can take weeks, months. We're inheriting a real person, a child with a personality. She could have a variety of reactions to being put with strangers, taken from the place she knows; or alternately, could succumb immediately to the personalized attention. I worry most about Joe's reaction and the effect of his reaction on me.*

I share none of my brooding with Joe. Though I'm now confident that he'll both come to China and return home afterward with baby and me, I'm no less certain that Joe would exploit any expression of doubt to pressure me to call the adoption off.

Instead, for the first time in this long process, I enlist his family's support. "If ever there was a time to express enthusiasm about this adoption, this is it," I tell Esme. "I'd appreciate your telling your parents, too."

Silent so long about our adoption, my in-laws prove worthy allies. They ask about the child waiting for us in Yangzhou, speak of what joy it will be to have a child at next year's Christmas celebration, say they can't wait to visit their new grandchild. Esme promises to meet her niece at the airport if we return home from China via Los Angeles, and offers to come to New Jersey to help with the baby. They all want to know what name we've settled on and how we picked it.

I explain that the Jewish tradition is to select a name in memory of a departed loved one. My great-grandmother was named Blanche. (I don't add that Blanche was the adult my mother most adored, and that we're doing this mainly to honor my mother's efforts on behalf of our adoption.) Joe and I have racked our brains for a "B" name and found only one we both like.

"We're naming her Rebecca," I say, "but we'll call her Becky."

"Rebecca?" My mother-in-law's eyes light. "That was the name of my great-grandmother." I look toward Joe and see his own expression brighten momentarily.

The time we spend with our West Coast friends also proves unexpectedly reinforcing. Parents all, each of them is excited about our pending adoption. At one home, Claudia teaches me how to diaper a baby and prepare a bottle while her husband, my college pal Evan, coaxes Joe to play with their two small daughters. At the home of Joe's college friends, the conversation is lively and engaging as the parents delight in the holiday return of their two grown daughters. At another house, two of our journalist friends talk with their usual bite about work, then turn to mush when their two preadolescent kids join the conversation. I watch Joe observe all these children with closer attention than usual, and I can only hope he's finally preparing to be an involved father.

If not, I have a backup plan. Many times over the last year, Joe and I have discussed whom we might ask to be godparents. Always, we've intended the request to signal our high regard; because we have many good friends, it's been hard to decide. In recent months, though, qualms about Joe have forced a change in my agenda. Now, my concern is to ensure that Becky has adoring, attentive men in her life, should Joe prove a remote presence. I know just the people. I just don't know if Joe will buy my idea.

I needn't have worried.

"Let's pick people who began as neither your friends nor mine," I try one day, "but rather whom we befriended together." From there, it's easy to get Joe to where I want us to be: Arthur and Ken, two of our closest friends and one of the most solid couples we know. I point out that since we see Arthur and Ken most weekends in the Endless Mountains, they'll not only be a constant presence in Becky's life, but will no doubt spoil her rotten. Joe likes the idea, and is only surprised that I would forego a godmother in favor of two godfathers.

"Since we're going to be a nontraditional family," I answer, "it seems appropriate that Becky should have nontraditional godparents."

Sold.

Home from the holidays, I consult with a pediatrician who comes recommended by parents belonging to the fast-growing local chapter of Families With Children From China. (WACAP warning: "It is very important that you consult with your pediatrician about medicine you and your child may need. You will not be able to obtain most Western medicines in China.") In addition, WACAP provides me with names of adoptive parents around the country who returned recently from Yangzhou. From them, I get an accurate weather report (cold, rainy) and useful packing tips like take a thermos (great for a daylong supply of formula while on the road), small gifts for your Chinese guides (chocolates are a favorite), and "comfort foods" (coffee, cookies, Pop Tarts).

Then, Joe and I make our first foray to Toys 'R Us. We load up a cart with eight cans of powdered baby formula, diapers (sizes two and three), wipes, cold and fever drops, remedies for dehydration, bronchitis and ear infection, rash ointments, diarrhea antidotes, skin creams, and plastic bottles with disposable liners.

Siblings and neighbors supply an assortment of used baby clothes, insisting it's foolish to shop before we get an accurate fix on Becky's size. The information we have is at least a month old. Kathryn provides a new baby blanket; Lynn lends a Sara's Ride, which returning travelers have advised is more versatile than other chest pouches and not as cumbersome as a backpack. Toys prove, for me, one of the bigger challenges. We've been warned that orphanage children tend to be "developmentally delayed." What will interest and entertain Saiming? I settle finally on a stuffed rabbit, two cloth rattles, a soft ball, a ring of plastic keys, and some blocks.

All this, along with Joe and my clothes, must be squeezed into two suitcases. (WACAP warning: "You are allowed to bring one checked bag [44 pounds max.] per person, plus one carry on and a camera case or purse on the flight into China.") It's so tight that I have to photocopy select pages from baby books so I can leave the texts behind. I do the same with our travel books after Joe fails to do this, his sole packing task beyond laying out his own clothes. I try very hard not to regard this as a harbinger of resistance to come and look instead for encouraging signs.

January 6: *Slowly, very slowly, he is coming around. Two days ago, he came in inquiring if I had purchased pacifiers and a snowsuit. He'd been talking to a colleague.*

Yet, for all our preparations, it still feels distant, unreal, otherworldly. It *is* otherworldly. Half a world away, I'm reminded now that word is out at work I'll be leaving soon for Yangzhou. "Is this your first trip to China? Are you excited?" colleagues ask. I don't know how to make it make sense to these fellow journalists that despite my twelve years as a writer of foreign affairs, I've barely given China a thought. According to my internal itinerary, I'm not going to China; I'm going to pick up my daughter.

It's finally beginning to feel like it's really happening, and yes, I'm excited, I write on January 12, two days before our scheduled departure. *Now that the shopping and packing are finished, I have little to do but happily anticipate. We still have no picture. It was supposed to arrive yesterday by express mail, but the weather apparently delayed delivery. Joe's starting to get into it. He called WACAP yesterday and got the U.S. Express number (then naturally dumped it on me to trace the package). I called this morning and was assured that package Tb231184987 was delivered to our house at 10:30 a.m. today.*

I arrive home before Joe, leaving me time alone to study the four visa-size color snapshots of Becky. Though they're all copies of the same picture, the longer I stare, the more her expression seems to shift subtly from one frame to the next.

What an adorable child! Becky's expression is charmingly alert, as if curious what's going on during the photo taking. She looks neither happy nor unhappy. Her cheeks are puffy and pink, coming down to a tapered chin. The mouth is so tiny and perfectly formed, narrow lips, the bottom thicker than the top. The nose also looks beautifully formed (far better than in the Martian shot!). The eyes are large and brown. Hard to tell if her left eye is slightly crossed . . . She has almost no hair in the picture, but it looks very dark . . . It looks like there may be a tiny beauty mark high on her forehead that will be covered when her hair comes in, but it's so sweet-looking (if that's what it is). The expression is wide-eyed, alert, content. I'm ecstatic!

My excitement swells when Joe phones from the office to ask what Becky looks like. A few hours later, joy overwhelms my doubts as I watch him study her picture for the first time. Though Joe's lips speak skepticism—"Where's her hair? Do you think she's bald? Do her ears look low-slung? Do you think she's got mongoloidism?"—the smile tickling their edges says something else. He is pleased. He is very, very pleased.

Later, as we lie in bed studying the pictures together, Joe thinks to consult our baby texts about the possible crossing in the left eye. He goes to the nursery and pulls books from the bookshelf, at present the room's only piece of furniture now that we've moved the guest couch to Joe's office. Dr. Spock and others assure us that an impairment of vision is unlikely; among infants, a slight crossing, typically self-correcting, is common. This tableau of two expectant parents pressed head to head, poring over baby-care books, is probably also common. But to me it's unexpected ambrosia. Here, finally, is the sweet togetherness we've lacked all along.

The next morning Joe and I each carry one of the tiny photos to work. Throughout the day, we remain in constant touch, sharing headlines. He reports that a Chinese-American colleague says that Becky's large head is a "sign of beauty" in Chinese children. I report that while getting the last of my travel shots, a jab of gamma globulin in my butt, the nurse remarked on the good placement of Becky's ears. "And I hadn't even brought up your cracks about mongoloidism, Wease." Joe reports that he's enlarged his picture on a photocopier and faxed the image to both sets of grandparents. I report Lynn's observation after seeing the picture at lunch: "She must be content because her brow isn't furrowed, and there's no strain in her face."

All day, I carry the picture in the left breast pocket of my vest. When colleagues enter my office, I ask, "Want to see my daughter?" then hover protectively, as if the picture might disappear.

I keep thinking that's her picture resting against my heart. My heart is so full. I can't wait! I can't wait! We're going!

XI

NEWARK TO SAN FRANCISCO. SAN FRANCISCO TO Hong Kong. Hong Kong to Nanjing. Destination: Yangzhou, a dot in China's vast geography, southwest of Beijing, northwest of Shanghai. By the time we land in Nanjing, we've crossed so many time zones and date lines that we have to consult our airline itinerary to fix our place in time. Ah, January 16. A Monday. Shortly after three in the afternoon.

As we step out of the terminal, a petite woman with a young boy in her arms rushes forward. "Jill? Joe? I'm Linda. We're all here and waiting for you." Then she plunges intrepidly back into the dense crowd, parting a path for us to our small band of fellow travelers. We all break the ice by whipping out the tiny photographs of our daughters-in-waiting. We're still cooing when Mr. Li, the translator and tour guide provided by WACAP, politely nudges us toward a waiting van. Though the WACAP itinerary indicates we're not to meet with provincial authorities until tomorrow, Mr. Li has somehow managed to move our appointment to an hour from now so that we can get an earlier start for Yangzhou.

On the ride to the provincial civil affairs office, Mr. Li, microphone in hand, offers an uninterrupted commentary about the historic sights we are passing. It's hard to converse, but we manage to learn a bit about the others in our group. Michael is a bank manager from a small town in Washington and his wife Lisa is a former second-grade teacher. Their new daughter, like ours, is seven months old. Linda is a grocery clerk and her four-year-old traveling companion Orion is her biological son; her husband, a retired cop, is waiting back home in Seattle. Her new daughter will turn one while we're in China.

At the entrance to the civil affairs office, we collide with an exiting troupe of Canadians who, we learn in hurried exchanges, are also here to complete adoptions. As we climb the dark stairs, Joe and I leading the way, I call over my shoulder, "I guess we begin our Lamaze breathing now." Mr. Li, a grandfatherly man with warm eyes and nicotine-stained teeth, looks baffled as the Americans burst out laughing.

Our giggles silence when we enter a chilly, bleak room with dirty windows and three officials, all in overcoats, seated around a rectangular table cluttered with papers and a full ashtray. Mr. Li gestures for us to sit in a row of foldout metal chairs, then summons Joe and me to the table. The officials, two men and a woman, begin posing questions that Mr. Li translates into staccato English. What are our occupations? Given that our application lies open on the table, the question seems odd. What are our salaries? This one seems both odd and awkward. Our Manhattan-inflated incomes may sound unreasonably large to our traveling companions. I murmur a sum; Mr. Li translates loudly.

"Ah." The notaries smile approvingly. "We need not worry about the child."

"You need not worry about the child because we will love her, not because of the money," I say.

"Good answer," Michael mutters behind me. I turn and we nod at each other in solidarity.

As the notaries push papers at Joe and me, they tell us that because our daughter was born in a hospital in the urban Yangzhou area, we can be confident of her birth date. Yang Saiming, they say, was taken directly from the hospital to the orphanage. I ingest this information as if it were manna. Many of China's adoptable babies are abandoned on streets, beneath bridges, in doorways, with money pinned to their clothes and messages, penned on red paper, beseeching strangers to find the child a home. Our daughter, it seems safe to conclude, was never exposed to hostile elements or left unattended, battling for survival.

"What does her name mean?" I ask Mr. Li.

"Yang is the last name of all abandoned babies in Yang-zhou," he explains. "Saiming means as bright and glorious as the sun and the moon."

I'm sinking into reverie about the beauty of her name when Joe's laugh yanks my attention back to the table. "She has six toes!" Joe's index finger is pointing to a red footprint on one of the pieces of paper.

"No, no," Mr. Li says, his expression amused. "The baby squirmed. Do not worry."

Joe and I sign assorted documents, one to procure a passport for Saiming, another a formal application for adoption, the last an agreement that Joe and I will never harm or abandon Saiming.

Stamp. Stamp. Stamp. Done. Next.

From the windows of our comfortable tour van, we inspect the streets of Nanjing. What would probably strike most American tourists is the density of construction projects with its attendant haze of soot and dust, the unexpectedly Western cut of the pedestrians' hair and clothes, and the huge, carefully pruned sycamore trees that serve as a canopy when Nanjing, one of the "three furnaces of China," heats up during the summer.

What the expecting parents see instead and comment on is the beauty of the women. Like the babies awaiting us in Yangzhou, these females are Han Chinese, the country's largest ethnic group. Each of us, I imagine, is thinking, Maybe my daughter will look like that. Or that. Or that. ("Not me," Joe will tell me later. "I was thinking, 'I'm not happy about this.'")

When we enter the restaurant where we have a reservation for dinner, we spot the same lively group of Canadians we saw earlier. Though they have their own bus and translator, these eight families will be traveling companions of a sort as we move through Jiangsu Province over the next six days, always staying in the same hotels, often eating in the same restaurants, always just minutes ahead of us in the adoption process. The size of the Canadian entourage is more typical of the large groups adoption agencies assemble for the trip to China. I imagine their boisterous banter is more typical, too.

Our group, so quiet by comparison, lacks a breezy intimacy. As waiters place delicious dish after dish on the lazy Susan at the center of the table, we have no trouble making conversation. But now and in the days ahead, our dialogue will never expand to include details about our lives back home, our jobs, even our journeys to this moment. Though there is probably much we could share about failed fertility procedures, bruising decisions, thwarted adoption searches, we don't. I'll take our polite restraint to reflect not only a mutual respect for each other's privacy, but a fatigue with all the inquisitorial inspections by doctors and nurses, social workers and adoption personnel. It's as if, by unspoken agreement, we've collectively decided to leave our pasts behind and celebrate a present that finally promises a future. We simply accept that we are people with nothing and everything in common.

Around eight-thirty, we arrive at the Ding Shan Hotel, an accommodation so Western that there are white terry cloth robes in the closets and little shampoo samples on the marble sink. I remain awake just long enough to discover that one of the cans of powdered milk has sprung a leak, snowing all over the contents of my suitcase. Then I pass out from exhaustion.

Four hours later, I'm wide awake, ready to move on. With hours to kill before the two-hour drive to Yangzhou, I go into the bathroom, sit on the toilet, and write. *Somehow, none of this feels terribly foreign. People are just people . . . I guess this is excitement, though I feel remarkably calm. I am so aware that our lives are going to change dramatically tomorrow. This, I guess, is the final hours of labor.*

Tuesday, January 17, dawns chilly and overcast. Joe and I, still jetlagged and unsettled in our new time zone, awaken early and roll toward each other. Our lovemaking has a clingy quality that suggests mutual awareness of how irrevocably our life together is about to be transformed.

Hand in hand, we go for a prebreakfast stroll, our conversation alternately absurd and serious. We debate the great questions before us: Should we call it pee or wee, poop or number two? Joe surprises me with a great idea for a baby announcement—a matter I have not yet considered. We share impressions of the others in our group. And, at this, the eleventh hour of the rest of our lives, I voice my concern that Joe may not rein in his job to make room for baby and family. Joe, in turn, admits his fear that he'll be jealous of the baby, that she may be the only one in the house who'll be allowed to have any fun.

When he's like this—playful, warm, open, candid—he's so wonderful. That's the Daddy Becky deserves. I hope she gets him.

Shortly before noon, our van pulls up in front of Yangzhou's Xiyuan Hotel. Mr. Li instructs that we will get lunch, then should rest. "The babies," he says, "will arrive at five o'clock."

We lug our suitcases, camera cases, and diaper bags up one flight of stairs. As we start down the dark hallway in search of our assigned rooms, we again bump into the Canadians. They've not only beat us here; they already have their babies. As the parents cradle their new children in the hall, they look both exultant and dazed.

Mr. Li leads us through an extensive maze of corridors and dining halls to a cozy room, reserved for the Canadian and American families. We try not to stare too obviously at our teenage waitresses, but it's hard to look away. These tall, slender girls, all dressed in pale pink jackets, are even more beautiful than the women we saw in Nanjing. They, in turn, try not to stare too obviously at us, but they are no less intrigued with our group, particularly Linda's son, Orion. Because Linda is Chinese-American and her husband is Caucasian, Orion's handsome features are hard to place. Again and again during our stay in China, people will stare at this poised four year old, then murmur amongst themselves or boldly inquire, "Chinese?"

After lunch, while Joe unpacks his suitcase, I convert the surfaces of our comfortable room into a makeshift nursery. I stack diapers, set up bottles, and fashion a changing table on the bureau top with a small plastic travel mat and towel.

We're so wired from the combination of exhaustion and excitement overlaid by jetlag that there's no hope of napping. "Let's go for a walk," Joe suggests. In the lobby we encounter Linda and Orion, Lisa and Michael, all of them as sleep-deprived and restless as we are. En masse, we venture out into the streets of Yangzhou, dodging the confusing traffic of bicycles, cars, and pedestrians. As we stroll, we pause here and there to point our cameras and shoot.

"Yangzhou," I read dutifully from my travel guide, "was once an economic and cultural centre of Southern China. It was home to scholars, painters, storytellers, poets and merchants in the Sui and Tang dynasties."

Ask us if, at this moment, we care.

When we happen upon the Literary Pagoda, my interest perks momentarily. This three-tiered structure, its graceful design a stark contrast to the surrounding drab gray architecture, is a monument to the artists who thrived in Yangzhou before Mao purged their minds and broke their spirits with hard labor. Perhaps, I think, our daughter will, like Joe and me, have a natural affinity for the written word.

"It's a positive omen," I whisper to Joe.

I've just kicked off my sneakers and am drifting off to sleep when a loud knock sounds at our door. It's three-fifteen, almost two hours before the anticipated arrival. When a voice calls from the hallway, "Are you ready for your baby?" I think groggily, No, not quite yet. Please. Go away. Come back later.

Then Mr. Li bursts into the room, trailed by three other adults. I bolt upright, trying to look alert as Mr. Li makes the introductions. The man with the tinted glasses and pleasant smile is Mr. Wei, deputy director of the orphanage. The other man and woman are the notaries we met in Nanjing less than twenty-four hours earlier. Mr. Li bustles with efficiency.

"Prepare the orphanage donation," he says to me. "Joseph! Go tell the others to get their money ready."

The notaries settle into the room's two easy chairs and pluck a few grapes from the courtesy fruit basket. Mr. Wei props on the edge of the bureau. All three smile at me expectantly. I smile back, trying to look composed. When their eyes spot my sneakers by the nightstand, I hastily cross my legs, Indian-fashion, to hide my socked feet. They laugh. I laugh. One of them gestures at the makeshift changing table. They nod. I nod.

I pull wads of one hundred dollar bills from my purse and Joe's wallet, and begin counting out neat stacks on the bedspread. WACAP has instructed that all adoption-related payments should be made in U.S. currency. There is the three thousand dollar orphanage donation (an abundantly reasonable request for the months of care that has been provided), a five hundred dollar charge for the document preparation, and an unexpected fee of two hundred and fifty dollars, whose purpose I can't remember.

When Joe slips back into the room, we exchange a look and try not to laugh. Between the loot scattered on the mattress and the strangers across the room babbling in a foreign tongue, it feels absurdly like a drug deal. Then we hear a commotion of giggles outside the door.

"Wait a minute, wait a minute," I whisper to Joe. Though these payments are both expected and legitimate, I'd assumed the cash transaction would be handled discreetly, before the baby's arrival. I gesture frantically at the money. "Not with this here."

Joe bends over my crossed legs and is still scooping up the bills (which will somehow exchange hands in the ensuing confusion, complete with a receipt) when five, perhaps six, women arrive at the edge of my bed.

I reach up and, in a confused moment, a pair of hands descends to place a squirming body swaddled in a royal blue snowsuit in my arms. She is smiling, her dark brown eyes taking everything in with excited interest. When I lower my head so that we are eye to eye, she surveys my face with alert curiosity.

"Hello, sweetheart," I coo. Then, not wanting to offend our Chinese hosts, I drop my voice and whisper the words I long to say. "Hello, Becky."

She twists in my arms, trying to see everything at once. Then, with a poise well beyond her seven months, she settles contentedly on my thighs, staking an instant and irrevocable claim on my heart, my mind, and my lap.

But there is no time for sentimental tears. Behind me, the

notaries fire off a series of questions. Do you promise to take good care of Saiming? Do you promise not to harm her? Startled, Joe and I look at each other. Are they serious? Surely they can see—then we see their smiles. Yes, yes, it is obvious: already we are smitten parents.

A moment later, another fanfare of giggles announces the arrival of six pink-jacketed hotel maids. They crowd around me, tapping Becky's cheeks with their forefingers and chirping, *"Nihao! Nihao!"* (Hello!). Through it all, Becky wiggles happily, offering not even a whimper of protest. Then— whoosh!—they are all gone, moving onto the next family and the next baby delivery.

Suddenly, Joe and I are alone in our strange hotel room in this strange country with this strange baby—parents at last.

We cradle her, ogle her, bow our heads, and inhale her.

"She needs a bath," I laugh.

As we unzip the snowsuit, Joe exclaims, "Wease, look at the pattern!"

"Oh, my God! Wait'll your parents hear about this!" The royal blue material is appliqued with dalmatians in firefighter garb. "Of all the designs she could have come in— This really *must* be our baby!"

Not stopping to think how comforting the orphanage smells may be for Becky, we peel off her scented layers. Beneath the snowsuit, we discover a peach hand-knit cardigan with one red sleeve (perhaps the knitter ran out of peach wool?), a white and purple polyester shirt, a pair of pink leggings slit at the crotch (to allow for quick diaper changes?), a cloth diaper tied at the waist with a fraying blue rag, and a pair of red and white kneesocks, each stitched with a tiny angel. Though later I will fold and carefully lay away the pieces as keepsakes for Becky— someday she'll want to see, she'll want to know—for now we toss each item carelessly, eager to caress the bundle inside.

Once she is naked, we look, we point, we touch. Then,

instinctually, we perform the ritual of new parents the world over: we count her fingers and toes.

Look, it doesn't matter how you get your baby or where you get your baby. A new parent is a new parent is a new parent.

We both strip to the waist to perform our first parental maneuver, Operation Bath. We approach the tub skittishly, as if it were a deep, booby-trapped ocean shaft. Slowly, slowly, Joe lowers Becky toward the water.

"Wait!" I stick my elbow in the water. I don't know why it's got to be the elbow or what precisely my elbow is supposed to tell me, but I know I've seen it in the movies. "Feels okay to me."

Slowly, slowly, Joe continues the download procedure. When Becky's buttocks touch water, she emits a tentative cry, her first. Joe and I shoot each other a panicky look. Oh, my God, is it too hot? Too cold? Is she drowning?

She stops. She looks around. She smiles. Apparently, it's safe to proceed.

Now entering one of the more tricky and treacherous sequences of Operation Bath, we shift to a full four-hand maneuver. Joe braces Becky's head and back while I hold her ankles with one hand and soap her gently with the other. When she doesn't balk, I feel emboldened. "Do you think I should wash her hair?" I ask. Joe nods. I reach for the shampoo. We're on a roll now.

Joe and I can't stop laughing at our clumsiness, our inexpertise, our unvarnished delight. The only grown-up in the room is Becky, quietly regal as she submits to our giddy ministrations.

A new wave of panic washes over us when it comes time to raise our soaked charge of not-quite eight pounds from the tub. What if one of us slips? What if she falls? What if—

"You do it!" I insist.

"No, you do it!" Joe counters.

"No, you."

Finally, Joe lifts Becky out of the tub. Behold! She still breathes! Joe holds her tight while I towel her dry. I nuzzle her neck and say triumphantly, "Now, she smells like a baby!"

The size three diaper swims on her. The size two seems about right, though we're not sure which is the front and which is the back. Joe splashes the powder. I seal the sticky tabs. I maneuver her limbs into one of the borrowed baby outfits. Joe closes the zipper. Joe holds and talks to her. I fix a bottle. Soy powder spills on the floor, boiled water drips from the insulated jug provided by the hotel staff. While we wait for the bottle to cool, Becky falls asleep in Joe's arms.

Carefully, Joe lays her on the makeshift "crib" of blankets he's laid in the narrow space between our twin beds. For a moment, we stand peering down at her, awed. Then we tiptoe backward, perform a silent Munch Scream, and collapse in a hug. We are raw recruits no more. Operation Bath has been a success.

She's here! She's sleeping . . . Joe is in wonderful spirits. He's staring at her as she sleeps. So far, so good. She is SO alert. And active. When I laid her down naked before the bath, she was kicking like crazy. Joe is impressed by how well she holds her head up. She has a big smile. Makes lots of sounds. Joe noticed that she liked it when I kissed her head. She's such a sweetheart.

At dinner, the babies sleep in our laps as the five parents compare observations and share our concerns with Mr. Li. Since there are no pediatricians around to answer our questions, we make do by pooling information. Mostly, we hang on Linda's every word; she's a seasoned mom.

Joe and I describe the bluish discoloration that covers large sections of Becky's back and buttocks. Is it from too much lying around in a crib? we wonder. Or, God forbid, from being struck?

"It's called a Mongolian spot," Linda says. "It's common among Asian children." Her baby, Noel, and Michael and Lisa's daughter, Rose, also have patches of bluish skin.

Mr. Li nods. "It will fade with time."

"Why are Becky and Rose still almost bald?" Lisa asks.

"Is, um, Chinese custom," Mr. Li says. "They shave heads of little girls so the hair will grow thicker."

Ah. We all nod appreciatively.

"The back of Becky's head is very flat," I tell Mr. Li. "Why is that?"

Mr. Li is not sure. He will ask. I don't know whom he consults, but minutes later he returns with an answer: the flatness is from lying on her back so much in the orphanage. Once Becky begins to sit up, her head, still infant-soft, will round out.

But Becky is showing no inclination to sit up. As best Joe and I can tell from our brief play session before dinner, she's not yet rolling over, though she can lift her head. We've consulted our photocopied baby-care guides and sense that Becky is two, perhaps three months behind developmentally. Michael and Lisa say they've concluded the same about Rose. Ditto, Linda, who reports that Noel isn't yet pulling up or walking.

We all nod, none of us particularly concerned. We've been told to expect a developmental delay of two to three months, the toll of orphanage life. We've also been assured that once our children have the constant, personalized attention that comes with family life, they'll catch up within months to their age group. It's evident our beautiful babies are active and healthy. So healthy, in fact, that Linda is worried that Noel, a lively handful, may be taken away from her. China's regulations specify that parents who already have children must adopt a special-needs child. Noel's only special need appears to be for Linda's attention.

As our daughters now begin to awaken, the half-dozen pink-jacketed waitresses working our dining room stare hungrily.

"These girls are not accustomed to seeing so many babies," Mr. Li explains. "In China, we keep our children at home until they are two. We worry about colds and infections." Given China's one-child policy, I surmise, these unmarried teenagers are probably the closest thing to babies in their own homes.

Michael stands and hands Rose to one of the waitresses. Instantly, the other waitresses surround the lucky girl, cooing and giggling, tapping Rose's cheek with their forefingers. The girl wrestles her way out of the huddle and, pressing Rose's face to her cheek, smiles into the body-length mirrors that panel the walls.

"They all want to be mothers," Mr. Li says.

Linda and Joe follow Michael's example, handing Noel and Becky to two other waitresses. "Don't tell anyone," Mr. Li murmurs to Joe and me, "but yours is the prettiest. You are very lucky."

No doubt, Mr. Li, ever the gentleman and diplomat, finds a moment to murmur the same to the other parents. But Joe and I vigorously nod our assent. Yes, it's true. Ours is the most beautiful child in the room. In the country. In the universe.

Back in our room, Joe and I place Becky on one of the beds, sit on either side, then watch her every move, spellbound. She's having no trouble communicating her needs and desires. When I lay her on her stomach, she whimpers. When I switch her to a seated position, propped by pillows and the head-board, she smiles and looks around excitedly.

"Must be a new view of the world for her," I say to Joe. We beam at each other.

Our child, the explorer.

She burbles contentedly, her sounds filled with meaningful inflection. Ba-ba. Da-da.

"Did you hear that?" Joe demands. "She said, 'Daddy!'" We beam.

Our child, the linguist.

I wrinkle my nose. "Ahem." We take her to the changing table, and after sucking in a deep breath, I open the diaper. Joe bends at the waist and gags. "Hey, Wease," I say, "it looks like green cheese." For some reason, this cracks us up. We laugh and laugh, and when Becky joins in, we beam.

Our child, the comedienne.

As we change her into pajamas, she accepts our clumsy attentions without protest. When I kiss the top of her head, she smiles contentedly. We beam.

Our child, the good-natured sweetheart.

Again on the bed, Becky is ready to show us her stuff. She grabs my hair, grips Joe's index finger, waves both hands energetically, kicks her feet. When she slides down the small mountain of pillows to her back, she begins rocking side to side in a determined effort to roll over. We beam.

Our child, the Olympic athlete.

I begin to sing softly. "Twinkle, twinkle, little star." Joe joins in. Becky's body relaxes as she listens intently. We beam.

Our child, the musical prodigy.

Now, her eyes are beginning to close. We place her on the blankets between the beds and watch. After lying still for a few moments, she purses her lips, rocks her head to and fro several times, followed by a hand gesture beneath her chin. She pauses, then repeats precisely the same sequence. Lips, head, hand gesture. The motions are balletic and mesmerizing as she repeats them over and over until she falls asleep.

"Do you think that's the way she rocked herself to sleep in the orphanage?" I whisper to Joe. We look at each other, confused, concerned, frustrated that we do not understand.

Our child, the mystery.

I climb into Joe's bed, and together we watch our daughter sleep. We make love gently. Passionately. Very, very quietly.

"I love you, Wease," Joe whispers.

"I love you, too, Wease."

Then we, the parents, sleep.

In the morning Joe has headlines. At two-thirty, he'd been awakened by Becky. He'd changed her diaper, tried to feed her some solids, which she'd rejected, then fed her a bottle. All this without waking me.

"Wow, Wease," I marvel.

More important, he's gotten a fix on Becky's ballet. "It means she's hungry." We dissect the gestures, one by one, speculating that the head shaking is how Becky attracted the attention of her nurses, the hand beneath her chin is how she propped the bottle, the pucker of her lips is the sucking. This image of Becky feeding herself tears hard at my heart.

"But why does she suck so furiously?" I ask. "She holds onto the bottle with a death grip."

"Maybe she had only so much time to finish the bottle before they took it away." I beam at Joe.

My husband, the genius.

During these magical days in Yangzhou, it seems as if the city's one hundred and sixty thousand residents have joined in a conspiracy to divide time between the pain of before and the exultation of after. We feel like rock stars as pedestrians crowd us on streets and in parks, shouting "Baby! Baby!" Fingers dart out to chuck the babies' cheeks and chins. Those who speak no English flash a thumbs-up. Many cluck phrases like "Beautiful!" and "Very lucky!" The people of Yangzhou, it's obvious, are crazy about babies.

"They all want more children," Mr. Li explains.

To our surprise and relief, people grow even more excited when they realize that the bundles in our arms are not Caucasian. "Chinese baby!" they yell, their cries drawing still more gawkers. As most people who adopt overseas know, not all populations are so tolerant, let alone so enthusiastic, about members of their youngest generation being removed from native soil. No country wants a reputation for "exporting" its babies. In some countries, improbable reports of an international traffic in baby organs have led to brutal attacks on innocent Americans.

Joe and I assume the warm, generous response of the Chinese people reflects their long-standing experience with Beijing's one-child policy and their concern that abandoned children find a loving home. But why do so many inquire, "Boy or girl?" Given China's entrenched preference for boys, surely it's well known that the country's orphanages are populated almost exclusively by girls.

On a late morning walk through Slander West Lake Park, the beautiful and sprawling Central Park of Yangzhou, I stroll alongside Mr. Li. Matter-of-fact to the point of brusque with Joe and Michael, Mr. Li is respectful, almost reverential, toward the three mothers. Though he is a parent, he never asserts his authority. When he wants to offer advice, he first confers with our female bus driver, then reports back, "Experienced mothers say—"

"Good physics," he says, pointing to Becky, who sleeps soundly against my chest in a pouch. "I would adopt this baby."

Sensing an opening for a candid exchange, I express my confusion about the gender issue. Chinese attitudes are changing, Mr. Li explains. The preference for boys was spawned by an agrarian society, where strong males were needed to tend the family farms. Now, with so many people migrating to the cities in search of work, the need is no longer so acute. The new urban lifestyle has also rearranged assumptions about females leaving their families upon marriage to become a member of their husband's extended clan. Today, a married daughter often remains as or more connected to her own family.

Mr. Li looks wistful. He has one child, a daughter, currently a college student. Plainly the light of his life. He longs for grandchildren and knows that someday there will be one. But that's all there will be. One.

Back at the hotel, life along the second-floor corridor resembles a college dorm where everyone is majoring in the same subject: parenthood. We swap supplies and information with the Canadians and get updates about the sickly child, so pale and frail that her new father, a physician, has insisted on having her examined at a hospital. (She's fine; he's fine. Both will return shortly.) All-nighters are a given. At any hour, the hall is trafficked by some exhausted Canadian or American walking up and down, up and down, trying to lull a baby back to sleep.

Even so, our group remains discrete. Though we still know little of each other's lives back home, we are becoming tightly woven by our shared impressions, ignorance, and intoxication with our daughters. Like an extended clan of aunts and uncles, we delight in each child's progress. Already, Noel is pulling up along the edge of the bed and beginning to take steps; Rose is rolling over; Becky is almost sitting by herself. Together, we fret about the things we don't understand. Why does Rose cry so much? Does she miss her orphanage caretakers or is it just teething? What is that small rash on Becky's neck? Are Linda's fears legitimate that Noel might be taken from her when we get to Guangzhou?

We're able to devote our full attention and energies to our daughters because just about everything else is done for us. Contrary to my assumption that life with a baby on the road in a foreign land would be a logistical nightmare, the people who surround us make our lives far easier than they would have been back home. Thermoses of boiled water appear in our rooms throughout the day, and garbage cans filled with soiled diapers are whisked away. No moment of our stay is unplanned. We have only to show up in the lobby at the hour designated by Mr. Li and another wonderful day unfolds: visits to shrines and parks, lacquer factories, and Communist monuments. Even our meals are prearranged. All we have to do is pick up our chopsticks and eat.

Some in the Canadian entourage find their own tightly scheduled itinerary stifling. They want more control of their hours, their days, their stomachs. But the adults in our group surrender to the regimen without resistance. We are grateful that Mr. Li is doing all the thinking and planning. That frees us up to focus on our daughters.

I'm feeling queasy when our van pulls up to the entrance of the Yangzhou Social Welfare Institute, an austere three-story building with a dirty facade the same color as the grayish sky. I've been fighting nausea since morning. Probably too much Chinese food.

Deputy Director Wei escorts us to an adjacent building where, on the second floor, we enter a large, modern room with a polished marble floor, overhung by a silvery *Saturday Night Fever* ball. Mr. Wei explains that this is a discotheque, open to the public on weekends to raise money for the institute, which rehabilitates ailing seniors in addition to caring for orphaned and abandoned children. We're then shepherded into a small, windowless room, with a huge overstuffed couch and TV, and served orange soda and oranges while we wait for Mr. Cao, the orphanage director. The stale smell of cigarettes deepens my nausea.

I'm fading fast when Mr. Cao arrives. He tells us that these three babies in our group were abandoned after delivery at a nearby hospital. We can be confident, therefore, that the birth dates we've been told are accurate. No one, he assures, will try to take these babies from us in the future; the orphanage holds children for three months to give birth parents time to change their minds.

He's in mid-sentence when I bolt from the couch, asking for a bathroom. A young woman in a red ski jacket escorts me quickly to another building and up a flight of stairs to a room with a porcelain bowl built into the floor. I get down on hands and knees, bend over the bowl, but can't vomit. Involuntarily, my throat has locked against the pungent stench emanating from the bowl.

We rejoin the group at the entrance to the orphanage. As we climb up the wide cement steps, tricky to the Western foot with their narrow spacing, the eye-watering stench of disinfectant does the trick. I flee back down the stairs and make it outside just in time to hurl my undigested lunch into a neatly trimmed hedge of bushes. I'm horrified, embarrassed. There's no way to clean this mess up.

I race back in and find Joe on the fourth floor in a darkened room with four cribs and peeling blue concrete walls. This is the room that houses seven month olds. There are three children to each crib, save the spots left vacant by recently adopted children, Becky and Rose among them. In the cribs where children are sleeping, they lie width-wise, head to head, making it instantly clear why Becky has not yet learned to roll over: there's no room to roll. Those children who are awake look well fed, warm, bored.

I watch carefully for Becky's reaction. I'm concerned she may think we're going to leave her here, and fear she may get upset. Quite to the contrary, Becky bursts into a wide smile when she sees Mrs. Ma, one of the room's three nurses who rotate eight-hour shifts. When Mrs. Ma takes Becky in her arms, the affection between them is evident. Thank God, I think. Becky was loved.

With Mr. Li in another room and not on hand to translate, Mrs. Ma offers only two words. "Best baby."

I'm still grinning when I feel another intense wave of nausea. Hastily excusing myself, I flee back outside, where I remain inhaling fresh air while the others complete their tour.

When they reemerge, they tell me they enjoyed free run of the orphanage. All the rooms they wandered into were spotless, albeit dark and unstimulating. All the children they saw appeared well nourished. And all the workers they met seemed, like Mrs. Ma, attentive and caring.

Their account and my own limited observations will contrast starkly with a lengthy report issued a year later by Human Rights Watch. Based largely on four-year-old information about a single orphanage in Shanghai, that report will broadly condemn China's orphanages as a "secret world of starvation, disease and unnatural death." It will suggest that "dying rooms" are the norm, and that only the few showcase orphanages toured frequently by foreigners offer good care. Yet this orphanage in Yangzhou, too far from any standard tourist route to be of use as a showcase, was clearly offering commendable care to its one hundred and twenty-one tiny tenants a full year before the release of the human rights report.

When Beijing officials, angered by the unfair report, close all orphanages to foreigners for a time, I'll feel for the adoptive parents who can neither see where their children had lived nor meet and thank the people who had cared for them.

Even so, an orphanage is no place for a child.

When Joe emerges, he says to me, "All I wanted was to get Becky out of there."

Over the next twenty-four hours, I'm still able to participate with Becky in what is fast becoming our favorite activity. We lay together on a bed, she on her back, I on my side, our heads on one pillow. We peer deeply into each other's eyes. She smiles. I smile. Her smile widens. My smile widens. As we stare and stare, I feel as if I'm hugging her soul.

Beyond that, I can do little more than vomit, sleep, and watch Joe with Becky as he attends to her every need.

I'm totally stunned by Joe. My best hope had been he'd be playful with her. But he's totally smitten. He frets every little mark on her body. Loves playing with her. Pulls his fair share of feeding, diapering, etc. He is being WONDERFUL with her. He is taking to fathering so naturally.

There is no strain between us, no jockeying for the upper hand. When I recover, we return to shared responsibility for Becky. When Joe is flattened a day or two later by the same stomach bug, I take over, then step back easily once he is better. *There is a joy between us that is something new, something more.*

Toward the end of our stay in Yangzhou, I move Becky's bedding from the narrow corridor between our twin beds to the far side of my bed. She's already becoming more active and needs a larger squirming space. In the middle of the night, I'm awakened by a rustling sound. I prop my head on an elbow and see Joe moving Becky and her pile of blankets back to the space between our beds.

"Joe?" I whisper.

"I don't like not being able to see her," he whispers, his tone protective.

In that moment, I grasp that Joe's ambivalence about parenthood has already evaporated. He *is* a father.

Still, I have no illusions about what awaits us back home. I know there will be an unbalanced division of labor. And I know there will be an unbalanced division of Joe's attention between office and home once work demands begin to press. What I no longer need fear is an unbalanced division of love. Becky will have the daddy she deserves.

The fourth day of our stay at the Xijuan Hotel, Noel turns one. When we arrive for breakfast, our young waitresses are particularly giggly. Unlike the Canadians, we let them hold and play with our babies; in return, there is nothing they won't do for us. On this morning, they gesture for us to sit. Then out comes a birthday cake and two dolls for Noel.

We know these girls are apprentices, which means they work

like slaves: long hours, no pay. "How did they pay for this?" we whisper frantically to Mr. Li.

"They got money from their parents to buy the gifts," Mr. Li says. "These gifts are because the girls love the babies."

As we'd been instructed by WACAP, we've brought small gifts for the hotel staff, tokens that will not embarrass. Pencils, boxes of chocolate. How can we give so little when they've given so much? We ask Mr. Li if we can tip them. He looks horrified.

"It is the expression of thanks that is most important," he explains. "It is the giving and words that have meaning, not the gift."

On our fifth and final day in Yangzhou, the breakfast staff numbers a dozen. This is crazy. The Canadians have already finished their meal. We occupy just one table.

"What's up?" we ask Mr. Li.

Apparently, he's promised our waitresses that we'll take pictures of them with our daughters, then later send copies. Waitresses have come from all parts of the hotel to watch this rare photo op. When Michael and Joe ready their cameras, the girls jostle for the babies. I see the sweet waitress who's attended us with the greatest diligence reach for Becky, only to have an unfamiliar waitress push her out of the way.

Appalled, I hurry over and, tapping our waitress on the shoulder, say loudly, "This one must hold a baby. She has been so helpful to us." As Mr. Li translates and I place Becky in her arms, the girl blushes with pleasure.

Quite by happenstance, it seems, I've found a giving and words that have meaning.

Later that morning, the solicitous Mr. Wei pays a final visit. Though this is our third encounter with him, it is our first and last chance to learn about our daughters and their birth parents. We don't have to pose the question uppermost in our minds. "Your adoptions are final," Mr. Wei offers. "If a birth mother showed up here, she wouldn't even know what the baby looked like. And I wouldn't tell her anything."

Becky, Noel, and Rose, he then tells us, were all born in Yangzhou's Northern Jiangsu People's Hospital. Each of their birth mothers was an unmarried college student; each of them registered at the hospital under a false name, then later slipped away, leaving her baby behind. He knows nothing about the fathers. As for the infants, each remained in the hospital for two months, then was delivered by policemen to the orphanage.

The parents glance at each other. All three, the same story? Politely, but firmly, we voice our skepticism. Mr. Wei, no less polite and firm, maintains there's nothing unusual about the similarity of the stories. "Single women in China," he explains, "are not allowed to keep their babies." We smile, nod, but remain unpersuaded. (Our skepticism will ease only somewhat when we later learn that the Canadians were not told the same one-size-fits-all story.)

Mr. Wei's familiarity with the children's personalities, however, is convincing as he explains how he matched each girl with her parents. Noel, he says, is bright and loves to mimic people. She will respond well to siblings. It's true. Already she's crawling around after Orion, aping his every gesture. Rose, by contrast, is quiet. "Your application," he says to Michael and Lisa, "stated that the father is quiet."

As for Becky, he says, "She is very verbal. That is why we thought she should be with two correspondents." Mr. Wei, it turns out, is a former army journalist. Our standing as journalists has not harmed us; it has brought us Becky. Without a trace of irony, Mr. Wei adds, "And she looks like Joe's picture."

Our parting with Mr. Li is emotional. The women especially feel toward this gruff but tender shepherd the sort of warmth and gratitude that I've heard biological mothers express when they speak of the doctors who delivered their babies. As I give

Mr. Li a ferocious hug that he returns with a gratifying lack of reserve, I know that though I am unlikely ever to see him again, I will adore this man forever.

The translator who awaits the arrival of our Chinese Southern Airlines flight in Guangzhou is another matter. Though just thirty-one, unmarried, and childless, Robert is full of advice from the moment we step off the plane in Guangzhou.

"It is important that she wear a tight dress," he says as we exchange handshakes in the airport. He tugs at Becky's pink snowsuit. "You don't want wind blowing down her clothes."

This Chinese mania for overswaddling is the only cultural difference that has begun to wear thin on our group as the days pass. Everywhere we go, strangers tug at the infants' snowsuits, trying to tuck them in tighter. Our own preference is to keep the children in clothes that breathe and permit a wider range of motion. As far as we're concerned, they've been cooped up long enough.

As Robert checks us into the White Swan Hotel, a swank Western-style monolith that he assures us is "five star," the lower lobby begins to fill with American parents and their Chinese children. Chatting with some of the adults, we learn that the hotel is host to groups from Pennsylvania, Georgia, California, and Tennessee, all of them, like us, in Guangzhou to obtain U.S. visas for their children.

Robert proves an efficient fixer. Over the next two days, he takes us to get visa photos of the babies, then buses us out to the skirts of Guangzhou for a tour of a beautiful monastery and the Sun Yatsen Memorial Hall. He packs our schedule with far more sight-seeing than any of us want, but we follow along, too tired to resist. One evening, he drops us in front of the hotel with instructions to be back in the lobby in twenty minutes— barely time enough to change the babies' diapers and clothes, and brush our teeth.

When we reassemble, Robert lectures us. "It is good to wash the babies."

That does it. We revolt. We'll get our own dinner, thank you. As the five adults huddle, stewing in our aggravation, Joe suggests, "It's a power struggle. We, the Americans, are saying, 'These are our children,' and the Chinese are saying, 'Not so fast.'"

Maybe he's right. Maybe not. At this point, none of us really care. We just want to go home.

The last task before our scheduled visit to the U.S. Consulate is a government medical exam. The clinic is packed and the procedure is inefficient. Babies are weighed here, measured there. There is still another station for inspecting ears, eyes, and throats. Each stop has long snaking lines.

Robert proves his value, navigating us rapidly through the throngs. At the final station, we encounter a doctor who speaks English. Anxiously, Linda explains her concern that Noel has no "special need." The doctor tells Linda not to worry; Noel's early history of ear infections qualifies her for that status. (Though none of us realize it, the point is moot; our adoptions were finalized before we left Yangzhou. We also can't know that within two years, Beijing will be far more vigilant and strict about which children are designated as having a special need.)

Joe and I then ask about the rash on Becky's neck. After a quick look, the doctor pronounces: "Too many clothes." When the Americans burst out laughing, his brows furrow in bewilderment.

With monthly requests for visas by this time averaging one hundred and fifty, the U.S. Consulate has long since established efficient procedures for moving adopted babies through quickly. But China's New Year's celebrations have disrupted the Consulate's usual schedule, causing a large backup of families.

Now, the Consulate is robbed of all dignity as scores of jean-clad parents and their children transform the reception rooms and corridors into a noisy, sprawling nursery. Smaller babies perch on chairs and tables; larger ones pull up on couches and scuttle across the floors, chasing after toys. There is no hastening our exit. Each family must be interviewed separately.

We wait and wait. Feed our babies. Wait some more.

As we idle, I make one more attempt to persuade Joe to reconsider Becky's name. This is our last chance to change our minds. Whatever name we announce to the consul will go on the exit visa and be final. Though we're in agreement on the first and last names, we remain divided about a middle one. Joe is bent on Rebecca Smolowe Treen, a name that to my ears sounds too large and clunky for one so small.

"What about Becky Saiming Treen?" I try. I've been pushing this option since Mr. Li told us the meaning of Becky's Chinese name. Though my politically correct twitchings quieted after learning that Mr. Wei chose the name Saiming, not Becky's birth parents, I still suspect that Becky might someday appreciate our acknowledgment of her heritage. "If nothing else, Wease, Saiming sounds a hell of a lot nicer than Smolowe."

"Smolowe," he answers.

"I know! What about Rebecca S. Treen? Then *she* can decide what the S stands for."

"Smolowe," he says, his smile friendly, his tone final.

Our group is one of the last to be called. The consul is exhausted. The interviews are brief.

"Her full name, please?"

"Rebecca Smolowe Treen," we answer in unison.

Stamp. Stamp. Stamp. Done. Next.

We can go home.

At the precise moment our Dragon Air flight lifts off the tarmac in Guangzhou—destination: Hong Kong—I unexpectedly start to cry. Until now, I haven't realized that during our ten days in China, I've been harboring fears that someone might take Becky away from us. Now that we're finally aloft and headed for home, tears of joy and relief stream down my face.

"You're ours," I whisper into Becky's ear. "Ours for life."

XII

THE FIRST FEW DAYS AFTER WE GET HOME, THE
well wishes come at us by post and E-mail, by telegram and
phone. Every hour, it seems, the mailman is back on our
doorstep with another parcel or fragrant arrangement of
flowers.

Then, the warm-hearted messages begin to arrive in person,
a stream of relatives and friends whose presence leaves little
time for sleep, much less thought. Almost every night, there's a
guest in Joe's office, maybe another on the pullout bed in the
living room, another on the sunroom couch. This constant
traffic and excitement catches me off guard. In all the time I'd
been focused on bringing a baby home, I'd never once imagined what the homecoming might be like.

The bigger surprise, though, is the effortlessness with which
Joe and I absorb Becky into our lives. During the first week
home, as we continue to hand her back and forth, I figure,
Better enjoy this while it lasts. It's not that I have some schema
in my head of what will or won't transpire once Joe returns to

work. I simply know that once the demands of the office resume, Joe's interest in Becky's every meal, expression, and breath will deflate. I know that my three-month leave (a combination of vacation weeks and unexpected paid time put together by a conspiracy of male editors at *Time* who were appalled to learn that adoptive mothers don't get a maternity leave) will become the excuse for pushing more and more child-care duties my way. I know that the explosion is coming, the one where Joe points to a squalling Becky and erupts, "You handle it! I don't have time!"

I don't know squat.

After Joe returns to *People*, our life as a threesome continues much as before, with only minor adjustment. Instead of sharing Becky throughout the day, I become the day person, Joe the self-proclaimed "night guy."

Early each morning while Joe is still sleeping, I answer Becky's awakening ba-baing and da-daing. Our routine rarely varies. When I enter the nursery, we greet each other with a mutually astounded look that says: You're still here! I carry Becky to the window, open the shade, give the weather report. Next, we dance to the closet where I select an ensemble from the ever-growing collection of beautiful clothes that keep arriving in gaily wrapped boxes. By the time we finish dressing, Joe is done with his shower and shave, and eager to spend the remaining minutes with Becky before he must leave for the office.

Throughout the day, Joe phones home, seeking the sort of information I never imagined would interest him. What did the pediatrician say about her cold? Did she poop today? Did I remember to shoot the camera when I saw her sitting up by herself for the first time? (Joe seems so disappointed to miss this milestone that I'll later be relieved when Becky takes her first tentative step on an evening when we're all home together.)

Most nights, Joe gets home earlier than has been his habit in the years I've known him. "It's Daddy!" I say, rushing Becky to the door to greet him.

There's the kiss. The hand-off. Then, Joe takes over.

Often, they begin on the living room couch, Becky sprawled on her back across Joe's lap. He looks down and makes faces; she stares up and giggles. The joy they take in one another is so uncensored, so unbounded, so mesmerizing. When her tiny hand comes up and cups his chin, the intensity of their interaction has a sensuality that sometimes, quite literally, takes my breath away.

Then they ascend the stairs to begin their nightly ritual. Usually, I remain below, eager to give them time alone together, no less eager to have time to myself. Over the next hour, I hear their sounds: Joe singing and laughing, Becky babbling and giggling. When it starts to quiet, I appear at Becky's door with a warm bottle. On nights when I stay to watch Joe rock and read to her, I'll sometimes gasp dramatically and say, "I think I see a brown hair. Return that child at once!" Always, Joe laughs and kisses the top of Becky's head where her hair (black, as it happens) is slowly growing in.

On those occasions when one of our guests asks to bathe, bottle, and burp Becky, Joe steps aside with a show of grace, later muttering to me, "I feel like I'm getting cut out." Always, though, it's Joe who places Becky in her crib, tucks her beneath the same pink, blue, and white patchwork quilt that once covered him, and delivers the final kiss goodnight.

Enchanting as I find all this, I remain skeptical. While I'm on leave, it's no hardship to arrange my time around Joe's schedule and step in when he's held late at the office. But what will become of this easy esprit once I return to work and there are competing demands on both our time that require one of us to flex? What will happen when the novelty of an infant in the house wears off and these rituals become routine?

As I settle baby-sitting arrangements and gird for the stressful juggling every working mother I know complains of, I begin a mental litany that resembles the Passover song reminding the Jewish people not to take their blessings for granted. Had Joe gone to China and returned home without squawking, *Dayenu* (it would have been enough). Had he cultivated only a modicum of tolerance for the disruptions of a baby in the house, *Dayenu*. Had he pitched in begrudgingly on, say, a third of the chores, say, a third of the time, *Dayenu*. If he continues to shower Becky with love and affection, it is more than I hoped for or expected; it is more than enough.

A small incident four weeks after my return to *Time* finally dispels my doubt. On the last Saturday of April, Joe and I are scheduled to attend the White House Correspondents' Dinner in Washington, D.C. For days, I've been making arrangements: a hotel room for all of us, a sitter for Becky the night of the dinner, lunch and brunch dates with friends eager to meet our daughter. But that Friday night, just as I'm completing a cover story on armed militias, Eric, my former Bosnia connection, phones from Michigan with word of a bizarre news development. When an editor asks if I can come in the next morning to update the story, I answer, "Sure. No problem." I'm not about to give anybody the impression I intend to let motherhood get in the way of my job.

By now, it's close to midnight. With several more hours of work ahead before I can leave, I call home and wake Joe to tell him what's happened. "I'm really sorry, Wease," I say. "I'd probably be furious if it was *your* work screwing up our plans."

"That's okay. I understand," he answers. "Why don't I take Becky to Washington? That way you'll be able to get some rest Sunday."

"That would be great," I say gratefully. "I'm exhausted, and it's only going to get worse tomorrow."

The next morning, my tired brain has little room for anything beyond the words on my computer screen. When a colleague phones from Washington to say, "I just saw Joe and Becky. Are you coming?" I think nothing of it.

Around dinnertime as I'm putting the final touches on the story, an editor enters my office with a guilty expression on his face. "Did you and your husband have plans this weekend in Washington?"

I shrug. "No big deal. How did you know?"

"I just heard from someone down there that they saw Joe and Becky, but not you." Apparently, the same colleague who had phoned earlier, a single mother as it happens, had been spreading the word that Joe had made the trip alone with Becky.

I still don't get it.

Late Sunday afternoon while I'm sitting on the back porch, my next-door neighbor Lorraine calls across the fence, "Where's Joe?" When I tell her, the expression on her face assumes an almost cartoonish look of amazement. "You trusted him to take Becky?"

"Yeah, sure." Assuming she's thinking of the nightmarish logistics that can attend air travel with a baby, I add, "Becky is a veteran traveler already. She handles plane rides well."

"That's incredible," Lorraine answers. "I could never leave my husband alone with our kids for a whole weekend."

Finally, I get it. This is headline news: DAD TRAVELS WITH BABY. BABY SURVIVES TRIP.

Until that moment, it hadn't crossed my mind to question whether Joe could handle the rigors of a thirty-six-hour solo trip with Becky. It hadn't even crossed my mind there was anything unusual about this arrangement.

Dayenu, my ass, I realize. Wease is so completely involved with Becky's care that I'm already taking him for granted.

"He must be an amazing father," Lorraine says.

"He is," I agree. Then I hear myself say something I never, even in my most optimistic fantasies, imagined myself saying. "Joe's a real Superdad."

* * *

Hello, Earth to Jill. Reality check, please. Your gear appears to be malfunctioning.

I sit a while longer, sorting through the days and nights of Jill and Joe. Since our return from China, I see, a disproportionate share of the household burden has fallen to me. I am, indisputably, the administrator of our two houses. I keep the lists, stock the food, tote up our financial ledgers, write the checks. Then again, I wouldn't want it any other way. Experience has taught me that Joe is dismal at taking care of the shopping, a disaster at taking care of the bills.

But none of that, really, has much to do with taking care of Becky. When it comes to her—the feeding and dressing, bathing and diapering, playing and holding, worrying and loving—I detect no imbalance at all.

That night when father and daughter return from Washington, I try the S-word out on Joe. "I knew you were smitten by Becky within three minutes," I say. "I just didn't know you would turn out to be a Superdad."

A smile spreads across his face. Yes, he is pleased. He is very, very pleased. And embarrassed. "It didn't take three minutes," he protests lamely. "It took longer."

"Yeah, right, Wease."

"No, really," he persists. "It wasn't until late the first night that we kind of—" He shrugs.

"What? Did something in particular happen?"

"Yeah. Becky woke up and started to cry. I didn't want her to wake you, so I took her into the hall and walked up and down. To quiet her down, I started singing. It wasn't until I got back to the room that I realized what I'd been singing." He pauses, his face reddening.

"Wease?"

"It was 'Yessir, that's my baby.'"

Now Joe seems determined to ensure that no one, anywhere, anytime, will be able to challenge that claim. Though it was I who started us along the paper trail, it's Joe who brings us to its conclusion. Joe's the one who prods us to get baby announcements made, returning twice to the stationery store to inspect and correct mock-ups of the card he'd conceptualized in Nanjing. (The front reads, "We finally figured out where babies come from . . ." then opens to a picture of Becky and the word "China!") It's Joe who hastens our trip into town to obtain a Social Security number for Becky, and Joe who remembers to submit her application for U.S. citizenship. Joe's the one who keeps us from stalling on a U.S. "readoption." (Though New Jersey recognizes the adoption we completed in China, some states do not.)

On the May morning that we drive to Newark to appear before a judge (aptly named Fillilove) and finalize the readoption, it's Joe who thinks to answer the judge's concluding "Do you have any questions?" with "Yes, Judge. Could we take some pictures of you with Becky for our scrapbook?"

And it's Joe who interrupts his work day one Friday to schlep out to Newark to pick up an envelope addressed to Becky and imprinted with the words "The White House" in the upper lefthand corner. Later, Joe and I will both have tears in our eyes as together we read the enclosed document, a letter signed by President Clinton that begins: "Dear Fellow American: I want to congratulate you on reaching the impressive milestone of becoming a citizen of our great nation—"

On a day when our baby-sitting arrangements fall through, I drop Becky at the child center on the ground floor of the Time & Life Building. As the lunch hour nears, I retrieve Becky from her play and take her up to Joe's office. For the next half hour, Becky does her thing. High-fives everyone in sight. Plays with the toys in people's offices. Giggles fetchingly. Joe's colleagues ooh and ahh to him about his daughter. To me, they murmur things like, "You should see the way Joe's face lights up whenever he talks about Becky" and "I always knew he'd come around."

Since I'd thought that Joe had pretty much given no thought to children except when I was pounding away at him, I'm struck by the number of people to whom Joe apparently had expressed his reservations. I also find it striking how many people had such confidence that Joe would take to fatherhood. During the years of tussling with Joe over children, I'd heard people's claim that "every man is like that, but put a baby in a man's arms and he turns to jelly" as just one more piece of misleading folk wisdom to add to my collection.

"I don't know why you find this so surprising," Joe says when I recount his colleagues' comments. "I always knew I'd come around to this parenting business."

Usually when Joe says something funny, he laughs loudest and longest. But he's not even smiling. He actually means this. "That's bullshit, Wease," I say. "That's complete and utter bullshit."

Or is it? More weeks have passed. The flow of guests, our audience, has slowed to a trickle. Yet, Joe remains a model father. Attentive. Patient. Loving. The sort of father who not only knows which songs and books are his child's favorites, but can recite the words of each by heart.

Had I been wrong all along? Had I felt greater resistance from Joe than had actually existed? Had I grossly misread my husband? Could I have avoided the depression tripped by my certainty that I would never be a mother? Were my dark ruminations about choosing between a live-in absentee dad and a divorce completely out of whack with reality? Irked and intrigued, I call the two people whom I knew to be Joe's confidantes throughout our extended drama. "Everyone keeps telling me that they knew Joe would come around," I say. "I sure as hell didn't. Did you?"

"No." Esme, too, is amazed by her older brother's transformation. "That morning I met you guys at the airport the day you came in from China, I could see something had changed. I'd never seen you looking so happy, and there was a new maturity in Joe that I'd never seen before. His sense of responsibility was incredible. I still remember the way he got down on all fours in LAX to play with Becky."

Esme tells me that when Joe and I were in Pasadena for Christmas, less than three weeks before our departure for China, Joe was still opposed to the adoption. "Joe expressed a determination to see the adoption through," she says. "He was afraid he was going to lose you."

"Did I think Treen would turn out to be a great father?" Kathryn answers my question. "No way."

Kathryn had heard more of Joe's reservations and questions about adoption than anyone, possibly me included. Joe respected not only her opinion, but her experience. She and her husband had tried for years to adopt. Three referrals had fallen through on them, one in the U.S., two overseas, before the unexpected pregnancy that gave birth to their daughter.

Kathryn can trace Joe's reluctance even closer to our departure date. After our return from Pasadena, she says, Joe called and went into his usual spiel: Didn't want a child. Never had. Never would. "Until then, I'd been trying to support Treen in his decision making," Kathryn tells me. "But now you guys had the referral for Becky. I told him, 'You *are* a father. Whether divorced or married, that child is yours. So grow up, Treen.'"

A few weeks after my conversation with Kathryn, Joe recounts a chat he'd just had with a man opposed to his wife's adoption plans. Joe had been trying to ease the guy's fears.

"Did you tell him how you resisted this adoption every step of the way?" I ask. "How you were indifferent to the outcome?"

"I wasn't indifferent," Joe answers. "I didn't want a baby."

Earth to Jill. Reality check complete. Your gear is working just fine.

In May, WACAP representatives come east to discuss their China program with prospective parents. Usually, such gatherings draw a few dozen people, but because the meeting has been mentioned that day in a *New York Times* article about overseas adoptions, the audience on this evening numbers well over one hundred. I'm fourth in a lineup of six former clients invited by WACAP to discuss our experiences. By the time the microphone is passed to me, most of what I'd intended to say has already been covered, so I begin to toss out ideas randomly.

"I have a husband who really wanted no part of an adoption," I say toward the end of my remarks. "He's older and felt we should be thinking about retirement, not raising kids. So, most of the way, it was me several steps ahead, hauling Joe like this." When I gesture, as if towing a sack of potatoes, there's nervous laughter, then an audible rustle as several men sit forward in their chairs. Their wives, I notice, are no longer looking at me; they're looking at their husbands. "Happily," I conclude, "Joe fell for Becky within about five minutes. But I assure you, that is *not* an outcome I would have predicted." After that, I duck out, unable to stay for questions.

The next night, the phone rings several times. "I think you really hit something when you talked about you and Joe," another panel member tells me. A Long Island woman wants to thank me for being so "honest." A New Jersey woman with an older husband who doesn't want to adopt asks if they can drop by on Saturday to see Becky and talk.

"I hate to say no. She sounded so desperate," I tell Joe. "But I have to work on Saturday."

"I'll handle this one," he volunteers. "They'll get a different view of adoption from me than they would from you."

When I return home from the office early Saturday evening,

Joe says he's confident the couple will adopt. He'd told them his Frank Rogers story, the one where Chinese peasant women return to the rice paddies after giving birth, an infant's piss almost hits the ceiling, and a reluctant father turns to mush over his kid. "There was something about the way the guy laughed," Joe says. "He'll come around."

As always, I find this story altogether annoying. "Do you think with men like you and this guy, the resistance is mostly ignorance? Mostly not understanding what parenting is about?"

"No. I knew what went into parenting," Joe answers. "That's why I didn't want it. And that's why most men balk. They *do* see what's coming."

"Then what causes them to change?"

Joe shrugs. "Something happens to men. They don't want a child, don't want a child, don't want a child. Then they suddenly have their own child, and they come around."

That's *it?*

The milestones come and go quickly. We celebrate Becky's first birthday. Our first anniversary as a family. Her second birthday.

On this evening in August 1996, we've just returned from food shopping and dinner at a Chinese restaurant. There's a plan: I'll put the groceries away while Joe gives Becky a quick bath, then we'll all settle on the couch to watch *The Aristocats*, the newest addition to our growing Disney collection.

I step outside for one of my favorite activities: eavesdropping on Joe and Becky. Through an open second-floor bathroom window, I hear Joe. "Becky, where aarrre you? Come out, come out." I can tell by the switching on and off of lights that Joe is now in our bedroom. I hear his jubilant, "There you are!" Her insistent, "Again!" His patient, "Okay, now you find me. Close your eyes. One, two, three." Then Becky's, "Daddy, where aarrre you? Daddy? Nope, not in there!"

A few minutes later, I hear, "Tic. Toc. Tic. Toc," then, "Bong! Bong! Bong!" Though I can't see them, I know that on the bongs, Joe is hoisting Becky up and down in front of the bathroom mirror. When Becky shrieks, then commands, "Again!" I settle into the lawn chair. So much for plans. This is going to be one of those *long* bath routines.

As I light a cigarette and gaze at the stars, I recall sitting in this very chair in this very spot two years earlier, smoking and contemplating the very real possibility that I might leave Joe. Now, as I inhale their happy sounds along with my smoke, I think, I like a happy ending as well as the next person, but even Disney wouldn't buy this one. What *is* it that caused Joe's startling transformation? The dad-turns-to-jelly theory only goes so far; I know plenty of marmalade fathers who are better acquainted with the family photos on their office desks than their kids' books and drawings, or even their kids, for that matter.

Sitting there, I assemble all the possibilities that have occurred to me over the months and see for the first time that each reason grows organically out of the adoption experience. The fact that Becky was seven months old, for instance, eased our transition into parenthood. Several biological mothers have told me that an infant's first six months are a haze of feedings and diaper changes, with few rewards to offset the constant exhaustion. Obviously, I don't know what Joe and I missed. But I do know that at seven months, Becky was already a little person with a distinct personality. Quick to enchant, impossible to ignore, she responded to us immediately (though it would take about three months before I felt it was us specifically and not just a generic response to any attentive adult).

That she responded to us, not just me, was also a factor. By circumstance, the relationship among the three of us was configured as an equilateral triangle from the start. During our first ten days together as a family, we were in each other's company round-the-clock. With no friends or relatives on hand to guide or relieve us, Joe and I had to attend all Becky's needs. Even if Joe hadn't been seduced by Becky's distinctive wiles, he couldn't have ignored her unrelenting appeals for bottles, dry diapers, and attention. There were also no competing claims on Joe's time to distract him from confronting the reality of what goes into a baby's care. Had we been home, he might have escaped to the office, then convinced himself that I was back in New Jersey eating bonbons and reading movie magazines.

It also helped that the environment in which we traveled was a constant celebration of parenthood. The warm response and excited interest of the Chinese people reinforced the primacy and joy of family. So did the other parents with whom we traveled, American and Canadian alike. Everyone was so wrapped up in their new children that if Joe had remained uninterested in Becky, he would have felt excluded from most conversations. I think, too, that the palpable joy of these new parents, fathers as well mothers, helped dissipate any reservation, awkwardness, or embarrassment Joe may have felt about taking pleasure in his new daughter.

Looking back, I even think it was serendipitous that I was flattened by a stomach bug so soon after we got Becky. During those twenty-four hours when Joe was solely responsible for her well-being, he saw that he could meet her needs. I think that bolstered his confidence enormously. By the time we left China, Joe and I not only had established a joint caretaking of Becky, but our experience as parents was precisely the same, so neither of us had cause to think we knew more than the other. We'd also seen how much we enjoyed doing it together, exchanging observations, sharing the delight. Perhaps as a result, neither was inclined to maneuver to be either more or less in charge.

Even with all of that, though, Joe still might have held out were Becky not the remarkable child she is. Although I don't doubt that I would have fallen hard for any child, Becky made our transition to parenthood remarkably easy. From the moment she was placed in my arms in Yangzhou, Becky was cheerful, sweet tempered, and affectionate. During our days in China when we were constantly on the road with no set schedule for feeding, sleeping, and play, she tolerated the confusion with a minimum of fuss. Had Becky been suffering infant grief over lost caretakers or wailing constantly from the pain of cutting teeth, I doubt that Joe would have been singing "Yessir, that's my baby" quite so fast.

It's as if Becky took the best of her orphanage experience with her and left the rest behind. While we'll never know how much of the Becky we met was nature and how much was nurture, I have little doubt that the months she spent sharing the attentions of her three nurses with eleven other infants fostered her easygoing temper and disinclination to be either rigid or exhaustingly demanding. The need to vie for attention and affection perhaps accounts for her appealing way of reaching out to people.

Whatever the reason, Becky arrived at our hotel room with an alert, excited curiosity about her new surroundings and new parents. Ready to burst upon the world and stake her place in it, she was engaged and engaging from the very start. If she hooked Joe with her beauty and smile, she reeled him in with her personality.

(Joe thinks my theories are hilarious. "Want to know the real reason I came around so fast? You were a klutz with that poor kid. You didn't have a clue how to feed her, how to bathe her. *Someone* had to save Becky." For a second, I bite. Then we both crack up.)

Through the bathroom window, I hear Joe crooning, "Baby Beluga-dooga," and Becky squealing, "More! I want more, Daddy!" I know this routine, too. Joe will continue swaying her back and forth until his arms give out. As I picture them in my mind's eye, I realize that I've forgotten the most important reason for Joe's metamorphosis. Joe always had the qualities required to be an outstanding father. All that was missing was the resolve.

In China, Joe made up his mind to be a father.

As I write these words, it is January 17, 1997. Two years to the day since Becky entered our lives. It doesn't matter to me anymore how or why Joe came around. What matters now is that Joe is a father, I am a mother, Becky is our daughter, and we are a family.

After all the ups and downs, the partnership of Weasel & Weasel, formed in 1982, incorporated before a judge in 1985, feels stronger than ever. Joe and I have emerged from this rough passage as each other's best friend. Favorite playmate. Most trusted confidante. Truest critic. Staunchest ally. With a new associate on board, our dialogue has never been livelier, our incentive for compromise greater.

That Wease. After fourteen years, I still find him interesting, intoxicating, irreplaceable.

None of this is to suggest Joe and I don't still find each other pretty intolerable at times. Last month after a particularly grinding commute, Joe phoned from his office, barked, "We're moving back to Manhattan," then called a realtor and ordered up a reappraisal of our house. This month, Joe bought a new desk for his home office, one far too large to fit into any New York apartment we might be able to afford.

That Wease. I really must stop taking him so seriously.

Joe has stepped up his campaign to curb my smoking. I've stepped up my campaign to curb his expansionist designs on new Jill-free zones where he can stack and litter without threat of my straightening up behind him. For both of us, though, there are no Becky-free zones. Our daughter invades and pervades every aspect of our life together, serving as a constant check on our power struggles.

It's pretty clear who's in charge, anyway. Though she stands just three feet one, she looms over our household, a gentle tyrant.

Predictably, there have been some changes in our lives. Joe and I have become one of those stay-at-home couples that finds an evening with our child more satisfying and entertaining than anything the screen or stage might offer. Pre-Becky, we logged perhaps three dozen films a year and maybe a dozen plays; post-Becky, we average two movies annually and see no plays at all. We've taken none of the sorts of vacations we used to count on, the kind where we laze on a beach or explore new sights. Neither of us thinks any longer of pursuing an overseas post. For now, parenthood is exotic territory enough.

We see more of our relatives these days. Aunts, uncles, young cousins, adult stepcousins all want their time with the Beckster. Both sets of grandparents have discovered a deep bank of points in their frequent flyer accounts, points that have closed the distance between New Jersey and Wisconsin and North Carolina. Now that Becky is talking, I don't even want to discuss what our phone bills look like.

We do each Christmas with Joe's family, each Passover with mine. We're still punting on the rest.

We are, in short, a family like any other.

And then we are, like every family, our own unique constellation. Intergenerational. Interdenominational. Interracial. InterWeasel.

People often ask if Joe and I plan to adopt another child. Certainly, it seems doable. Earlier this year, both of the families we traveled with to Yangzhou returned to China and brought home second daughters. Yet, I doubt Joe and I will return to China until Becky expresses an interest in her native land. Joe is now fifty-four, I am forty-one. When I calculate the time required to complete an adoption, our ages worry even me.

But that isn't the largest obstacle. Nor is Joe, whom I sense would yield if I expressed interest. It's me and my aversion to risk. Things have worked out so much better than I ever dreamed or hoped. I don't want to chance the disturbance and disequilibrium a new star might bring.

I won't pretend that I think Becky is better off without the tortures and comforts of siblings. But there are substitutes. A six-year-old boy, who lives down the street, introduces Becky to everyone as his "second sister" and supplies the sort of ecstatic hugs and irreverent affection my own brothers offer me. His younger sister, our daughter's most frequent companion, tussles with Becky over toys, teaching her far more about sharing than Joe or I ever could. And when Becky's cousins boss her around with siblinglike authority, our daughter is transported.

People also ask if we remain in touch with the families we traveled with in China. Yes, we do. With other adoptive families, too. Though I'd assumed, upon our return from Yangzhou, that we were done with adoption networks, I was quickly set straight by a local father of two daughters from Taiwan, when he urged, "Come over and bring Becky. I want my girls to see a family that looks like ours."

With time, my appreciation of that statement has deepened. Joe and I would be deluded to think there won't be issues for Becky connected to her adoption and to the biracial composition of our family. As yet, there are only hints of the challenges ahead. Mostly, they are small grace notes, too faint for Becky to hear but enriching to my own symphony. I've noticed, for instance, that when I grocery shop with Becky, adults of all races are more likely to strike up a conversation with me. Something about the juxtaposition of Becky's face and mine makes me more approachable.

Recently, an elderly Asian clerk at the A&P checkout counter asked if Becky was my daughter. When I nodded, the woman wagged her index finger in my face and said, "Don't spoil her." Then she patted Becky's cheek and said to me, "God bless you." I loved that unexpected encounter.

The more familiar ones have begun to grow a bit stale. When Becky first came home, I thrilled everytime someone ogled her and asked about our adoption. Back then, it seemed a wonderful affirmation that I was her mother, she my daughter. But as the days, months, and years have passed and my need for such affirmation has evaporated, it's become a persistent reminder that most people see us as a novelty, not a mother and daughter.

It's a point that's hard to make vivid to a nonadoptive parent. I tried recently with Elizabeth, a new Montclair friend who has three biological children. "It's this feeling of always being watched and observed," I said. "When Becky and I are in public, we're never allowed to move beyond the adoption."

"People mean well," Elizabeth responded. "I think you're being overly sensitive."

"No doubt," I laughed. "But let's say that you had a particularly bad labor with one of you kids. Say, it was thirty-six hours, and after all that pain, you landed up having a cesarean. So, of course, after the delivery, everyone wanted to know how you were, how quickly you were recovering." She nodded. "Now, suppose more than two years have passed," I continued, pointing to her youngest. "Your daughter is involved in all sorts of interesting things you'd be only too happy to talk about. Nursery school. Potty training. Whatever. But the only thing people ask is—"

Elizabeth smiled and together we said, "How was your C-section?"

"Okay," she laughed. "I get it."

When I repeat the conversation to Joe, he renders his own verdict: "You're being hypersensitive."

Yeah, I probably am. But I hope my hypersensitivity is little more than the natural instinct of a mother to defend her young. I bristle at the thought of Becky having adoption constantly thrust at her as if it were the organizing principle of her life. Maybe it will be. Maybe it won't. I'd like Becky to decide.

I feel the same way about race. And again, it's a growing familiarity with certain comments that makes me want to remain alert to what may be heading Becky's way. Initially when people gushed, "She's so cute," I thrilled; Becky is, undeniably, an adorable child. But over time, I've come to realize that Caucasian parents of Asian-born children hear that comment far more often than biological parents. Often, I think, it's a reflection of the discomfort people feel around mixed-race families and an expression of their need to deny that discomfort by saying, in effect, "It's okay with me that you're a family."

An overexcited interest can also be a sign of understandable confusion or discomfort. When people ask, "Is she going to learn Chinese?" then rush ahead with uninvited advice, it can feel intrusive. Sort of like if they were to ask whether we intended to have Becky bat mitzvahed, then weighed in with unwanted opinions.

Who knows? Maybe Becky's Chinese heritage *will* be of central importance to her. Around her second birthday, Becky took to insisting, "My name is Ming." Joe and I were baffled. Was this a memory from Yangzhou of being called Saiming, or was she identifying with Min, the Asian-American girl on *Barney*? Should we follow her lead and call her Ming? After about two weeks, she reverted to calling herself Becky, and the issue passed.

A few months later while Joe and I were watching a *60 Minutes* segment shot in China, Becky pointed at a street scene of pedestrians and shouted, "Me!"

"Yes, sweetheart!" I said excitedly. "That's China. That's where you were born."

I don't know what part of my statement, if any, Becky

understood at that moment. I don't know what part of it, if any, will be important to her in the future. I just know that Becky should be allowed to decide that for herself.

All this is difficult to explain, which may be why I enjoy getting together with other members of Families With Children From China. With them, I don't have to explain at all. Nor do I run into the sorts of comments that typically leave adoptive parents gnashing their teeth. "Who are her real parents?" (We are, thank you.) "She's a China doll." (No, she's a Chinese-American girl.) "She's very lucky." (No, it is we who are the lucky ones.) Instead, conversation starts where we are, in the present, and tends to focus on the issue of interest to all of us: our children's futures.

Far more importantly, Becky is building friendships with kids who will be able to rant about, laugh at, and address the issues particular to adopted Chinese daughters of Caucasian parents. No matter how sensitive Joe and I may (or may not) prove to be, I remain convinced that parents are, by definition, neanderthals. Every kid needs an ally. So, yes, we remain in contact with families that look like ours.

But we don't confuse anyone else's family with ours.

Everyday, Joe and I see a little more of us in Becky. From Joe, Becky gets her wonderful laugh and wit. From me, her love of dance, music, and footrubs. From both of us, she's inherited a passion for books and a tendency to talk everything to death. She is, as Mr. Wei promised, a very verbal child.

"What are Grandma and Papa D doing? What are they eating?" she grills. "Can you make Tigger talk? Can Pocahontas give me a bath?" Given her inquisitorial bent, she may, God help her, grow up to be a journalist, like her parents.

And if her parents are lucky, they'll grow up to be more like Becky. Not a day goes by that she doesn't teach us something about the art of living and the art of loving.

Thanks to Becky, Joe and I are learning a more generous give and take that doesn't tote up quid pro quos. Because Becky is evenhanded in her affections, we can joke without resentment, "You're the parent du jour," on those days when she favors only Joe with her dirty diapers or permits only me to zip up her coat. On matters of safety and discipline, Joe and I are a united, unyielding front. Otherwise, Joe has his relationship with Becky, I have mine, and we don't interfere with each other's choices of clothing, feeding, or expressions of love. Because Becky's magnetic pull is so strong, the zone shared by all of us keeps enlarging.

If Joe is not the live-in absentee dad I anticipated, I think it's fair to say that I'm not the control-freak mother that was once Joe's dread. I've been surprised by the number of friends who have commented, "I can't believe what a relaxed mother you are." Of course, that may be a polite way of saying, "Thank God, you've finally chilled out."

Still, I'm pretty sure that, like Joe, I'm a better parent now than I would have been had our original baby plans proceeded on schedule. I think the long wait for motherhood has left me more patient and less prone to sweat the little things that can occasionally make parenting hell; more receptive to others' input and less disposed to hover overprotectively; more respectful of Becky's unique qualities and less inclined to try to mold her to my own needs. Then again, that may just be a wish list of parenting qualities I'd like to achieve.

Of this much, though, I'm certain. The effort that was required to bring our family into being has made me less inclined to take my daughter for granted and more appreciative of her father who, far from draining the pleasure out of motherhood, enhances my delight. Even on those days when Becky and I are out of sorts with each other—she frustrated with me for spending too much time at the computer, I annoyed with her for testing her expanding boundaries one too many times—I can still feel deeply moved as I watch Joe and Becky together, aware that I'm experiencing a joy I was once certain would never be mine.

"What's amazing," my friend Jan said recently, "is that you knew what you wanted, and you got it."

"No," I answered without forethought. "What's amazing is that I thought I knew what I wanted, and it turned out I was right. It *was* what I wanted."

Priorities shift, needs change. What seems important to me right now is to savor both this precious time with Becky and the unexpected sweetness and contentment that has bridged the once-unnavigable distance between Joe's dreams and mine.

I still plan my work, and work my plan. Some things, I guess, never change. But these days I'm trying to allow more room for improvisation. Recently, I traded my full-time job at *Time* for a part-time contract to pursue a writing career of my own design. I work as many hours as I ever did, probably more. But I relish the new flexibility in my schedule that enables me to be a co-op mom in Becky's nursery school, to nap beside her in the late afternoon, to see what is unfolding, unplanned, before my eyes every day.

After so much waiting, waiting, it's all happening so quickly. Already Becky is beginning to show interest in the story that began her journey as it ended Joe's and mine. Often, now, she says, "I want to read *that* one," and points insistently at the blue scrapbook, impressed along the spine with the gold letters REBECCA SMOLOWE TREEN, until I take it down from the shelf.

"That's Mommy! And that's Daddy!" she says excitedly, pointing at the pictures on the first page, the visa shots of Joe and me that attended our adoption application.

Quickly, we turn past the pages and pages of paperwork documenting the twisty path that brought our three lives together. When we get to the first pictures of Joe and me, still Beckyless, in China, I begin to narrate: "Here we are in Yangzhou, having just flown halfway across the world to get you. And we are eager, sweetheart, so impatient and eager to hold our Becky. And—" Turn the page. "There you are! There you are! And see? You're smiling. And your Daddy and me, see our smiles? We are so happy. So very, very happy—"

02/04/10